OXFO

T

RUMI, known in Iran and Central Asia as .... oddin Balkhi, was born in 1207 in the province of Balkh, now the border region between Afghanistan and Tajikistan. His family emigrated when he was still a child, shortly before Genghis Khan and his Mongol army arrived in Balkh. They settled permanently in Konya, central Anatolia, which was formerly part of the Eastern Roman Empire (Rum). Rumi was probably introduced to Sufism originally through his father, Baha Valad, a popular preacher who also taught Sufi piety to a group of disciples. However, the turning-point in Rumi's life came in 1244, when he met in Konya a mysterious wandering Sufi called Shamsoddin of Tabriz. Shams, as he is most often referred to by Rumi, taught him the most profound levels of Sufism, transforming him from a pious religious scholar to an ecstatic mystic. Rumi expressed his new vision of reality in volumes of mystical poetry. His enormous collection of lyrical poetry is considered one of the best that has ever been produced, while his poem in rhyming couplets, the *Masnavi*, is so revered as the most consummate expression of Sufi mysticism that it is commonly referred to as 'the Koran in Persian'.

When Rumi died, on 17 December 1273, shortly after completing his work on the *Masnavi*, his passing was deeply mourned by the citizens of Konya, including the Christian and Jewish communities. His disciples formed the Mevlevi Sufi order, which was named after Rumi, whom they referred to as 'Our Lord' (Turkish 'Mevlana'/ Persian 'Mowlana'). They are better known in Europe and North America as the Whirling Dervishes, because of the distinctive dance that they now perform as one of their central rituals. Rumi's death is commemorated annually in Konya, attracting pilgrims from all corners of the globe and every religion. The popularity of his poetry has risen so much in the last couple of decades that the *Christian Science Monitor* identified him as the most published poet in America in 1997.

JAWID MOJADDEDI, a native of Afghanistan, read Middle Eastern Studies at the University of Manchester. He has taught Arabic and Islamic Studies at the University of Manchester and the University of Exeter, and has served as an editor of *Encyclopaedia Iranica* at the Center for Iranian Studies, Columbia University. He is currently Assistant Professor of Religion at Rutgers University. Dr Mojaddedi's books include *The Biographical Tradition in Sufism* (Richmond, 2001) and, as co-editor, *Classical Islam: A Sourcebook of Religious Literature* (London, 2003).

OXFORD WORLD'S CLASSICS

*For over 100 years Oxford World's Classics have brought
readers closer to the world's great literature. Now with over 700
titles—from the 4,000-year-old myths of Mesopotamia to the
twentieth century's greatest novels—the series makes available
lesser-known as well as celebrated writing.*

*The pocket-sized hardbacks of the early years contained
introductions by Virginia Woolf, T. S. Eliot, Graham Greene,
and other literary figures which enriched the experience of reading.
Today the series is recognized for its fine scholarship and
reliability in texts that span world literature, drama and poetry,
religion, philosophy and politics. Each edition includes perceptive
commentary and essential background information to meet the
changing needs of readers.*

OXFORD WORLD'S CLASSICS

══

JALAL AL-DIN RUMI

The Masnavi

BOOK ONE

══

Translated with an Introduction and Notes by
JAWID MOJADDEDI

OXFORD
UNIVERSITY PRESS

OXFORD

UNIVERSITY PRESS

Great Clarendon Street, Oxford OX2 6DP

Oxford University Press is a department of the University of Oxford.
It furthers the University's objective of excellence in research, scholarship,
and education by publishing worldwide in

Oxford New York

Auckland Bangkok Buenos Aires Cape Town Chennai
Dar es Salaam Delhi Hong Kong Istanbul Karachi Kolkata
Kuala Lumpur Madrid Melbourne Mexico City Mumbai Nairobi
São Paulo Shanghai Taipei Tokyo Toronto

Oxford is a registered trade mark of Oxford University Press
in the UK and in certain other countries

Published in the United States
by Oxford University Press Inc., New York

© Jawid Mojaddedi 2004

The moral rights of the author have been asserted
Database right Oxford University Press (maker)

First published as an Oxford World's Classics paperback 2004
Reissued 2008

British Library Cataloguing in Publication Data

Data available

ISBN 978-0-19-955231-3

21

Typeset in Ehrhardt
by RefineCatch Limited, Bungay, Suffolk
Printed in Great Britain by
Clays Ltd, Elcograf S.p.A.

This translation is dedicated to the memory of

MR NIKTAB

(d. 12 May 2003)

and

JERRY CLINTON

(d. 7 November 2003)

ACKNOWLEDGEMENTS

I SHOULD like to express my gratitude to all those who have helped to make it possible for me to produce this translation of Rumi's *Masnavi*. The teachings of Dr Javad Nurbakhsh have given me the essential background knowledge to understand and appreciate the message of this Persian Sufi masterpiece. Edmund Herzig, Paul Luft, and Colin Turner taught me Persian language and literature at the University of Manchester. The late Norman Calder taught me to appreciate traditional verse forms and convinced me that the *Masnavi* should be translated into iambic pentameters. With remarkable sensitivity and patience, the late Jerry Clinton taught me how to translate into verse. I received invaluable encouragement from J. Christoph Bürgel, Dick Davis, Simin Nabavi, Alireza Nurbakhsh, and Michael Sivori. Julie Scott Meisami offered many insightful criticisms and suggestions that have helped to improve this work significantly, as well as to increase my own understanding of the poetry. Andrew Rippin generously took on the lion's share of the responsibility for a project in which I collaborated at the same time as producing this translation and working as a full-time editor of *Encyclopaedia Iranica*. My colleagues at the Center for Iranian Studies of Columbia University helped make that experience rewarding. After I discovered Rumi when I was a teenager, it was my mother who first nurtured my enthusiasm and interest in his poetry and the Sufi tradition which he represents. I would also like to thank my brother Anis, who has been a major source of inspiration over the past year, and Negin for her loving support and companionship.

CONTENTS

x   *Contents*

Why the Prophet Conquered Mecca Yet Said,
'The World is a Carcass'   240

INTRODUCTION

Rumi and Sufism

Rumi has long been recognized within the Sufi tradition as one of the most important Sufis in history. He not only produced the finest Sufi poetry in Persian, but was the master of disciples who later named their order after him. Moreover, by virtue of the intense devotion he expressed towards his own master, Rumi has become the archetypal Sufi disciple. From that perspective, the unprecedented level of interest in Rumi's poetry over the last couple of decades in North America and Europe does not come as a total surprise. Once his poetry finally began to be rendered into English in an attractive form, which coincided with an increased interest in mysticism among readers, this Sufi saint who expressed his mystical teachings in a more memorable and universally accessible form than any other started to become a household name.

Rumi lived some 300 years after the first writings of Muslim mystics were produced. A distinct mystical path called 'Sufism' became clearly identifiable in the late tenth and early eleventh centuries with the compilation of the manuals and collections of biographies of past Sufi saints. The authors of these works, who were mostly from north-eastern Persia, traced the origins of the Sufi tradition back to the Prophet Mohammad, while at the same time acknowledging the existence of comparable forms of mysticism before his mission. They mapped out a mystical path by which the Sufi ascends towards the ultimate goal of union with God and knowledge of reality. More than two centuries before the time of the eminent Sufi theosopher Ebn Arabi (d. 1240), Sufis began to describe their experience of annihilation in God and the realization that only God truly exists. The illusion of one's own independent existence began to be regarded as the main obstacle to achieving this realization, so that early Sufis like Abu Yazid Bestami (d. 874) are frequently quoted as belittling the value of the asceticism of some of his contemporaries when it merely increased attention to themselves. An increasing number of Sufis began to regard love of God as the means of overcoming the root problem of one's own sense of being, rather than piety and asceticism.[1]

The Sufi practice that is discussed the most in the early manuals of Sufism is listening to music, commonly referred to as 'musical audition' (sama'). Listening to music, which often accompanied the love poetry and mystical poetry that Sufis themselves had begun to write, while immersed in the remembrance of God and unaware of oneself induced ecstasy in worshippers. The discussions in Sufi manuals of spontaneous movements by Sufis in ecstasy while listening to music and the efforts made to distinguish this from ordinary dance, suggest that already this practice had started to cause a great deal of controversy. Most of the Sufi orders that were eventually formed developed the practice of making such spontaneous movements while listening to music, but the whirling ceremony of the followers of Rumi is a unique phenomenon.[2] Although it is traditionally traced back to Rumi's own propensity for spinning round in ecstasy, the elaborate ceremony in the form in which it has become famous today was established only in the seventeenth century.[3]

The characteristics of the Sufi mystic who has completed the path to enlightenment is one of the recurrent topics in Sufi writings of the tenth and eleventh centuries, but students of Sufism at the time would tend to associate with several such individuals rather than form an exclusive bond with one master. By the twelfth century, however, the master–disciple relationship became increasingly emphasized, as the first Sufi orders began to be formed. It was also during this century that the relationship between love of God and His manifestation in creation became a focus of interest, especially among Sufis of Persian origin, such as Ahmad Ghazali (d. 1126) and Ruzbehan Baqli (d. 1209).[4] The former's more famous brother was

---

[1] Translations of representative samples of the key texts of early Sufism are available in M. Sells, *Early Islamic Mysticism* (Mahwah, 1996).

[2] Concerning the contrast between the Mevlevi *sama'* and other forms of Sufi *sama'*, see J. During, 'What is Sufi Music?' in L. Lewisohn, ed., *The Legacy of Medieval Persian Sufism* (London and New York, 1992), 277–87.

[3] See further C. W. Ernst, *The Shambhala Guide to Sufism* (Boston, 1997), 191–4.

[4] See further C. W. Ernst, tr., *Teachings of Sufism* (Boston, 1999), 82–94 and A. Ghazali, *Sawanih: Inspirations from the World of Pure Spirits*, tr. N. Pourjavady (London, 1986).

responsible for integrating Sufism with mainstream Sunni Islam, as a practical form of Muslim piety that can provide irrefutable knowledge of religious truths through direct mystical experience.[5]

In this way, by the thirteenth century diverse forms of Sufism had developed and become increasingly popular. Rumi was introduced to Sufism through his father, Baha Valad, who followed a more conservative tradition of Muslim piety, but his life was transformed when he encountered the profound mystic Shams-e Tabriz. Although many of the followers of the tradition of his father considered Shams to be totally unworthy of Rumi's time and attention, he considered him to be the most complete manifestation of God. Rumi expressed his love and utter devotion for his master Shams, with whom he spent little more than two years in total, through thousands of ecstatic lyrical poems. Towards the end of his life he presented the fruit of his experience of Sufism in the form of the *Masnavi*, which has been judged by many commentators, both within the Sufi tradition and outside it, to be the greatest mystical poem ever written.

Rumi and his Times

The century in which Rumi lived was one of the most tumultuous in the history of the Middle East and Central Asia. When he was about ten years old the region was invaded by the Mongols, who, under the leadership of Genghis Khan, left death and destruction in their wake. Arriving through Central Asia and north-eastern Persia, the Mongols soon took over almost the entire region, conquering Baghdad in 1258. The collapse at the hands of an infidel army of the once glorious Abbasid caliphate in Baghdad, the symbolic capital of the entire Muslim world, was felt throughout the region as a tremendous shock. Soon afterwards, there was a sign that the map of the region would continue to change, when the Mongols suffered a major defeat in Syria, at Ayn Jalut in 1260. Rumi's life was directly affected by the military and political developments of the time,

---

[5] The chapter of Mohammad Ghazali's autobiography which describes his experience on the Sufi path is available in translation in N. Calder, J. Mojaddedi, and A. Rippin, eds. and trs., *Classical Islam: A Sourcebook of Religious Literature* (London, 2003), 228–32.

beginning with his family's emigration from north-eastern Persia just two years before the Mongols arrived to conquer that region. Although the family eventually relocated to Konya (ancient Iconium) in central Anatolia, Rumi witnessed the spread of Mongol authority across that region too when he was still a young man.

In spite of the upheaval and destruction across the region during this century, there were many outstanding Sufi authors among Rumi's contemporaries. The most important Sufi theosopher ever, Ebn ʿArabi (d. 1240), produced his highly influential works during the first half of the century. His student and foremost interpreter, Sadroddin Qunyavi (d. 1273), settled in Konya some fifteen years after his master's death and became associated with Rumi. This could have been one channel through which Rumi might have gained familiarity with Ebn ʿArabi's theosophical system, although his poetry does not suggest the direct influence of the latter's works.[6]

The lives of two of the most revered Sufi poets also overlapped with Rumi's life: the most celebrated Arab Sufi poet, Ebn al-Farez (d. 1235), whose poetry holds a position of supreme importance comparable with that of Rumi in the Persian canon;[7] and Faridoddin ʿAttar (d. 1220), who was Rumi's direct predecessor in the composition of Persian mystical *masnavi*s (see below), including the highly popular work which has been translated as *The Conference of the Birds* (tr. A. Darbandi and D. Davis, Harmondsworth, 1983). It is perhaps not surprising that the Sufi poet Jami (d. 1492) should want to link Rumi with ʿAttar directly by claiming that they met when Rumi's family migrated from Balkh; ʿAttar is said to have recognized his future successor in the composition of works in the mystical *masnavi* genre although Rumi was then still a young boy. Soon afterwards ʿAttar was killed by the Mongols during their conquest of Nishapur.

As the Mongols advanced westwards, Anatolia became an increasingly attractive destination for the inhabitants of central parts of the Middle East who wished to flee. A number of important Sufis

---

[6] On the relationship between the theosophy of Ebn ʿArabi and the poetry of Rumi, see W. C. Chittick, 'Rumi and *wahdat al-wujud*', in A. Banani, R. Hovannisian, and G. Sabagh, eds., *Poetry and mysticism in Islam: The Heritage of Rumi* (Cambridge, 1994), 70–111.

[7] See further T. Emil Homerin, *From Arab Poet to Muslim Saint: Ibn al-Farid, his Verse, and his Shrine* (Columbia, SC, 1994).

and influential scholars chose this option, including Hajji Bektash (d. *c.*1272), the eponym of the Bektashi order, which became one of the most influential Sufi orders in Anatolia in subsequent centuries, and Najmoddin Razi (d. 1256), whose teacher, Najmoddin Kobra (d. 1221), the eponym of the Kobravi order, had been killed during the Mongol invasion of Transoxiana.

From shortly after his death many works have been written about Rumi's life in Konya, but contradictions in these sources, and the hagiographic nature of most of the material compiled, mean that a number of important details remain uncertain. The recent landmark study by Franklin Lewis, entitled *Rumi, Past and Present, East and West* (Oxford, 2000), has considered this problem at length. By examining the sources critically, Lewis has clarified what precisely can be learned from them and what still cannot be confirmed beyond any doubt. His study is therefore indispensable for any serious academic investigation, and is likely to inspire many revisionist accounts in the future. None the less, the general outline of the life of Rumi seems to be presented relatively consistently in the sources, and remains helpful for putting the *Masnavi* into context.

Rumi was born in September 1207 in the province of Balkh, in what is now the border region between Afghanistan and Tajikistan.[8] His father, Baha Valad, was a preacher and religious scholar who also led a group of Sufi disciples. When Rumi was about 10 years old his family emigrated to Anatolia, having already relocated a few years earlier to Samarkand in Transoxiana. This emigration seems to have been motivated primarily by the approach of Genghis Khan's Mongol army, although rivalries between Baha Valad and various religious scholars in the region may have also played a part. Instead of moving westwards directly, Rumi's family first made the pilgrimage to Mecca, and it was only a few years after arriving in Anatolia that they decided to settle permanently in Konya. By this time, Rumi had already married (1224) and seen the birth of his son and eventual successor in Sufism, Soltan Valad (1226).

In Konya Baha Valad found the opportunity, under the patronage of the Seljuk ruler Alaoddin Kay Qobad I (r. 1219–36), to continue

---

[8] Concerning the precise location of Rumi's birth, see F. D. Lewis, *Rumi, Past and Present, East and West: The Life, Teachings and Poetry of Jalal al-Din Rumi* (Oxford, 2000), 47–8.

his work as a preacher and to teach students in a religious school. He had been grooming Rumi to be his successor, but died only a couple of years after settling in Konya, in 1231. Although the original reasons for his arrival remain unclear, it seems that one of Baha Valad's students, called Borhanoddin Mohaqqeq, arrived in Konya from north-eastern Persia soon afterwards to take over the management of his school. He also took responsibility for overseeing the continuation of Rumi's education and training. Within a few years, Borhanoddin sent Rumi to Aleppo and Damascus to continue his education in the religious sciences. It is possible that during his stay in Damascus he may have heard the lectures of Ebn 'Arabi, who was living there at the time. Rumi returned to Konya in about 1237 as a highly accomplished young scholar, and took over leadership of Baha Valad's school from Borhanoddin.

After his return to Konya Rumi's reputation as an authority on religious matters became firmly established there, and he reached the peak of his career as a scholar, achieving what his father seems to have hoped for him. In November 1244, after seven years of excelling as a highly respected religious teacher, Rumi experienced a challenging encounter that would prove to be the most significant event of his life. As one would expect, an event as important as this has generated many competing accounts.[9] However, most versions at least share the same basic element. According to one popular and relatively simple account, Rumi is asked about his books by an uneducated-looking stranger, and responds by snapping back dismissively, 'They are something that you do not understand!' The books then suddenly catch fire, so Rumi asks the stranger to explain what has happened. His reply is: 'Something you do not understand.'

Rumi was immediately drawn to this mysterious figure, who turned out to be a wandering mystic called Shamsoddin from Tabriz (known popularly as Shams, or Shams-e Tabriz) in north-western Persia. The two began to spend endless hours together in retreat. What was shared by the pair during this time remains a mystery that can only be guessed from the volumes of poetry that it inspired. Even in the *Masnavi*, where Rumi makes painstaking efforts to communicate his teachings as clearly as possible for the benefit of his

---

[9] For translations of all the main descriptions of this meeting, see Lewis, *Rumi*, 154–61.

students, he none the less expresses his unwillingness to disclose anything about his experiences with Shams, despite the persistent requests from his deputy at that time, Hosamoddin Chalabi; Rumi explains that those experiences were beyond the capacity of others to understand: 'Please don't request what you can't tolerate | A blade of straw can't hold a mountain's weight' (v. 140).

What is reported consistently about the period of about a year and a half that Rumi spent with Shams is that it provoked intense jealousy and resentment among his disciples, who also feared that their highly respected master was risking his reputation by mixing with someone so unworthy in their eyes. These disciples eventually drove Shams away, but, on hearing reports of sightings of him in Syria, Rumi sent his own son, Soltan Valad, to ask him to come back. Although Shams did return a year later, in 1247, he soon disappeared forever. According to tradition, Shams was killed by Rumi's disciples after they had seen that driving him away had failed to separate him permanently from their master, but, as Lewis has pointed out, there is little external evidence to substantiate this claim.[10]

The transformation of Rumi as a result of his relationship with Shams cannot be emphasized enough. Although he was already a respected religious authority in Konya and had trained in a tradition of Sufi piety under his father, whom he had even succeeded as master, Rumi was led by Shams to a far loftier level of Sufi mysticism. His poetry, for instance, emphasizes the importance of love to transcend attachments to the world, and dismisses concerns for worldly reputation, literal-mindedness and intellectualism. From dry scholarship and popular piety, Rumi turned his attention to mystical poetry, and he became known for his propensity to fall into an ecstatic trance and spin around in public. It is clear that Rumi recognized Shams as a profound mystic, the like of whom he had never encountered before, and that for him Shams was the most complete manifestation of God. Rumi innovatively named his own collection of *ghazals*, or lyrical poems, as 'The Collection of Shams' (*Divan-e Shams*) rather than as his own collection, and also included Shams's name in place of his own at the end of many of his individual *ghazals*,

[10] See ibid. 185–93.

where by convention the poet would identify himself. This can be seen as Rumi's acknowledgement of the all-important inspiration that Shams had provided for him to write such poetry.[11] Rumi chose a plain, descriptive name for his *Masnavi* (*masnavi* is the name of the rhyming couplet verse form used; see further below), which he started composing some fifteen years after Shams had disappeared, but it does not take long before he digresses in this work to his praise, at the mention of the word *shams*, which means 'sun' in Arabic (vv. 124–42).

After the final disappearance of Shams, Rumi remained in Konya and continued to direct his father's school. However, he chose to appoint as deputy, whose responsibility was to manage many of the affairs of the school in his place, a goldsmith called Salahoddin. Like Shams, he was disliked by many of Rumi's disciples, who considered him uneducated. A colourful story about the first encounter between the two describes Rumi as falling into ecstasy and whirling, on hearing the rhythmic beating of Salahoddin at work in his market stall. After Salahoddin's death in 1258, Rumi appointed Hosamoddin Chalabi in his place. At the time when Hosamoddin had become a disciple of Rumi he was already the head of a local order for the training of young men in chivalry. He had brought with him his own disciples, the wealth of his order, and the expertise he had acquired in running such an institution. However, the most important contribution of Hosamoddin was serving as Rumi's scribe and putting the *Masnavi* into writing as Rumi recited it aloud. Rumi praises Hosamoddin profusely in the introduction to the *Masnavi*, which on occasion he even calls 'the Hosam book', indicating the vital importance of his role for this work.

In addition to Rumi's poetry, three prose works have also survived. They reveal much about aspects of his life that have been neglected by most biographers. The collection of Rumi's letters testifies to his influence among the local political rulers and his efforts to secure positions of importance for his disciples through letters of recommendation. This contradicts the popular image of Rumi withdrawing completely from public life after the disappearance of Shams. His collection of seven sermons attests to the fact that he was highly

---

[11] See further ibid. 329–30.

esteemed by the local Muslim population. It reveals that he delivered
sermons at the main congregational mosque on important occasions,
and that he used such opportunities to give Sufi teachings, albeit
within the rigid constraints of a formal sermon.[12] Rumi's most
important prose work, however, is the written record of his teaching
sessions, which was compiled after his death by his students as sev-
enty-one discourses. This work, called 'In it is what is in it', probably
on account of its diverse and unclassified contents, provides intimate
glimpses of Rumi as a Sufi master. The content of this work is com-
parable with his didactic poem, the *Masnavi*, in that it contains many
of the same teachings. A reference to a specific verse in the second
book of the *Masnavi* confirms that the discourses represent Rumi's
teaching activity towards the end of his life.[13] However, a relatively
long time-span seems to be represented in this work, for another of
its component discourses refers to the opposition faced by Salahoddin
when he was serving as Rumi's deputy.[14]

Rumi died on 17 December 1273, probably very soon after the
completion of the *Masnavi*. Tradition tells us that physicians could
not identify the illness from which he was suffering, and that they
suspected he had decided to embrace his physical death, fulfilling
sentiments often expressed in his poetry. His death was mourned not
only by his disciples but also by the large and diverse community in
Konya, including Christians and Jews, who converged as his body
was carried through the city. Many of the non-Muslims had not only
admired him as outsiders, but had also attended his teaching ses-
sions. The 'Green Dome', where his mausoleum is found today, was
constructed soon after Rumi's death. It has become probably the
most popular site of pilgrimage in the world to be visited regularly
by members of every major religion.

Hosamoddin Chalabi served as the leader of Rumi's school for the
first twelve years after Rumi's death, and was succeeded by Soltan
Valad. Rumi's disciples named their school 'the Mevlevi order'
after him, for they used to refer to him by the title 'Mevlana' (in
Arabic *Mawlana*, meaning Our Master). It became widespread and

[12] One of Rumi's sermons is provided in translation in Lewis, *Rumi*, 130–3.
[13] Rumi, *Signs of the Unseen: The Discourses of Jalaluddin Rumi*, tr. W. Thackston, Jr.
(Boston, 1999), 205.
[14] Ibid. 99–101.

influential, especially under the Ottoman empire, and remains an active Sufi order in Turkey as well as many other countries across the world. The Mevlevis are better known in the West as the Whirling Dervishes because of the distinctive dance that they perform to music as the central ritual of the order.

The Masnavi

Rumi's *Masnavi* holds an exalted status in the rich canon of Persian Sufi literature as the greatest mystical poem ever written. It is even referred to commonly as 'the Koran in Persian'. As already mentioned, the title Rumi himself chose for it is simply the name of the form of poetry adopted for it, the *masnavi* form. Each half-line, or hemistich, of a *masnavi* poem follows the same metre, in common with other forms of classical Persian poetry. The metre of Rumi's *Masnavi* is the *ramal* metre in apocopated form (-◡--/-◡--/-◡-/), a highly popular metre which was used also by ʿAttar for his *Conference of the Birds*. What distinguishes the *masnavi* form from other Persian verse forms is the internal rhyme, which changes in successive couplets according to the pattern *aa bb cc dd* etc. Thus, in contrast to the other verse forms, which require a restrictive monorhyme, the *masnavi* form enables poets to compose long works consisting of thousands of verses. Rumi's *Masnavi* amounts to about 26,000 verses altogether.

The *masnavi* form satisfied the need felt by Persians to compose narrative and didactic poems, of which there was already before the Islamic period a long and rich tradition. By Rumi's time a number of Sufis had already made use of the *masnavi* form to compose mystical poems, the most celebrated among which are Sanaʾi's (d. 1138) *Hadiqatoʾl-haqiqat*, or *Garden of Truth*, and Faridoddin ʿAttar's (d. 1220) *Manteqoʾt-tayr*, or *Conference of the Birds*.[15] According to tradition, it was the popularity of these works amongst Rumi's disciples that prompted Hosamoddin, Rumi's deputy, to ask him to compose his own mystical *masnavi* for their benefit.

Hosamoddin served as Rumi's scribe in a process of text-production that is described as being similar to the way in which the Koran was produced. However, while the Sufi poet Rumi recited the

[15] See e.g. F. Attar, *The Conference of the Birds*, ed. and tr. A. Darbandi and D. Davis (Harmondsworth, 1983).

Masnavi orally when he felt inspired to do so, with Hosamoddin always ready to record those recitations in writing for him as well as to assist him in revising and editing the final poem, the illiterate Prophet Mohammad is said to have recited aloud divine revelation in piecemeal fashion, in exactly the form that God's words were revealed to him through the Archangel Gabriel; those companions of the Prophet who were present at such occasions would write down the revelations and memorize them, and these written and mental records eventually formed the basis of the compilation of the Koran many years after his death.

The process of producing the *Masnavi* was started probably around 1262, although tradition relates that Rumi had already composed the first eighteen couplets by the time Hosamoddin made his request; we are told that he responded by pulling a sheet of paper out of his turban with the first part of the prologue, often called 'The Song of the Reed' (see below), already written on it. References to their system of production can be found in the text of the *Masnavi* itself (e.g. v. 2947). They seem to have worked on the *Masnavi* during the evenings in particular, and in one instance Rumi begs forgiveness for having kept Hosamoddin up for an entire night with it (v. 1817). After Hosamoddin had written down Rumi's recitations, they were read back to him to be checked and corrected.

The crucial role played by Hosamoddin as Rumi's assistant in this process, as well as an inspiration, is highlighted not only by the fact that Rumi refers to the *Masnavi* on occasion as 'the Hosam book', but also by the fact that its production was halted completely after Book One was finished because of the death of Hosamoddin's wife, as indicated at the beginning of Book Two. The devastated Hosamoddin spent almost a year, between 1263 and 1264, mourning his deep loss before they could resume their work. However, the hyperbolic praise that Rumi lavishes on Hosamoddin in the prose introduction to Book One, the very start of the *Masnavi* (pp. 3–4), should be understood as a token of his generosity in extolling the virtues of his deputy, rather than at face value.

Rumi's *Masnavi* belongs to the group of works written in this verse form that do not have a frame narrative. In this way, it contrasts with the more cohesively structured *Conference of the Birds*, which is already well known in translation. It is also much longer; the

Conference is roughly the same length as just one of the six component books of the *Masnavi*. Each of the six books consists of about 4,000 verses and has its own prose introduction and prologue. There are, however, no epilogues, and the fact that the sixth volume ends somewhat inconclusively has prompted suggestions that the work may never have been completed, as well as claims that there was a seventh volume. Book One stands apart from the rest, because of the pause for approximately a year before work was started on Book Two.

The component narratives, homilies, and commentaries on citations which make up the body of the *Masnavi* are signalled by their own separate headings. The text of longer narratives tends to be broken up into sections by further headings. Sometimes the headings are positioned inappropriately, such as in the middle of continuous speech (e.g. vv. 348–9), revealing that they were inserted only after the text had been prepared and therefore do not represent some form of organizational framework. The tendency for the given headings to refer only to the immediate start of the subsequent passage of text suggests that they were designed to serve primarily as markers for the benefit of reciters. However, occasionally the headings are actually longer than the passage that they represent (e.g. vv. 2813–16), and serve to explain and contextualize what follows. It is as if, on rereading the text, further explanation was felt necessary in the form of an expanded heading.

The diversity of the contents of Book One of the *Masnavi* is representative of the work as a whole. It includes stories with characters ranging from prophets and kings to beggars and tramps, as well as animals. The citations which receive commentary are taken primarily from the Koran, the traditions of the Prophet (*hadith*), and the works of Rumi's precursors in Sufism. The homilies cover, in addition to specifically Sufi issues, general ethical concerns based on traditional wisdom. Rumi drew on his knowledge of a vast range of both oral and literary sources in the composition of his work,[16] as well as his familiarity with a wide range of disciplines, including theology, philosophy, the exegesis of the Koran and *hadith*, philology, literature,

---

[16] Since most of the literary sources drawn upon for Book One are unavailable in English, references have been provided only to the Koran and to those *hadith* that have been translated in Nicholson's commentary. A useful list of the sources for the main stories of Book One is provided in Lewis, *Rumi*, 288–91.

jurisprudence, and medicine. Most of his stories are very humorous at least in parts, and he does not hesitate to use whatever may convey his point in as memorable a way as possible to his contemporaries, including jokes about sexuality and ethnic and gender stereotypes.

The arrangement of material in Book One, as in the *Masnavi* as a whole, does not suggest the use of a plan or a single principle of order. Rather, juxtaposed material is associated by virtue of a common theme, a key word, or an association between the characters of narratives. Moreover, these associations tend to be between the very final part of one section and the very beginning of the next one, reinforcing the traditional view that Rumi produced the *Masnavi* extemporaneously. This could also account for Rumi's propensity to explain and illustrate specific details of a passage, even at the cost of breaking off in the course of a narrative, to resume it only after the explanations (and any other material that they may have generated) have been completed. This tendency has made parts of the *Masnavi* multi-layered (as indicated by means of indentation in the Contents of this translation).

The frequency of breaks in the flow of narratives in the *Masnavi* reveals that, although Rumi has earned a reputation as an excellent storyteller, none the less his primary concern was to convey his teachings as effectively as possible to his Sufi disciples. The *Masnavi* leaves the impression that he was brimming with ideas and symbolic images which would overflow when prompted by the subtlest of associations. In this way, free from the constraints of a frame narrative or a strict principle of order, Rumi has been able to produce a work that is far richer in content than any other example of the mystical *masnavi* genre. That this has been achieved often at the expense of preserving continuity in the narratives seems to corroborate Rumi's opinion on the relative importance of the content of his poetry over its form, as reported in his discourses.[17] If it were not for the fact that his digressive 'overflowings' are expressed in simple

---

[17] In a famous passage among Rumi's discourses, he is reported to have compared writing poetry with serving to a guest something which one finds unpleasant like tripe, because that is what the guest wants (Rumi, *Signs of the Unseen*, 77–8). The main theme of the sixteenth discourse (pp. 74–80), in which this passage is found, is the relationship between form and content, and it includes Rumi's response to the charge that he is 'all talk and no action' (p. 78). The statement should therefore be understood in its proper context, rather than as evidence that Rumi disliked the art of writing poetry.

language and with imagery that was immediately accessible to his contemporary readers, they would have constituted an undesirable impediment to understanding the poem. Where this leads Rumi to interweave narratives and to alternate between different speakers and his own commentaries, the text can still be difficult to follow, and, for most contemporary readers, the relevance of citations and allusions to the Koran and the traditions of the Prophet will not be immediately obvious without reference to the explanatory notes that have been provided in this edition. None the less, it should be evident, not least from the lengthy sequences of analogies that Rumi often provides to reinforce a single point, that he has striven to communicate his message as effectively as possible rather than to write obscurely and force the reader to struggle to understand him.

By far the best-known passage in the entire *Masnavi* is the prologue of Book One, where one finds what is often called 'The Song of the Reed'. Dick Davis has pointed out that the form this prologue takes is highly innovative; in preference to following the established convention of beginning mystical *masnavi* poems with an invocation of the Transcendent and Omnipotent Creator and His Prophet, Rumi chooses to focus on the humble reed-flute, and addresses the reader in the second person, with 'Listen!' (v. 1).[18] These initial eighteen verses have been thought by many to contain the essential message of the entire work.[19] There is some validity to this point, since the *Masnavi* is a poem that repeats in a kaleidoscope of different ways and with ever-increasing nuances the same message about the human condition and the means of recognizing this reality and achieving fulfilment through Sufi mysticism.

The reed that mourns having been cut from the reed-bed may be understood as a symbol representing the mystic who feels inwardly a strong sense of separation from his origin with God, and yearns to return to that state. Love is the force that intensifies this yearning in the mystic (v. 10), increasing his perception of reality, from which he has become veiled through his attachment to the world of phenomenal existence. Rumi further illustrates the power of this divine love

[18] See D. Davis, 'Narrative and Doctrine in the First Story of Rumi's *Mathnawi*', in G. R. Hawting, J. A. Mojaddedi, and A. Samely, *Studies in Islamic and Middle Eastern Texts and Traditions in Memory of Norman Calder* (Oxford, 2000), 93–6.

[19] See e.g. E. Turkmen, *The Essence of the Masnevi* (Konya, 1992).

as an all-consuming force, with reference to the crushing of Mount Sinai before Moses's eyes, making him fall in a swoon (v. 26). Through divine love, the lover is effaced and only God, the beloved, lives on (v. 30). Rumi often describes Man's relationship with God by using the scholastic language of Islamic theology and philosophy. God is described as Absolute Being, while humans are non-beings who merely imagine that they have their own independent existence. They are urged to recognize their non-existence and to strive to become effaced in God, in order to truly exist through Him.

Another well-known story in the *Masnavi* is the brief and simple tale in Book One about the lover who knocks on the door of his beloved's house (vv. 3069–76). When she asks 'Who's there?' he answers, 'It is I!' and is consequently turned away. Only after being 'cooked by separation's flame' (v. 3071) does he learn from his mistake and perceive the reality of the situation. He returns to knock on her door, and this time, on being asked, 'Who's there?' he answers, 'It is you', and is admitted to where two I's cannot be accommodated. This story is found among a cluster of passages which illustrate effacement in God. In the preceding story, a fox learns not to think about himself but only for his king, the lion, when dividing up what they had caught while hunting, while in the subsequent story Joseph's visitor can think of nothing better to present to him as a gift than a mirror in which he can admire his own beauty. The mirror is in fact one of Rumi's favourite images for the soul; it is tarnished by the rust of attachment to phenomenal existence, which must be scraped away by the breaking of those attachments, through discipline under the guidance of a Sufi master. Only once it has become completely clear can it become receptive to the light of God and contain nothing but His reflection.

The very first story of the *Masnavi* appropriately expands on the message of the prologue that immediately precedes it, by its differentiation of contrasting kinds of love. In order to cure his sick slave-girl, the prayers of a devout king are answered with the arrival of a divine healer. On discovering that she is lovesick, the healer reunites her with her sweetheart, but after they are married he poisons her husband so that she can slowly observe him rotting away in front of her and losing his former good looks. In this way, all the love she once had for him leaves her heart. The powerful force of divine love thus takes effect through the holy healer who cures the slave-girl by murdering her lover with poison. Rumi makes it clear through this harsh lesson that the love discussed in the prologue as an annihilating force is divine love, by contrasting it with the fickle love of a pair of superficial lovers.

Just as Rumi recognized that his frequent high praise of love could be misinterpreted, he saw the same risk in his expression of the experience of witnessing God in all of creation. While this is possible for an experienced mystic like himself, the novice is more in danger of loving creation for its own sake and thereby becoming increasingly veiled from reality through such attachments (see e.g. vv. 2813–16). God is made manifest most clearly to them through mediating figures such as prophets and Sufi masters, or saints, who fulfil the same specific role of leading human beings back to Him.

The overriding importance of the Sufi master for Rumi's understanding of Sufism is evident in the fact that he is represented by a character in at least nine of the dozen or so major narratives in Book One, while his role and characteristics are frequently discussed in homilies and commentaries on citations. This figure is perhaps represented most clearly by the divine healer in the first story. In other stories, he is represented by religious and political leaders, such as prophets, saints, and caliphs, as well as by animals. Among the many homilies about this figure there is a lengthy one urging the reader to choose a Sufi master as guide and follow him wholeheartedly and unconditionally (vv. 2947–93), as well as many further passages explaining specific characteristics of such a master. The fact that Rumi also includes a section on impostors who claim to be Sufi masters (vv. 2275–98) only underlines further the importance for him of the genuine mediator figure, a fact which comes as no surprise in view of his own transformation to a Sufi mystic through his devotion to Shams-e Tabriz.

Rumi made painstaking efforts to convey his teachings as clearly and effectively as possible, using simple language, the *masnavi* verse form, entertaining stories, and the most vivid and accessible imagery possible. The aim of the present translation is to render Rumi's *Masnavi* into a relatively simple and attractive form which, with the benefit of metre and rhyme, may enable as many readers as possible to read the whole book with pleasure and to find it rewarding.

NOTE ON THE TRANSLATION

Rumi put his teachings into the *masnavi* verse form in order that, with the benefit of metre and rhyme, his disciples might enjoy reading them. I have therefore decided to translate Rumi's *Masnavi* into verse, in accordance with the aim of the original work. I have chosen to use rhyming iambic pentameters, since this is the closest corresponding form of English verse to the Persian *masnavi* form of rhyming couplets. These are numbered and referred to as verses in the Explanatory Notes and Introduction.

Book One of the *Masnavi* consists of some 4,000 couplets, the continuity of which is broken up only by section headings. For the sake of clarity, in this translation further breaks have been added to those created by the section headings. In order for the Contents to fulfil its function effectively, alternative headings have been employed there, albeit at corresponding points to the major section headings in the text, which were designed principally as markers for reciters and therefore refer in many instances to merely the first few subsequent verses rather than representing the section as a whole.

Although the *Masnavi* is a Persian poem, it contains a substantial amount of Arabic text. This invariably takes the form of citations from Arabic sources and common religious formulas. It also includes the entire prose introduction. Italics have been used to indicate Arabic text, except in the section headings, which are fully italicized. Many Arabic terms and religious formulas have become part of the Persian language, and have therefore not been highlighted in this way. Capitalization has been used when reference is made to God. This includes, in addition to the pronouns and titles commonly used in English, the ninety-nine names of God of the Islamic tradition, as well as certain philosophical terms.

Most of the sources of the *Masnavi* are not widely available in English, if at all, and so references have been provided in the notes only for citations of the Koran. Verse numbering varies in the most widely available translations of the Koran, some of which do not in fact number individual verses, but since this variation is very slight (maximum of a few verses) the reader should still be able to find the relevant passages without difficulty. The notes also identify those passages in the translation which represent the sayings and deeds of the Prophet Mohammad (*hadith*) without this being made self-evident in the text (e.g. by 'the Prophet said'). It should be pointed out that citations in the original *Masnavi* are very often variants of the original sources, including the Koran, rather than exact renderings, due to the constraints of the metre that is used. The same applies in this verse translation.

This translation corresponds exactly to the text of the first volume of the edition prepared by Mohammad Estelami (6 volumes and index, Tehran, 2nd edn., 1990). This is by far the best critical edition that has been prepared, since it offers a complete apparatus criticus, indicating the variant readings in all the early manuscripts more comprehensively and transparently than any other edition. Although R. A. Nicholson's edition of the text is more widely available, because it is published in Europe, its shortcomings for today are widely recognized and outweigh the advantage of having his exactly corresponding prose translation and commentary to refer to.

As far as possible, the English equivalents of technical terms have been provided, in preference to giving the original in transliteration and relying on explanatory notes. Where it is provided, the transliteration of names and terms has been simplified to such a degree that no diacritics are used. It is designed simply to help the reader use Persian pronunciation, especially where this would affect the metre and rhyme.

SELECT BIBLIOGRAPHY

General Background

J. T. P. De Bruijn, *Persian Sufi Poetry: An Introduction to the Mystical Use of Classical Poems* (Richmond, 1997).

C. W. Ernst, *The Shambhala Guide to Sufism* (Boston, 1997).

C. W. Ernst, tr., *Teachings of Sufism* (Boston, 1999).

L. Lewisohn, ed., *Classical Persian Sufism: From its Origins to Rumi* (London and New York, 1993).

J. Nurbakhsh, *The Path: Sufi Practices* (London and New York, 2002).

A. Rippin, *Muslims: Their Religious Beliefs and Practices*, 2nd edn. (London and New York, 2001).

M. Sells, ed. and tr., *Early Islamic Mysticism* (Mahwah, 1996).

Reference

Encyclopaedia Iranica, ed. E. Yarshater (New York, 1985– ; in progress; also available online at www.iranica.com).

Encyclopaedia of Islam, ed. H. A. R. Gibb *et al.* (Leiden, 1960–2003).

J. Nurbakhsh, *Sufi Symbolism*, 16 vols. (London and New York, 1980–2003).

On Rumi

W. C. Chittick, ed., *The Sufi Path of Love: The Spiritual Teachings of Rumi* (Albany, NY, 1983).

F. Keshavarz, *Reading Mystical Lyric: The Case of Jalal al-Din Rumi* (Columbia, SC, 1998).

F. D. Lewis, *Rumi, Past and Present, East and West: The Life, Teachings and Poetry of Jalal al-Din Rumi* (Oxford, 2000).

Rumi, *Mystical Poems of Rumi*, 1 and 2, tr. A. J. Arberry (New York, 1979).

Rumi, *Signs of the Unseen*, tr. W. M. Thackston (Boston, 1994).

A. Schimmel, *The Triumphal Sun* (London, 1978).

Editions of the Masnavi

Masnavi, ed. M. Estelami, 7 vols., 2nd edn. (Tehran, 1990). The seventh volume is a volume of indices. Each of the six volumes of text contains the editor's commentary in the form of endnotes.

The Mathnawi of Jalalu'ddin Rumi, ed. and tr. R. A. Nicholson, E. J. W.

Gibb Memorial, NS, 8 vols. (London, 1925–40). This set consists of the Persian text (vols. 1–3), a full translation in prose (vols. 4–6) and commentary (vols. 7–8).

Masnavi, ed. T. Sobhani (Tehran, 1994).

Masnavi-ye maʾnavi, ed. A.-K. Sorush, 2 vols. (Tehran, 1996).

Interpretation of the Masnavi

W. C. Chittick, 'Rumi and *wahdat al-wujud*,' in A. Banani, R. Hovannisian, and G. Sabagh, eds., *Poetry and Mysticism in Islam: The Heritage of Rumi* (Cambridge, 1994), 70–111.

H. Dabashi, 'Rumi and the Problems of Theodicy: Moral Imagination and Narrative Discourse in a Story of the *Masnavi*', in A. Banani, R. Hovannisian, and G. Sabagh, eds., *Poetry and Mysticism in Islam: The Heritage of Rumi* (Cambridge, 1994), 112–35.

R. Davis, 'Narrative and Doctrine in the First Story of Rumi's *Mathnawi*', in G. R. Hawting, J. A. Mojaddedi, and A. Samely, eds., *Studies in Islamic and Middle Eastern Texts and Traditions in Memory of Norman Calder* (Oxford, 2000), 93–104.

M. Mills, 'Folk Tradition in the *Masnavi* and the *Masnavi* in Folk Tradition', in A. Banani, R. Hovannisian, and G. Sabagh, eds., *Poetry and Mysticism in Islam: The Heritage of Rumi* (Cambridge, 1994), 136–77.

P. Morewedge, 'A Philosophical Interpretation of Rumi's Mystical Poetry: Light, the Mediator and the Way', in P. J. Chelkowski, ed., *The Scholar and the Saint* (New York, 1975), 187–216.

J. Renard, *All the King's Falcons: Rumi on Prophets and Revelation* (Albany, NY, 1994).

E. Turkmen, *The Essence of the Masnevi* (Konya, 1992).

Further Reading in Oxford World's Classics

The Arabian Nights' Entertainments, ed. Robert Mack.

The Koran, translated and edited by Arthur J. Arberry.

The Qurʾan, translated and edited by M. A. S. Abdel Haleem.

A CHRONOLOGY OF RUMI

1207	Rumi is born in Balkh, north-eastern Persia
c.1216	Rumi's family emigrate from Persia
1219	Alaoddin Kay Qobad ascends Seljuk throne in Anatolia
1220	Death of Faridoddin Attar
1221	The Mongol army conquers Balkh
c.1222	Rumi's family settle temporarily in Karaman, Anatolia
1224	Rumi marries Gowhar Khatun
1226	Birth of Soltan Valad
c.1229	Rumi's family relocate to Konya
1231	Death of Baha Valad
1232	Borhanoddin Termezi arrives in Konya
c.1233	Rumi begins his studies in Syria
1235	Death of Ebn al-Farez in Egypt
1237	Rumi returns to Konya as leader of Baha Valad's school
	Ghiyasoddin Kay Khosrow II ascends Seljuk throne in Anatolia
1240	Death of Ebn Arabi in Damascus
1243	The Mongols extend their empire to Anatolia
1244	Rumi meets Shams-e Tabriz in Konya for the first time
1246	Shams leaves Konya
1247	Shams returns to Konya
c.1247–8	Shams disappears
	Salahoddin the Goldsmith begins tenure as Rumi's deputy
1258	Death of Salahoddin
	Hosamoddin Chalabi begins tenure as Rumi's deputy
	The Mongols conquer Baghdad, the Abbasid capital
1260	The Mongols are defeated in Syria by the Mamluks
c.1262	*The Masnavi* is started
c.1264	*The Masnavi* is resumed after a pause on account of the death of Hosamoddin's wife
1273	(17 December) Death of Rumi in Konya

THE MASNAVI

BOOK ONE

Prose Introduction

This is the Masnavi, the roots of the main tenets of theology regarding the unveiling of the secrets of certain knowledge and union. It is the greatest creed and the most luminous of holy laws, as well as the most manifest of proofs of God—His light is like a niche in which there is a lamp* that shines more brightly than the dawn. This book's the paradise of hearts with boughs and springs, one known as Salsabil* by travellers on this path; to those with mystic stations who know miracles it is the very best of stations and of resting places.* The godly here both eat and drink; the free feel joy and mirth through it. It is, like Egypt's Nile, a wine for patient worshippers, but an affliction for all Pharaoh's people and those who don't believe—as He has said: Many He leads astray by it, while many others God will guide with it.* It is the cure for breasts, the purge of sorrows, the Koran's unveiler, and a vast profusion of Man's sustenance and purest qualities. And it was written by the hands of noble, pious scribes,* who in this way ordain that none shall touch it but the purified, a revelation from the Lord of both the worlds!* Falsehood does not approach it from the front or from behind;* God watches it and oversees it too: He is the best of guards and the most merciful of all.* And it has other titles given to it by the Lord. We've just provided this brief summary—a token which points to much more: a mouthful tells of a whole pool, a handful indicates a threshing-floor of wheat.

This slave in need of mercy from the Lord, Mohammad Ebn Mohammad Ebn Hosayn from Balkh, may God accept him, says: I've striven in composing this long work of rhyming couplets which comprises wonders, rarities, enlightened sayings, pearls of guidance, the path of the ascetics, and the garden of the pietists—concise in form but rich in terms of meaning—to answer the request of my chief and support, the location of the spirit in my body and my provision for today and for tomorrow, chief and exemplar for the mystics, leader to certainty and guidance, helper of mankind, trustee of hearts and intellects, who was established by the Lord among His creatures, His choice among created beings, the aim of the injunctions given to the Prophet and the secrets shared with just His chosen one, the key to all the treasures of the empyrean, trustee of treasures in this world too: that's Abu'l-Faza'el

Hosamo'l-Haqq-wa'ddin, named Hasan Ebn Mohammad Ebn Hasan Akhi Tork, the Abu Yazid of his time, Jonayd of this age, veracious like his father and his grandfather, may God be pleased with him and them.* Originating from Orumiya, from the lineage of that noble shaikh who said, 'Last night I was a Kurd, but now I've woken up an Arab!'* God bless his soul and those of his successors too. How blest the ancestor as well as the successor!

His is a lineage on which the sun has cast its mantle and before which stars have shone down their bright beams. Their courtyard has not ceased to be the qebla* of good fortune, towards which sons of saints all face—hope's Kaaba which is circumambulated by those whose aim is the obliterated ones. May it not cease to serve this way, so long as one star rises and the sun appears on the horizon, as a refuge for those with insight, the divine, the holy and the spiritual, enlightened and celestial ones—the silent observers, absent and present ones;* the kings in rags, the notables of all the races, those with many virtues, the guiding lights.

Amen, Lord of the worlds! This is a prayer that will not be turned down, for it's a prayer for every kind of creature. Praise be to God, who is One, and blessings on our chief Mohammad and his family. God suffices for us; He is a generous protector.

Exordium: the song of the reed

Now listen to this reed-flute's deep lament
　　About the heartache being apart has meant:
'Since from the reed-bed they uprooted me
　　My song's expressed each human's agony,
A breast which separation's split in two
　　Is what I seek, to share this pain with you:
When kept from their true origin, all yearn
　　For union on the day they can return.
Amongst the crowd, alone I mourn my fate,　　　　5
　　With good and bad I've learnt to integrate,
That we were friends each one was satisfied
　　But none sought out my secrets from inside;
My deepest secret's in this song I wail
　　But eyes and ears can't penetrate the veil:

Body and soul are joined to form one whole
    But no one is allowed to see the soul.'
It's fire not just hot air the reed-flute's cry,
    If you don't have this fire then you should die!*
Love's fire is what makes every reed-flute pine,   10
    Love's fervour thus lends potency to wine;
The reed consoles those forced to be apart,
    Its notes will lift the veil upon your heart,
Where's antidote or poison like its song,
    Or confidant, or one who's pined so long?
This reed relates a tortuous path ahead,
    Recalls the love with which Majnun's heart bled:
The few who hear the truths the reed has sung
    Have lost their wits so they can speak this tongue.
The day is wasted if it's spent in grief,   15
    Consumed by burning aches without relief—
Good times have long passed, but we couldn't care
    When you're with us, our friend beyond compare!
While ordinary men on drops can thrive
    A fish needs oceans daily to survive:
The way the ripe must feel the raw can't tell,
    My speech must be concise, and so farewell!

Unchain yourself, my son, escape its hold!
    How long will you remain a slave of gold?
You've tried to fit inside a jug the sea—   20
    It only has a day's capacity:
A greedy eye is never satisfied,
    Shells only when content grow pearls inside,
While men whose clothes are ripped to shreds by love
    Are cleansed of greed like this to rise above.
Be joyful, love, our sweetest bliss is you,
    Physician for all kinds of ailments too,
The cure for our conceit and stubborn pride
    Like Plato here with Galen,* side by side;
Through love the earthly form soars heavenward,   25
    The mountain dances nimbly like a bird:

Love made Mount Sinai drunken visibly,
 So *Moses fell and swooned** immediately!
With my own confidant if I'd been paired,
 Just like the reed, such stories I'd have shared:
Without a kindred spirit there to hear
 The storyteller's voice must disappear,
And if the rose should vanish from its sight
 The nightingale* will keep its beak shut tight—
The loved one's all, the lover's just a screen,   30
 A dead thing, while the loved one lives, unseen.
When shunned by love you're left with emptiness,
 A bird without its wings knows such distress:
'How can my mind stay calm this lonely night
 When I can't find here my beloved's light?'
Love wants its tale revealed to everyone,
 But your heart's mirror won't reflect this sun,
Don't you know why we can't perceive it here?
 Your mirror's face is rusty—scrape it clear!

How a king fell in love with a sick slave-girl and tried to cure her

Now here's a tale for you to contemplate,   35
 It tells the truth about our present state:
There was a king, most glorious and refined,
 With spiritual and temporal power combined;
Once he was riding on his favourite steed
 Out hunting with his friends, whom he would lead,
When he beheld a slave-girl near the fray—
 His soul became her servant straight away!
His old heart fluttered like a caged young bird,
 He met the asking-price without a word,
But just when he had signed and sealed this trade   40
 By fate an illness overcame the maid:
Like buying saddles for your mule one day
 To find that wolves have chased it far away!

Or fetching water with your finest pot
 For it to smash, as if there's been a plot!
The king brought healers from all distant lands:
 'Our lives are both now in your expert hands,
My life is over till she's well again,
 For she's my medicine, distinguished men;
Light of my life, whoever makes her well 45
 More treasure wins than he could ever sell.'
As one they said, 'Our lives we'll sacrifice,
 We will confer and seek from all advice,
We're the messiahs for the world's distress,
 A salve for every wound we each possess.'
They skipped 'If God wills' through their arrogance
 So God revealed through them Man's impotence:
I mean omission from inside one's heart
 Not just the utterance—that's the lesser part—
Many have failed to say, 'If God should will,' 50
 Although their souls were in accordance still.
The more these men produced a salve or cure
 The more distress the girl seemed to endure:
That girl became much thinner than a hair,
 The king wept tears of blood in his despair,
The drugs they gave her made her feel more ill
 And almond oil just made her drier still,
Fruit made her constipation even worse,
 Water increased the flames, as if a curse.

The inability of the healers to cure the slave-girl becomes
apparent, and so the king turns to God at the mosque,
where he subsequently dreams about a saint

After he watched them fail each single day 55
 The king ran barefoot to the mosque to pray,
Confessing at the prayer-niche all his fears
 He drenched the rug beneath him with his tears;
When from annihilation's trance he woke
 With prayers the Lord he started to invoke:

'O you whose smallest gift is the whole world,
    Words can't describe this mystery you've unfurled!
Our refuge when we find ourselves in need,
    Once more we've strayed by failing to take heed;
You did say, "Though I know your secrets well   60
    It doesn't mean I don't want you to tell!"'
When from his inmost depths he raised a scream,
    The sea of bounty surged and sent a dream:
In tears, the king was overcome with sleep,
    An old man then appeared whose voice was deep:
'Greetings, your wish is granted, humble king,
    Tomorrow to your aid our man we'll bring,
Trust him, as one who's mastered how to cure,
    Accept his word for he's sincere and pure,
Witness amazing magic and applaud,   65
    See in his temperament the might of God.'

The next day came, the promised meeting neared,
    The sun shone bright, the stars had disappeared,
The king gazed from the watchtower eagerly
    To see what had been promised secretly,
Beyond the crowd he saw a virtuous one,
    Among the shadows he was like a sun!
Just like a crescent moon he came to view—
    A non-existent image seen by you,
In form existing only in one's mind—   70
    The world is turned by forces of this kind:
Their war and peace are based on fantasy,
    And shame and pride are both illusory,
While images that saints may often love
    Are visions of the moon-faced ones above;*
The image which while dreaming he'd just seen
    The king saw in him just as it had been,
And so, instead of chamberlains he went
    Himself to greet this guest who had been sent.
Both swimmers used to seas of union,   75
    Their souls without a thread were sewn as one:

'The one I love is not that maid but you;
   One thing led to another, as they do,
You're Mostafa and I'm Omar your friend,*
   Prepared to serve you till the bitter end!'

*From God, who grants success, we ask for success in
maintaining good manners always; explanation of the
harm in being ill-mannered*

Let's pray to God for manners in their place
   Since those who lack them lose out on his grace,
It's not as though it's just themselves they harm,
   They set the world on fire, disrupt the calm:
A feast was sent down from above one day   80
   Without demands or any price to pay,
Moses had men who still bemoaned their lot,
   'Why weren't some lentils spiced with garlic brought?'
The host then cleared the feast that had been laid
   And each was forced to farm with scythe and spade;
Jesus once interceded for a man,
   A bounteous feast was sent down in God's plan,
But then some greedy brats who lacked respect
   Like beggars grabbed the most they could collect,
Even though Jesus cried, 'It's infinite,   85
   You greedy fools, you'll not run out of it!'*
Regard this lust and faithless attitude
   Before God's feast as sheer ingratitude:
When blinded by their greed these low ingrates
   Cause God to shut to all his mercy's gates:
If you withhold *zakat*,* then rain won't fall
   And fornication spreads a plague to all,
So what's the source of your deep misery?
   Acting without respect conceitedly!
Whoever fails to show respect to God   90
   For robbing other men deserves the rod!
Good manners are what made the heavens bright
   And angels sinless, purer than the light,

Irreverence caused eclipses of the sun
    And Satan, through his pride, to be undone.

The meeting of the king with that saint who had
appeared in his dream

The king embraced his guest and wouldn't part,
    He welcomed him like love inside his heart;
Kissing his hand and forehead fervently
    He asked about his home and family
Then led him to his dais with this thought: 95
    'The greatest treasure patience here has brought!
The light of God, defence against all harm,
    Showed *patience is the key to joy and calm*:
The answer to our needs is meeting you,
    All faults you fix before we ask you to,
Translating what we keep inside our souls,
    Stretching your hand to lift those trapped in holes.
O chosen one with whom God's pleased, *don't leave,*
    For then you'd make us suffocate and grieve!
Since you're our master, he who shows disdain   100
    Will be destroyed if he does not refrain.'*
They served the feast, the king then took his hand
    And led him to the harem as was planned,

The king leads that doctor to the patient so he can see how she is

Recounting all the sick girl had been through,
    He sat him down so he could witness too;
Her pulse and pale complexion first he checked,
    Discovering the cause through its effect.
The drugs that they'd prescribed were like a curse,
    Sapping her strength and making her feel worse:
They'd failed to see the ailment deep within—   105
    God save us from what they are dabbling in!
He saw her pain, her secret was revealed,
    But from the king he kept it all concealed,

Her pain was not from bile the doctor learned:
    The scent of wood is from its smoke discerned;
Her grief revealed that it was from her heart—
    Physically fine, her heart was torn apart:

Being a lover means your heart must ache,
    No sickness hurts as much as when hearts break,
The lover's ailment's totally unique,   110
    Love is the astrolabe of all we seek,
Whether you feel divine or earthly love,
    Ultimately we're destined for above.
To capture love whatever words I say
    Make me ashamed when love arrives my way,
While explanation sometimes makes things clear
    True love through silence only one can hear:
The pen would smoothly write the things it knew
    But when it came to love it split in two,
A donkey stuck in mud is logic's fate—   115
    Love's nature only love can demonstrate:
Sunshine reveals its nature in each ray,
    So if it's proof you want just look this way!
Shadows can indicate what's shining bright
    But it's the sun which fills your soul with light,
Shadows like late-night chat make people doze,
    *The moon was split** when that divine sun rose!
Eternal sun—there's nothing quite so strange,
    The soul's sun has no past, it doesn't change,
There's only one sun there before your eyes   120
    But similar suns you still can visualize,
The soul's sun though is from a loftier sphere,
    You'll not find any similar suns down here—
How can his essence ever be perceived
    For things comparable to be conceived!
When news about my Shamsoddin* first came
    The heaven's highest sun withdrew through shame!

I'm now compelled through uttering Shams's name
    To tell you of his gifts and spread his fame:
Hosamoddin has flung me by my skirt   125
    So I can breathe in scent from Joseph's shirt:*
He asked me, 'Life-long friend, please share with me
    From your rich stock a single ecstasy,
To raise a smile from both the land and sky,
    To make each person's soul expand and fly.'
'Don't give me duties now I've passed away,
    My senses dulled, I've no clue how to pray,
For anything a drunk might sing is wrong
    Whether he's meek or boastful in his song:
Since all my veins now pulse with drunkenness*   130
    How can I represent his loftiness?
Describing separation's torture then
    Is best postponed until we speak again.'
He said, '*I'm hungry and must now be fed!*
    "Time is a cutting sword" the Prophet said,
The sufi is the present moment's son,
    Talk of "tomorrow" sufis learn to shun—
Are you not then a sufi as I'd thought?
    Delaying payment turns your wealth to naught!'
'The loved one's secret's best kept veiled,' I said,   135
    'Listen to it in ecstasy instead,
The lover's secret that's been kept concealed
    Is best through tales of other loves revealed.'
'Tell it unveiled and naked, candidly,
    You tricky man, don't try distracting me!
Be frank and lift the veil, you ditherer,
    I wear no nightshirt when in bed with her!'
I said, 'If the beloved strips for you,
    You'll be effaced, your waist and body too!
Please don't request what you can't tolerate: 140
    A blade of straw can't hold a mountain's weight,
And if the sun which gives us light should near,
    All things would burn and leave no traces here—
Don't try to make more strife for everyone,
    Ask nothing more about Tabriz's Sun!'

The tale is incomplete, begin anew,
　Narrate the rest, as only you can do!

The saint asks the king to let him spend time
alone with the slave-girl in order to
discover her ailment

The doctor said, 'Vacate your house today,
　Even your family must be sent away,
So no one's listening from the corridors   145
　While I interrogate the girl indoors.'
The house was emptied, no one else remained,
　Alone now with the girl who looked so pained,
He gently asked, 'From which town did you come?
　The cure depends on where the patient's from;
Which relatives do you have living there,
　Who's family? Whose friendship do you share?'
Feeling her pulse he went through one by one
　Questions about the course the stars must run:

When someone stumbles barefoot on a thorn   150
　He stops and checks what he has trod upon,
To use a needle to dislodge its head,
　Or failing that, by moistening it instead:
If in your foot it proves so hard to find
　Imagine one that's pierced your heart and mind!
If such thorns could be traced by any fool
　How then could sorrow ever hope to rule!
If someone pricks a donkey near its tail
　The helpless beast will buck and start to wail,
But this will serve to drive it further in—   155
　A sage is needed to remove the pin;
The donkey would continue with its fit
　And prick itself a hundred times with it!
Our thorn-removing doctor is the best,
　He presses first all over as a test:

Through sharing stories with the poor sick maid
    He asked about her friends and where she'd stayed,
And she divulged to him the history
    Of all her past friends and her family;
While listening to what the girl would share   160
    He monitored her pulse with utmost care—
Whoever's name would raise her pulse would be
    The one for whom she suffered constantly.
Once she had named her friends from home, he'd then
    About another town inquire again:
'After you left your home where did you go?
    Where did you stay the longest, let me know!'
She mentioned further places by their name,
    Her pulse and her complexion stayed the same,
She listed every detail of each town   165
    From local bread to features of renown—
Of town by town and home by home she'd speak
    Without a quiver in her veins or cheek,
Her pulse felt stable to his knowing hand
    Until he asked the girl of Samarkand—
Her pulse increased to rates beyond compare,
    She'd been kept from a certain goldsmith there!
Once the physician solved this mystery
    He found the source of her deep agony.
'So where precisely is this man's abode?'   170
    'It's near the bridge, on the Ghatafar road.'
'I recognize your illness, count on me—
    My magic will provide the remedy,
Be joyful, maiden, carefree and secure,
    As rain revives the grass, I'll find the cure!
I'll take your suffering on, so grieve no more!
    I'm kind like fathers who their girls adore,
Make sure to keep this secret safe with you,
    I mean in case the king should ask you too,
For if a soul entombs its secret love   175
    Fulfilment comes more quickly from above.
The Prophet said, "Whoever hides his dream
    Attains it sooner through the Lord Supreme":

When seeds are hidden deep beneath the ground
　　Their secret turns to verdure all around,
Silver and gold are hidden in the mine
　　To nurture them and purify their shine.'
The doctor's soothing words and promises
　　Relieved the girl of countless illnesses:
True promises give pleasure constantly,   180
　　False promises increase anxiety,
The promise of the pure's hard currency,
　　The promise of the base brings bankruptcy!

The saint identifies the affliction and explains it to the king

Then he stood up and headed for the king
　　To share a bit of what was happening:
'What you must do is summon here that man,
　　To cure her pain this is the wisest plan:
Summon the goldsmith from that distant town,
　　With gold and robes of honour, bring him down!'
After this speech the king chose to obey   185
　　Each word that he had heard the healer say.

The king sends messengers to Samarkand to bring the goldsmith

The king then sent two men to Samarkand,
　　Both shrewd, experienced men at his command,
As soon as they arrived there they began
　　To read this message to the wanted man:
'O gentle master, pure intelligence,
　　Talk everywhere is of your eminence!
Our king requests you for your peerless skill,
　　This vacancy no other man can fill,
Accept this robe of honour and this gold,   190
　　When you arrive a special rank you'll hold.'
On seeing robes and wealth he was beguiled,
　　He left his townsfolk, even his own child,
He set off on the journey feeling thrilled
　　Without a clue the king would have him killed,

He proudly mounted an Arabian stud,
    Not knowing that the price was his own blood:
Conceited fool, you failed to comprehend,
    So eagerly you raced to your own end!
He dreamt of majesty that wouldn't cease,   195
    As Azrael said, 'Come and grab your piece!'

He was escorted, after entering,
    Up to the royal throne to meet the king,
The escorts treated him with special care,
    They knew his love of pomp—it was a snare!
The king embraced him like a friend of old,
    Entrusting to him all his stores of gold,
The doctor urged, 'There's more you can award:
    Why don't you give the girl as a reward?
Through union with this man she could be nursed,   200
    Love's waters might revive her, quench her thirst.'
The maiden then received a wedding band—
    They joined the couple just as they had planned!
The first six months together how they thrived,
    The servant girl soon totally revived!
But then the groom was poisoned in a plot,
    She saw the doctor's potion make him rot:
Through sickness he lost all his youthfulness,
    Each day his looks got worse, her love grew less,
He soon became so ugly, pale, and old   205
    That she could feel her heart becoming cold—
Love which is based on just a pretty face
    Is not true love, it ends in sheer disgrace.
Would that he'd been all over so debased
    And therefore spared the judgement he has faced!
Instead of tears his eyes gushed blood in streams,
    His face became his enemy, it seems:
Feathers became the peacock's bitter foe
    And kings were killed by their own love of show.
He said, 'I'm like the deer for whose musk scent   210
    Hunters desire to catch and then torment;

The desert fox, which when they capture her,
    They chop her head off just to keep the fur;
That elephant who's beaten savagely,
    They shed his blood just for his ivory,
Those who would kill for secondary goals
    Should know I'll take my vengeance on their souls,
I'm now the victim, your turn's coming soon,
    Those hungry for my blood are not immune!
A lengthy shadow though a wall can cast;   215
    That shadow will return to it at last:
The world's a mountain, actions like a shout,
    Your echo will return to you, watch out!'
These were his final words when he was slain,
    The slave-girl now was purged of love and pain.

Love of the dead is not a lasting love
    Because the dead don't come back from above,
Love of the living in your soul and blood
    Each moment makes you fresher than a bud,
Save love for him, eternal and divine,   220
    The Saqi with the soul-expanding wine!
Choose love of him, from whose resplendent face
    The prophets find their mission and their grace—
Don't tell me 'From that king we have been barred,'
    Dealing with noble men is not that hard !

*Explanation of how the goldsmith's murder by poisoning was in
accord with God's instruction, not due to the passions and corrupt
wishes of the carnal soul*

Although the healer's killing seems severe,
    Be sure he didn't act through greed or fear,
Nor to placate the king's desire instead—
    Divine command decreed he should be dead.
Think of the child whose jugular Khezr slit,*   225
    Most people failed to see the good in it:

For those in deep communion with their Lord
   Their every deed's correct, in full accord,
He who gives life may kill, we must condone
   His deputy's act like his very own;
Like Ismail* lay your neck before his blade
   And smile for this brave sacrifice you've made,
So that your soul will live on joyfully
   With God, like Ahmad's* soul, eternally;
Each lover drinks the wine of his own soul   230
   When slain by his beloved that's his goal.
The king did not start scheming through desire—
   Now throw that false suspicion in the fire!
You still think he committed sin, don't you?
   When God refines, no flaws can filter through;
Religious discipline and suffering loss
   Is so the furnace burns the silver's dross,
That's why for good and bad we scrutinize
   And gold is boiled so that the scum may rise—
So if his deeds from heaven didn't spring   235
   He'd be a dog that bites and not a king!
Already he's been purified from greed,
   His righteous act just seemed a wicked deed:
When Khezr destroyed that boat out in the sea
   What seemed destructive was true piety,
Moses stayed veiled,* though he was wise and good—
   Don't jump without wings, till you've understood!
This red's a rose and not a bloody stain,
   He's drunk with gnosis, don't call him insane,
If shedding Muslim blood was his sole aim   240
   I'd be an infidel to bless his name!
When evil's praised the highest heavens shake,
   If pious men applaud that's their mistake!
He was a glorious king, and circumspect,
   Hand-picked by God, one of the pure elect,
Whoever such a king should choose to slay
   More grace and status soon will come his way.
If good could not be caused through violence
   How could his soul have shown such vehemence?

When children tremble near the barber's blade,*   245
  Their mothers smile with joy though they're afraid:
For half a life he gives a hundred more,
  Such gifts beyond your dreams he has in store,
So stop comparing him with your low state,
  Reflect on this before it gets too late!

The tale about the grocer and the parrot: the parrot spills oil in the store

A grocer kept a parrot in his stall,
  The bird was green and talked, amusing all,
Perched on a bench it watched the passers-by,
  Sharing a word with those who caught its eye,
It knew how to pronounce all human words,   250
  Spoke fluently with men as well as birds.
The parrot hopped down from the bench one day,
  Spilling a flask of rose oil on its way;
And when the grocer came back to his store,
  When he sat down he stained the clothes he wore.
On seeing the spilt oil a rage took hold—
  He struck the parrot's head and left it bald!
The next few days the bird refused to speak,
  The grocer grieved, repentant now and meek,
He tugged his beard, 'Alas!' he cried aloud   255
  'My sun of bounty's hidden by a cloud!
Would that my hand had broken then instead
  Of striking my most precious parrot's head!'
He then gave gifts to all the needy men,
  Hoping to hear the parrot speak again.
After three nights, perplexed and desperate
  He sat down on the bench, disconsolate,
Then showed the parrot wondrous tricks galore
  To coax it into talking back once more;
A monk then strolled by on his daily route,   260
  In woollen garb and balder than a coot—

This made the parrot talk again at last.
    It shouted at the monk as he walked past:
'How did you end up such a slaphead, friend?
    Did you like me a flask of oil upend?'
At this assumption everybody laughed,
    It thought the monk its equal—it was daft!
Don't you compare yourself with God's élite,
    Remember 'souls' just sounds like 'soles' of feet!
Because of this the whole world's gone astray,   265
    Few recognize God's chosen saints today:
Themselves the prophets' equals some proclaim
    And that from saints they differ just in name,
'We're all mere human beings,' they will say,
    'They too must eat some food and sleep each day.'
Their blindness stops them from discerning it—
    Between the two the gap is infinite:
Both wasps and bees those flowers are nourishing,
    Bees give back honey, wasps a painful sting!
All grazing deer look similar when they're young   270
    But some give musk, while others just leave dung!
They're like the canes that you see growing there—
    One's sugar-filled, the other just holds air!
With false comparisons this world is packed,
    Notice how different each one is in fact:
For one, the food he eats just turns to shit,
    Another shines the light of God with it;
One eats and grows more envious and tight,
    Another one bestows God's purest light.

Contrast this good land with that marshy patch,   275
    Don't claim this angel and that demon match!
When opposites to us the same appear
    Like sweet and bitter water, both being clear,
Who can discriminate between the two?
    None but a man who's tasted truth* will do.
Magic and miracles some view the same
    For both to them are just a clever game:

Magicians challenged Moses, friend of God,*
    Producing their own versions of his rod—
The difference was vast, like night and day,   280
    Their deeds contrasted, they were poles away!
Their actions earned them curses from the Lord,
    While Moses earned more grace as his reward.
Such unbelievers are just apes, no more,
    Their lying breasts are rotten to the core!
Whatever men should do, apes imitate,
    They try to copy every human trait,
Thinking, 'We've copied them so faithfully.'
    Deluded, apes can't sense the way we see.
His actions were from God, theirs just a game,   285
    Those who keep picking fights should all feel shame!
Although the hypocrites attend the prayer,
    It's just so they can start a quarrel there,
In fasting, prayer, the pilgrimage, and alms,
    These hypocrites make good men take up arms!
Believers will be led to victory,
    While hypocrites will pay eternally!
Although it's the same game these two groups play,
    They're chalk and cheese, like those from Merv and Reyy.*
Each one where he belongs at last you'll find,   290
    Since each fulfils the name he's been assigned,
If called *believer*, he'll end up much higher;
    Those labelled *hypocrite* just feed the fire!
His essence earns the first *loved one* as name,
    His failings give the next, *the loathed*, all blame.
The name 'believer' is itself worth naught,
    It only signifies a person's thought;
Call someone hypocrite and he'll protest
    As if a scorpion's stung him in his chest,
'If this vile name has not emerged from hell,   295
    Why then does it possess its taste and smell?'
The word's referent letters don't decide—
    Don't blame the bowl for what's contained inside!
The bowl's mere form, its content meaning, look!
    All meaning's from *the Mother of the Book*:*

The planet's different seas aren't joined as one,
    God's fixed *a gap they don't encroach upon*,*
Their origin however's still the same,
    Transcend them all and make their source your aim!

To check that it's not counterfeit you'll need   300
    A touchstone to be sure it's gold indeed:
If God should place a touchstone in your heart
    You'll then tell doubt and certainty apart,
Like when a hair gets in your mouth you know
    To spit it out before it slips below,
Among a hundred morsels just one hair,
    Each man can sense it if he should take care!
These senses are the ladders of this world,
    From heaven separate ladders God has hurled.
Physicians treat and keep your body well   305
    But just God's friend can save your soul from hell,
Good health's equated with a strong physique,
    A healthy soul will make your body weak;
Bodies are wrecked along the mystic way,
    For their destruction treasure's brought as pay:
For gold your house is knocked down to the ground
    To be rebuilt, foundations deep and sound,
He cuts off water, drains the river bed,
    With purest water fills it up instead;
He flays your skin to find the blade inside,   310
    Fresh skin will heal the wound, however wide;
He'll raze the castles of those faithless powers
    But then rebuild them with a thousand towers.
Who can discern when acts seem arbitrary?
    What I've just said shows that it's necessary:
Sometimes like this, and then the opposite,
    God's way bewilders those who're travelling it,
Not the false ways of those whose backs are turned,
    But the amazement that love's drunks have learned:
One faces the beloved constantly,   315
    The other chooses just himself to see—

Observe which way the people choose to turn,
  While serving others learn how to discern!
The devils make themselves look just like men—
  Don't shake hands with just anyone again:
The hunter blows a whistle near his prey,
  Deceiving thus the bird, who's led astray,
It hears what sounds like calling from a friend
  And lands inside his trap to meet its end;
A wretch may steal the words of dervishes   320
  To chant tall tales to simple audiences:
The actions of the genuine spread light,
  While false pretenders just distort what's right.
Low beggars with stuffed dolls they feel no shame:
  'Ahmad', some claimed, was Bu Mosaylem's* name:
He was called 'liar' soon, and entered hell,
  While Ahmad gave the world *those who know well.**
The wine of love's flask smells of musk that's pure,
  While other wines all stink of foul manure!

The story about the Jewish king who out of fanaticism would kill Christians

There once was an oppressive Jewish king,   325
  A foe of Jesus and his following
During the period of his prophethood,
  Succeeding Moses, as we've understood—
The cross-eyed king saw them as miles apart
  Although as prophets they were one at heart:

A teacher told a cross-eyed boy one day,
  'Go fetch for me a bottle straight away!'
The boy returned, 'Which bottle did you mean
  Of that exactly matching pair I've seen?'
The teacher said, 'There's only one you fool!   330
  Have you not learned to add up yet at school?'

The boy protested, 'Sir, don't laugh at me!'
    The teacher said, 'Try smashing one to see!'
A single bottle looked to him like two
    But when one broke, both vanished from his view!
When he smashed one the other broke as well,
    Desire can make you cross-eyed in its spell!
And lust and rage don't just affect your sight,
    They agitate your soul, set it alight,
Virtue's forgotten when your heart feels lust,   335
    Veils block your heart and eyes like layers of dust,
So when a judge lets bribery win his heart
    He can't tell guilt and innocence apart.

This king became so cross-eyed through his hate,
    The Christians prayed, 'Save us from his dictate!'
He slew believers, claimed it was correct,
    Said, 'Moses's faith I have to protect!'

The vizier informs the king of his plot

He had an infidel vizier, so sly
    That he convinced men even when he'd lie!
He said, 'The Christians want to save their lives,   340
    They see that he who hides his faith survives—
Don't round them up, that method won't work well,
    You can't tell people's faith just by their smell!
They've hidden their beliefs inside a sheath,
    What smiles at you opposes you beneath.'
The king said, 'Tell me what you recommend
    To wipe out those who play-act and pretend,
To rid this world of every Christian soul,
    Hidden or in the open—that's my goal!'
He said, 'Cut off my nose and hands, dear king,   345
    And split my lip to show my suffering,
Then hang me from the gallows publicly
    Till someone comes to intercede for me,

Set all this up inside the market square
　　So people flock to see from everywhere,
Then banish me to exile far away
　　And I'll make mischief for them from that day!

How the vizier deceives the Christians

I'll say, "I've been a Christian in disguise—
　　All-knowing God will prove these are not lies:
When he found out my true identity   350
　　That bigot of a king came after me!
To keep my faith a secret from that king
　　I'd mimic his own brand of worshipping,
But when he did get wind of my belief
　　Of wicked crimes he charged me like a thief,
Saying, "Your words are needles in my spine!
　　A window lies between your heart and mine
Through which upon your secrets I can spy,
　　And so your false claims I'll no longer buy."
If Jesus had not saved me from that Jew   355
　　He would have butchered me, I swear to you,
For Christ I'd therefore sacrifice my head
　　And pay back all my debts before I'm dead;
Though I would gladly die for our Lord's sake,
　　I've studied, so it would be a mistake—
To risk the future of our faith's not right
　　Though under heathens we have such a fight!
Thanks be to God and Jesus, this I pray,
　　That I've become a guide to lead the way,
That I've escaped the cruel, oppressive Jews   360
　　To wear my Christian girdle when I choose!
This is the epoch of our Holy Lord,
　　Hear now his secrets, live in full accord!"'
The king did what was needed to destroy
　　All Christian families with their hidden ploy:
He started to expel them from his land
　　When the vizier began to preach, as planned.

The Christians are taken in by the vizier's plot

A thousand Christians gradually thus converged
    Around his home, where they all finally merged,
He'd teach them secretly, the old and youths,   365
    About the gospel, prayer, and hidden truths;
Although he seemed to teach mere ordinances
    He led to hidden traps his audiences:
That's why a few Companions* would enquire
    About the self's tricks and its true desire,
'Dear Prophet, tell us what's its hidden goal
    In worship and in purifying one's soul?'
From the self's piety they sought no grace
    But errors in its acts they sought to trace,
Its every lie they quickly learned to see,   370
    To tell rose stems from sticks of celery!
Companions who knew how to scrutinize
    The prophet's sermons still would mesmerize.

The Christians follow the vizier

So all the Christians gave their hearts to him
    Too ready to obey another's whim!
Submission to him they thought piety,
    Imagining he was Christ's deputy:
He was the one-eyed Antichrist within—
    Please help us God, protector from all sin!
He's set for us a hundred thousand traps   375
    And we're like hungry birds in search of scraps,
Each moment caught in yet another snare
    Though we be phoenixes who rule the air,
You free us, but repeatedly we fall,
    Entrapped, 'O Needless One', for you we call:
Like bringing wheat inside a farmhouse store
    But at the same time losing it once more!
Why can't we work this out now with our brains?
    A mouse keeps sneaking in to steal the grains!

This mouse has dug a hole to creep inside,   380
   It's ruined every storehouse far and wide—
Defend against the mouse first, that's the plan,
   Then come and gather all the wheat you can!
Now listen to the Prophet of Mankind:
   '*No prayer's complete without a present mind.*'
Tell me, If there's none left inside your store
   Then where's the stock of forty years and more?
Why isn't every grain of daily prayer
   Still in the storehouse, since you put them there?
The anvil sent up sparks at rapid pace,   385
   Impassioned hearts received them in embrace,
But then a thief crept in when it was dark
   And placed his finger over every spark:
He put each spark out in this heart of mine
   Until the heavens could no longer shine,
But even if such snares encircle me
   I feel no fear when you stand next to me:
When constantly your favour gives relief
   How can I fear at all that wretched thief!

Out of the human body's trap each night   390
   To serve as tablets for the truths you write:
You free our spirits from confinement's cage,
   No longer slaves, they reach the highest stage!
Prisoners at night forget about their chains
   And sultans think no more of their domains,
No loss or profit, nor a moment's stress,
   About our foes one couldn't now care less!
The mystic's in this state while wide awake:
   God said, '*They're sleeping*',* so make no mistake!
Asleep to worldly things all night and day,   395
   Just like a pen, God's hand he must obey—
Those who don't see the movement by His hand
   Think that the pen moves by its own command.
Some clues about the mystic God's made plain
   Since sleeping also stills the simple brain:

Their souls transcend to realms beyond compare
  Where souls and bodies rest without a care,
Though with a whistle He will call them home
  When they'll be judged and can no longer roam.
Once dawn's first light from heaven should appear   400
  The golden sun would overwhelm this sphere,
Like Esrafil, *He who makes each dawn break**
  Brings back all human spirits wide awake,
Inside their bodies they are trapped by day
  As if the body's pregnant in this way.
Thus he strips trappings off the spirit's steed—
  '*Brother of death*' for sleep is apt indeed!
In order that by dawn they all come back
  He's tied a tether round them, though it's slack,
To draw them in from meadows to their pen   405
  Where they are burdened with their loads again;
Protected like Companions of the Cave,*
  Or safe, on Noah's ark, from every wave,
If only souls were spared from being aware
  Of what our mind and senses see out there!
Companions of the Cave today are found,
  They're right before you and heard all around
In song with the beloved constantly—
  Your eyes don't have the power though to see.

The tale about the caliph* seeing Layli

The caliph said to Layli, 'You're the one   410
  Who's left Majnun bewildered and undone,
But you don't seem remarkable to me!'
  She said, 'You need Majnun's own eyes to see!'
To be awake to this world means to sleep,
  It's worse than sleep in fact, and much more deep!
Asleep to God, awake to spectacles—
  This represents the worst of obstacles;
We're kicked and punched by fantasies all day
  From fear of loss to hope of higher pay,

Our souls thus lose their grace and purity   415
   To block the path above for you and me.
The one asleep believes in fantasies
   And dozes off seduced by what he sees:
A demon for a houri* he'll mistake,
   In lust ejaculating for its sake!
Once he has spilt his semen thus in vain
   He'll wake up, but his dream shall not remain—
His weakness his own body has defiled,
   So he'll regret that he had been beguiled.
A bird flies past, its shadow slides below   420
   As if it can itself move to and fro,
A foolish hunter chases this all day,
   Thinking it's real he seeks it as his prey,
Not knowing it's a shadow of the bird—
   About this simple fact he had not heard—
He shoots this shadow with his hunting bow,
   Empties his quiver for a phantom show!
Just like his quiver soon his life runs dry,
   Wasted pursuing shadows, days pass by!
But when the shade of God heals like a nurse   425
   It frees one from that empty shadow's curse;
This shade's beneath each of God's chosen slaves,
   To this world dead, his life for God he saves,
Forget your doubts and follow this man's lead
   So at the end of time you might be freed!
How he makes shadows stretch* shows this is right
   For saints are proof of the Divine Sun's light;
Without a saint as guide, don't enter yet,
   Like Abraham *don't love the ones that set*;*
Leave shadows for the sunshine, and then seize   430
   The cloak's hem worn by King Shams-e Tabriz!
If you can't find the banquets where he's been
   Then ask the light of truth, Hosamoddin!
But if sheer envy grabs your throat, beware,
   The devil's the most envious one out there!
Through jealousy, he's shown contempt for Man,
   He'll try to end our joy if he still can;

No harder road's on this itinerary,
  You're blessed if from this jealousy you're free!
The body serves as home for jealousies   435
  When what's inside is struck by this disease;
Although it's home to jealousies, be sure
  That God has made the body to be pure,
For *Sanctify my house** confirms it's right
  And earthly talismans can bring you light.
Don't cheat those free from envy in their souls,
  Your heart will blacken like the darkest coals,
Become instead the dirt on which they tread,
  Bury, like us, your mean and envious head!

Explanation of the vizier's jealousy

That base vizier, the spawn of jealousies,   440
  Wasting his faculties on vanities,
Hoped that his bitter envy's poisonous breath
  Would make the souls of poor men meet their death:
If out of envy men turn up their nose
  They'll lose their nose for striking such a pose,
Each person's nose is there to breathe in scent
  And one can send you to the firmament:
Whoever lacks it must forsake his nose,
  This holy scent through which the spirit grows,
And should he catch a whiff, but not sing praise   445
  His nose will be devoured for his sick ways,
Therefore give thanks and serve all grateful folk,
  To live on, be as dead as dust and smoke!
Don't waylay others like this sly vizier,
  From ritual prayer don't tempt away those near!
He acted holy, but he was a fake,
  Like using garlic on an almond cake!

The perceptive Christians see through the vizier's plot

Judging his words with taste-buds well refined
  A few sensed sweet and bitter were combined:

He'd mixed the words of saints with those of cheats, 450
    Like hiding poison in amongst the sweets,
He seemed to say, 'Stand firm while on the way!'
    But to their souls, 'Be weak!' he'd really say:
Although the silver's surface shines like new
    It makes your hand turn black, your jacket too,
Though fire by yellow flames each man discerns
    Watch how it turns to black all things it burns,
Though lightning helps us see by shining bright
    It's also known for robbing men of sight.
For those who didn't know how they could check 455
    His words became a halter round their neck!
The six years he spent absent from his king
    To Christians he claimed safety he would bring—
People surrendered heart and soul to him,
    They would have died to satisfy his whim!

The king corresponds secretly with the vizier

But with the king he still would correspond,
    The king wrote secretly, thus kept their bond:
With this aim finally he wrote: that they
    Like worthless dust should soon be blown away:
'Of all my ministers you are the best, 460
    Now it's the time to put my mind at rest.'
He answered, 'Please observe, your majesty,
    The strife I've caused for Christianity.'

Explanation of the twelve divisions of the Christians

The Christians had agreed a leading role
    For twelve of them to whom they gave control:
Each Christian group chose one and then obeyed
    Expecting that through him they'd be repaid;
But through their leaders, whom they'd all revere,
    They also came to follow this vizier:
Trusting that through his teachings they'd be saved 465
    They'd imitate the way this man behaved,

And every leader would have gladly died
  To please this man whom they all glorified.

The vizier deliberately mixes up the ordinances of the Bible

To every tribe he sent a document,
  But what each scroll contained was different:
They each set separate rules to be obeyed
  And contradicted points the others made:
In one it said, 'The fast and discipline
  Are needed for repentance to begin.'
The next said, 'Discipline's no use to you: 470
  Resort to being liberal, as I do.'
Another: 'Fasting and asceticism
  Both really are a form of polytheism,
You should have trust in fate, abandon cares!
  In ease and hardship, all you'll find are snares!'
In one he wrote, 'God's service is a must
  To prove beyond a doubt your total trust.'
The next said, 'End proscription and command,
  It's just to show we're weak that things are banned:
Once we've observed our weakness through their light   475
  We'll then appreciate God's power and might.'
The next one said, 'Ignore your weaknesses,
  Don't be ungrateful for God's kindnesses:
Give thanks for strength and sing his praise aloud,
  Of God's most generous gifts you should be proud!'
The next one said, 'Don't look at either one:
  Things visible are idols you must shun.'
The next said, 'Don't blow out this candle's flame,
  Vision of union shines bright just the same:
Your mental visions mustn't be wiped out,   480
  At midnight no one blows the candle out!'
The next one said, 'Just blow it out, don't grieve,
  And in return great visions you'll receive:
Extinguish it to make your soul expand,
  Layli will ask Majnun then for his hand:

Renounce the world now on your own accord
    And it will seek you out to be its lord!'
The next one said, 'What God has brought to view
    He's made look good especially for you:
It's for your sake, accept it happily,   485
    Don't choose to wallow in your misery!'
The next one said, 'Abandon what you own,
    Since what the self desires you can't condone!
Each path seems easily followed to the goal
    So each one loves his sect more than his soul,
But if the path were open to each creed
    Then Jews and Magians also could succeed.'
The next said, 'This is all I know for sure,
    The soul's food is what makes your heart endure:
Our sensual tasting's transient, like blown sand,   490
    And nothing ever grows from barren land:
Its produce is regret for farming it,
    Its sale results in a huge deficit,
It gives no beneficial fruit at all
    So as 'deficient' it is known to all,
Choose what is favourable from what is not
    To know the end-result before it's sought!'
'Seek out a trusty guide,' the next one said,
    'You can't tell what's in front just by your head!
Each sect had thought that they could see the goal   495
    Then fell in error deep inside a hole!
If everyone could know what to expect
    There wouldn't be disputes between each sect.'
The next said, 'You're the perfect guide, please rise,
    For others only you can recognize,
Become a man, don't be a foolish clown,
    Hold up your head, don't turn your gaze back down!'
The next said, 'All around is unity,
    Just cross-eyed wretches see duality!'
The next said, 'How can millions equal one?   500
    That's just what madmen like to claim for fun!'
And so their rivals' views each group would blame,
    One's meat and poison never judged the same:

Until you can transcend the differences
    You'll never breathe in union's fragrances;
Such different scrolls, each written in this style,
    The foe of Jesus wrote with all his guile.

*Explanation of how the differences are apparent in form,
but not in the reality of the way*

Not seeing Jesus's one-colouredness
    About his vat of dye he didn't guess:*
A multi-coloured garment placed in there   505
    Comes out one-coloured, clearer than the air,
Not that one-colouredness which seems a bore
    But like pure water which all fish adore:
A thousand colours decorate the land
    But dryness on the shore no fish can stand,
So who's the fish and what is water here
    That the Almighty should like them appear!
Thousands of fish and seas lie down prostrate
    Before the Lord, obeying his dictate!

How many rains have poured down filled with grace   510
    And scattered pearls up from the ocean's base,
And through His grace how many suns have shone
    The clouds and seas with care to smile upon:
A ray of knowledge shone on soil and clay
    To teach them how to nurture seeds this way,
Such ground is pure no matter what you sow,
    Without a defect plants will quickly grow,
Its soundness comes from the primordial trust*—
    That's why it gets its light from the All-Just,
But spring must give a signal from the Lord   515
    Before the soil reveals its hidden horde.
He's given to inanimate things too
    Knowledge, a trust and rectitude—it's true!
His grace schools even things without a mind,
    His wrath leaves educated scholars blind!

Your heart and soul can't take the heat at all,
　No ears to hear these truths, whom shall I call?
He changes every ear into an eye
　And every stone into a gem you'd buy,
Compared with this what then is alchemy!　　　　　520
　Next to His miracles what's sorcery!
My uttering praise is really ceasing praise,
　It proves my being—what I must erase!
Before His being please leave yours behind!
　What is our own existence, blue and blind:
Except the blind, all melt before his feet
　The moment that the sun emits its heat,
And if from mourning it has not turned blue*
　How come it's freezing standing next to you!

How the vizier lost his way in his plot

The king's vizier, like him a heedless fool,　　　　525
　Sought to contest divine eternal rule,
To punch Almighty God, who out of naught,
　In moments, worlds like ours to life has brought!

A hundred worlds in seconds He'll display
　When your own eyes, through Him, can look this way;
To you this world seems vast and limitless,
　To Him compared with atoms it's worth less.
This world's a gaol, your souls are locked inside,
　Head that way for the open countryside!
This world has limits, that one's limit-free,　　　　530
　Form is a barrier to reality:
The thousand spears of Pharaoh Moses knew,
　With just one rod how to split them in two;
Medical sciences once Galen taught
　But next to Jesus's breath* they're worth naught;
The finest poetry was put to shame
　The day illiterate Mohammad came—

With such an overwhelming lord, how then
　　Can you not die unless you're wretched men!
Men's hearts like Sinai fall drunk at His words,   535
　　He hangs up by their claws such clever birds—
To hone the intellect is not the way,
　　The destitute alone the king will pay!
Truth's treasure-hunters with their stores of gold
　　The foolish thought were donkeys they could scold:
How can a donkey be compared with you,
　　As if you have a tail and four legs too!
Sins made a woman's olive face turn white,
　　But God made her like Venus shining bright:*
This change in her was a great transformation,   540
　　While turning back to clay is degradation!
Your spirit urged you to the highest sphere,
　　You've turned to clay instead by falling here,
Transformed yourself by sinking from above
　　From an existence that great men would love;
The value of this change of course below
　　Compared with her change is extremely low:
You urged ambition's steed towards the sun
　　But then snubbed Adam, the most honoured one,*
Despite the fact you're Adam's progeny—   545
　　How long will you think baseness majesty!
'I'll rule a world,' how long will you declare,
　　'And let my massive ego fill the air!'
The world each year gets covered up with snow
　　Until it's melted by the sun's warm glow:
His sins, like those of any sly vizier,
　　With just one spark from God soon disappear;
To wisdom God can turn what idiots think
　　And poisoned water to a wholesome drink!
The cause of doubts He turns to certainty,   550
　　To love He changes spite and enmity,
Like saving Abraham from flames that roar*
　　He'll change fear to security once more;
He burnt all logic, leaving me ecstatic,
　　While idle fancies just made you a sceptic!

The vizier devises another plot to lead the people astray

Then the vizier devised another plot,
    Retreated from the Christians whom he'd taught
And set his students' longing hearts ablaze
    By staying there for more than forty days.
Pining for him the people all went mad,   555
    Missing tales of experiences he'd had;
They'd all lament and then they'd supplicate
    While in seclusion he would simply wait:
They said, 'Without you we have lost the light,
    With blind men lacking guides we share this plight!
For God's sake and to spare us, we implore,
    Don't keep your distance from us any more!
We're children needing you as nursing-maid,
    Spread over us your calm, protective shade.'
He said, 'Dear lovers, though my soul is near,   560
    It's not permitted to step out of here.'
The twelve group-leaders tried to intercede
    While his disciples wept in desperate need:
'Master, what a misfortune for us all,
    Orphaned of love and faith, and left to fall!
You give excuses while we suffer pain,
    Our burning hearts breathe desperate sighs in vain;
Accustomed to the marvellous way you teach
    We now need daily doses of your speech—
For God's sake, please don't torture us this way,   565
    Our needs until tomorrow don't delay!
Have you the heart to leave us in this strife,
    Barren without you, robbed of our own life?
Don't leave us writhing just like fish on land,
    Open the floodgates with your generous hand!
Since in this age you're totally unique,
    For God's sake, give your people what they seek!'

The vizier's rebuttal of the disciples

He said, 'Heed well you easily influenced men
   Longing for preaching and advice again,
Plug up your baser senses' ears, be wise,   570
   Unbind the senses' blindfold from your eyes!
Ears in your head plug up the spirit's ear
   So that those ears themselves no longer hear,
Hearing, all thought and senses you must spurn
   So you will hear when God tells you, "*Return!*"*
If you pay heed to what the idle say
   You'll have no clue what truthful dreams convey:
While outward travelling lies in words and deeds
   Beyond the sky the inner journey leads,
While bodily senses only know things dry,   575
   Like Jesus, over water souls pass by;
The body's journey takes place on dry land
   While souls dive into seas when they expand,
But since the land is all you've ever known,
   The barren mountains, desert sand, and stone,
You'll not find Water of Eternal Life,*
   Nor part the waves like butter with a knife;
From dryness come vain thoughts and contemplation,
   From seas effacement, thanks, annihilation,
While you are drunk you're far from ecstasy,   580
   The actual goblet drunks can't even see,
Your outward talk's worth less than dust, take heed—
   Maintaining silence now is what you need!'

The disciples ask him again to end his seclusion

They said, 'O sage who loves such loopholes, please
   Stop torturing us like this, and please don't tease!
Give every mule a load that it can bear,
   Observe the limits of the weak, be fair!
Each bird's own seed provides its every need,
   For birds you don't put out your figs as feed!

Instead of milk if you give babies bread   585
   You're bound to find the helpless creatures dead,
But later when each baby's teeth have grown
   They'll ask for bread and eat it on their own;
When fledglings start to practise how to fly
   They're easy prey for cats they hobble by,
But once their wings have grown they'll fly in peace
   Without the need for prompting or release.
Demons are stunned to silence by your speech,
   Your words bring wisdom's truths within our reach,
When you should speak our ears hear consciously,   590
   Since you're the ocean we become a sea!
Earth's better now than heaven since you're near,
   It's you who makes the world so bright and clear—
For us, without you heaven has no light,
   To be compared with you it has no right!
Though heaven has the form of loftiness,
   Its essence only spirits can possess,
Though outward greatness is each body's aim,
   Next to the essence, form is just a name.'

The vizier's answer that he won't end his seclusion

'Cut short your proofs,' the sly vizier then said,   595
   'Let these words penetrate your skulls instead:
If I'm the truthful one, abandon doubt,
   Even if, "Sky is land!" you hear me shout!
If I am perfect, you can't disagree,
   And if I'm not, then why keep pestering me?
I won't leave my seclusion from all cares,
   I'm busy now with spiritual affairs!'

The disciples object to the vizier's seclusion

They said, 'It's not that we're refuting you,
   Our words don't give a stranger's point of view;
Deprived of union mournfully we cry,   600
   In unison our tortured spirits sigh:

A child which never argues with its nurse
   Cries, but can't tell what's better and what's worse.
We're like a harp you pluck in various ways,
   This sad lament's not ours, it's you who plays,
We're like the flute whose music you blow out,
   The mountain which must echo what you shout,
Chess-pieces, winning now, and now in mate:
   It's you, majestic one, who seals our fate!
Who are we, soul of souls, that we should sit   605
   Beside a man like you when we're unfit?'

Non-entities, we're forced to fade away,
   Eternal One, our transience you display,
We're just like lions men paint on their flag
   Who only charge when wind should make it sag:
Our charge is visible, while wind is not—
   May that which is invisible be sought!
This wind, our very being, blows from You,
   You brought to life our whole existence too:
When You showed non-existence Being's light,   610
   It gave itself to You, love at first sight!
Such great attractions please don't gather up,
   Nor take away the wine and drinking-cup,*
For if You take them who can challenge You—
   Paintings can't tell their artist what to do!
Don't gaze at us, nor look on secretly,
   Witness instead your generosity:
We were not there, and we made no demands,
   You heard our prayer before we raised our hands!
The fabric hanging in the weaver's loom   615
   Is helpless like a child inside the womb,
The people at the court before His might,
   Like cloth before the needle, cannot fight:
Sometimes it sews a demon, then a man,
   Sometimes sheer joy then pain is in its plan,
Cloth has no hands to save itself from it,
   Nor tongue to tell its harm and benefit.

Read out from the Koran that verse we know
    Where God says, *When you threw you did not throw!**
When we fire arrows don't give us the blame—   620
    We're just the bow, it's God who's taking aim!
Don't dwell on our compulsion, but His might,
    To know humility keep this in sight,
Our wretchedness confirms this further still
    While feeling shame just proves we have free will:
If we're not free to choose then why feel shame,
    Express regret and grief, and take the blame?
And why should students strive and teachers guide,
    Why does the mind shove fate's decree aside?
And if you say, 'He's blind to fate and proud,   625
    The moon of truth is covered by a cloud',
This is the answer if you've ears to hear—
    Quit unbelief, and faith will make things clear:
When you fall ill you grieve and feel so low,
    You're then awake to what you need to know,
When starting to feel sick your prayers begin,
    You beg forgiveness for a life of sin,
Its ugliness the Lord to you displays
    So you'll resolve to follow righteous ways:
You swear to God that you'll at last take heed   630
    And make your every act a pious deed,
That being sick can heal you thus makes sense,
    It wakes you with increased intelligence!
So heed this principle and never doubt,
    Whoever's suffering pain has worked this out:
The more awake they are the worse their plight,
    Their suffering turns their tortured faces white!
Before His power where's your humility,
    Admit that you're a slave to His decree!
How can a man who's chained feel joy and ease   635
    Or prisoners do exactly as they please?
And when your feet are shackled like a slave
    While officers make sure that you behave,
Don't proudly seek from weaker men respect—
    For poor souls being humble's more correct!

When you don't see His power, don't claim you do!
  Or prove it if you really have a clue!
In every act with which you're satisfied
  You give yourself the credit with such pride,
But when your actions make you blush with shame   640
  You say, 'He forced me; God's the one to blame!'
Prophets in this world follow God's command
  While infidels receive in hell what's planned:
In heaven, prophets have free will, that's clear,
  But fools will claim it for themselves right here!
Since every bird will fly to its own kind,
  Its soul ahead, the body dragged behind,
Hell's dungeons are where infidels belong
  For in this world the prison's where they throng;
Prophets belong to heaven, that's their goal,   645
  That's why they seek the depths of every soul—
This talk is incomplete, but anyhow
  Let's finish the main narrative right now.

The vizier makes the disciples give up hope of his ending his seclusion

Then the vizier cried out from his locked cell,
  'Now listen well to what I have to tell:
Jesus has issued this command to me
  To separate from friends and family,
To face the wall and sit here all alone,
  Renouncing life, and that includes my own:
From now on I've no right to even speak   650
  Let alone teach the wisdom that you seek,
I'm dead from now on, friends, so it's goodbye,
  I'm taking my belongings to the sky!
In order not to burn like wood in hell,
  Enduring blame and hardship there as well,
I'll sit with Jesus from now on up there
  In heaven's summit, like a perfect pair.'

The vizier's appointment of each one of the group-leaders as his successor

He summoned each group-leader on his own
    To privately divulge what Christ had shown:
He said to each one, 'Christ has chosen you   655
    As my sole heir and God's own spokesman too;
The other leaders are your deputies,
    You should consider them your own trainees,
If one of them should grumble or protest
    Kill him, or put him under house-arrest!
But don't disclose this while I'm still the head,
    Don't seek my role until I'm finally dead,
Until that time, act like you haven't heard,
    Don't make a claim, nor breathe a single word!
Inside this scroll is Jesus's decree—   660
    Recite it then to his community!'
To each of them he said, 'This is your role,
    There's no one else who can assume control.'
He treated each one like a special king,
    And promised each of them the same old thing;
To each he gave a separate scroll he'd signed
    With different rules as if God changed his mind!
Discrepancies in them were easily read,
    As different as the letters A to Z,
Each contradicted what the rest declared,   665
    Already news about this ploy I've shared.

The vizier's suicide in seclusion

He stayed apart a further forty days
    Then killed himself to flee his own vile ways,
When people heard the news they moaned and screamed,
    For some, the end of time had come, it seemed:
Towards his grave they came in disbelief
    And pulled their hair, and ripped their clothes in grief!

Who knows how many came in those first weeks,
　　Including Arabs, Turks, the Kurds, and Greeks!
They kissed his grave's soil, thinking it was pure,   670
　　Redemptive suffering they sought as their cure:
For one whole month the crowds wept tears of blood,
　　Creating round his grave a massive flood.

The followers of Jesus ask their leaders,
'Which one of you is his successor?'

After a month had passed in bitter grief,
　　The people asked, 'Who now can serve as chief?
Which one do we consider up to it
　　To swear allegiance to him and submit?
We've roasted, but the sun has left no trace—
　　Don't we now need a torch to take its place?'

When union with the Lord has left our sight   675
　　We need to be reminded of His might,
Like when the fragrant rose's life is spent
　　Rose water lets us still breathe in its scent;
God won't reveal himself although He lives
　　So prophets serve as representatives,
They're not apart from what they represent—
　　That's incorrect, it's not what I first meant:
They seem distinct if to their form you're tied,
　　Discerning eyes can tell they're unified.
You're seeing double if their form's your aim,   680
　　Observe their light, you'll see that it's the same!
Who can discern his own eyes' share of light
　　When it's this light which gives each man his sight:
If you light up ten lamps when there's a storm
　　Each differs from the other in its form,
But no one still can separate their light
　　Which makes the space around you clear and bright;
You now see countless apples in the cart
　　But once they're crushed you can't tell them apart:

The spirit's realm has no plurality,   685
  Division, individuality;
This union of the lovers waits for you,
  Hold on, don't let its form obstruct your view,
Melt stubborn form through hardship and be bold
  And you'll find unity beneath like gold!
If you don't melt it, then his kindness will,
  The master of our hearts supports us still:
He shows his face inside your happy heart
  And sews the Sufi cloak that's torn apart.
Like one expansive whole was our past state,   690
  Beyond one could not differentiate,
The same throughout in form just like the sun,
  Like water, clear and still as if it's one;
When it took form that pure light multiplied
  Like shadows of the battlements outside—
Demolish all of them my faithful troop,
  Erase the differences among this group!
I would have clarified this all, my friend,
  Had I not feared you wouldn't comprehend,
These points are finer than a sabre's tip,   695
  Escape, if you've no shield yet in your grip!
Without a shield don't try to hold your own,
  In murder this cruel blade no shame has shown,
I've put my own sword in its sheath again
  So my intentions aren't misread by men;
Now let's complete the story rapidly
  About those godly Christians' loyalty:
After their teacher died they tried to find
  Someone to fill the role he'd left behind.

The struggle between the leaders over successorship

One of the leaders stepped up, tall and proud,   700
  Before the faithful and expectant crowd,
He said, 'I'm the successor of that sage
  To represent Lord Jesus in this age,

This scroll is evidence for all to see
    That his inheritance belongs to me!'
But from the crowd another leader came,
    His claim to be successor just the same:
He held a scroll too under his right arm—
    In rage they cursed and wished each other harm!
In turn, the other leaders made their way,   705
    Drawing their gleaming swords to join the fray,
Each held a scroll and sabre in the maul,
    Like drunken elephants they'd swing and fall;
Thousands of Christian bodies soon lay dead
    And mounds were formed by gathering each one's head,
Just like a flood their blood spilled all around,
    Enormous clouds of dust rose from the ground.
Dissension's seed which that vizier had sown
    Produced such tragedies that chill the bone;
Their walnut bodies soon were split and cracked,   710
    Only the purest kernels stayed intact.

Death's what the body's nature seems to fit
    As pomegranates must be crushed and split:
The sweet ones turn to syrup, pure and good,
    The rotten just make sounds like lumps of wood,
Those with pure spirits finally see His face
    While rotten ones will only find disgrace.
Don't worship form, but look for loftier things
    Because the spirit gives the body wings,
Keep company with those who're spiritual   715
    To gain His grace and be more liberal.

A body which does not contain a soul
    Is like a sheath that holds a wooden pole,
While hidden in the sheath it might seem good,
    But burning is the only use for wood,
With just a wooden sword don't join this fight,
    Check first, or you'll regret your wretched plight:

If yours is wooden, change it straight away,
    But if it's razor-sharp then join the fray!
Saints have such swords among their armory,   720
    Just seeing them for you is alchemy—
Listen to this description once again:
    He is *a mercy to the world of men.**
Buy pomegranates that the grocer's split
    So that its mouth will show the seeds in it,
For generous laughter shows us openly
    The heart, a pearl within the spirit's sea,
The tulip's laughter though displays its sin—
    Its mouth reveals the darkness deep within.
Whole gardens bloom when pomegranates smile: 725
    To be like mystics stay with them awhile,
For even if you should be made from stone,
    Through mystics as a jewel you'll soon be known;
Plant love of saints now firmly in your heart,
    Submit your soul to those who'll never part,
While there's still hope don't wallow in despair,
    Why choose the dark when there's a sun up there?
Your heart will lead you to the mystic way,
    Your body drags you to its cell of clay,
So give your heart food from those in accord—   730
    Seek fortune from the ones who know their lord!

Veneration of the description of the Prophet Mohammad which was included in the gospels

Inside the gospel was Mohammad's name,
    The soul of prophecy who's free from blame:
Accounts of his appearance it contained,
    His battles, fasts, and diet it explained;
A Christian sect, for their own benefit,
    On reading his most glorious name in it
Would kiss the text and raise it to their head,
    Respecting what the holy gospel said:

In all this latest strife that group were saved   735
    From terror, for the good way they behaved,
And from the evil of that sly vizier,
    Protected by his name, which they held dear;
Their offspring flourished, fortune didn't end,
    Mohammad's light became their helpful friend.
The other Christian groups made no attempt—
    They held the name Mohammad in contempt,
So they met shame and suffering so severe
    From seeds of evil sown by that vizier:
Their faith was tampered with,* it's not the same,   740
    Those false, misleading scrolls are all to blame!
From Ahmad's name you can gain such support,
    His light gives help of a much higher sort,
His name's a fort that foes can't penetrate—
    Imagine then his truthful spirit's state!

The story of another Jewish king who tried to destroy the religion of Jesus

After this bloodshed with no remedy
    Caused by that sly vizier's sheer cruelty,
Another king descending from that Jew
    Attempted to destroy the Christians too,
If you desire to learn of this attack   745
    Recite, *By heaven and its zodiac!**
The former king's bad precedent, by fate,
    This other king now tried to imitate;
Those who established evil customs still
    Receive each hour a curse which makes them ill,
While habits of the good don't fade away,
    From wicked men oppression's what will stay,
Until the end of time this latter kind
    Towards their fellow tyrants are inclined.
In parallel veins different waters passed   750
    And they'll continue till the trumpet blast,*

Sweet water reaches good men in the end,
   What is it? *To the good the Book we send.**

When you express your need, that is a flame,
   From prophethood's home straight to you it came,
Like flashes always circling round their source
   They'd head back there if they could find the force;
Light from the window circles round within
   Because the sun from star to star must spin.
If you're associated with a star,   755
   You'll share your journey home, however far,
With Venus as ascendant, what delight!
   You'll be disposed to love, and want what's right;
But if it's murderous Mars, then all will see
   That what you seek is war and enmity;
Beyond them there's another universe
   Where stars don't burn out, nor seem ominous,
In other heavens such stars circle round,
   Not those that we can gaze at from the ground,
Bathed in the light of God, immaculate,   760
   Not joined together, nor kept separate—
If for ascendant you have one of these
   Your soul will burn each infidel you seize!
It's not the rage of Mars, so don't be fooled,
   It doesn't change from mastery to being ruled,
This ruling light which God helps keep alight,
   By shielding it with fingers curled up tight;
Over all souls God lets His radiance fall,
   The lucky lift their skirts to catch it all,
Appreciating their small share of light   765
   From all apart from God they blind their sight;
Whoever lacked a skirt acquired through love,
   Could not catch any radiance from above:
Round Universal Being contingents turn
   While roses make each nightingale's heart burn.
The ox has on the outside coloured skin,
   Colours in humans are found deep within:

Bright colours from the vat of purity
  And ugly ones from brooks of cruelty:
The colouring by God* is rated first,   770
  The filthiest is called *what God has cursed*;
All flotsam on the sea must run its course
  But in the end it goes back to its source,
Like rapid torrents in the peaks above
  And human souls returning through their love.

The Jewish king makes a fire and places an idol next to it, saying 'Whoever prostrates himself before this idol will escape the fire'

Now witness what that Jew tried to conspire,
  He placed an idol right beside the fire,
Saying, 'Bow down before this to be free
  Or else you'll burn in fire eternally!'
Not dealing with his own self's vile abuse   775
  An idol form's what he let it produce;
Such forms the mother of all idols makes:
  Your dragon-self produces countless snakes!
Idols are sparks your flint-like self sends out,
  Water is what you need to put them out,
But water can't defeat that stubborn stone
  So safety's what no selfish man has known.
The idol is foul water in a bowl,
  Its source is nothing but the carnal soul;
The idol is just like a filthy flood,   780
  The self produces it like its own blood;
A stone can break a hundred cups and more,
  But nothing stops the fount's relentless pour:
To break an idol is an easy task,
  To smash yourself is hard—you need to ask?
To know the self's form, read what he dictates
  Concerning hellfire and hell's seven gates:
Each moment there's a plot, dear travellers,
  Drowning more pharaohs with their followers*—
To Moses and his God escape today,   785
  Don't spill faith's water—that's the pharaoh's way!

Cling to the Prophet and his God, take pride,
   Your body's ignorant, cast it aside!

A child begins to talk from inside the fire, urging people
to throw themselves into it

This Jew then brought a woman with her child
   Before the idol while the flames grew wild,
Then grabbed her child and quickly threw it in
   So she, in fear, would swap her faith for sin:
He wanted her now to bow down her head,
   But then her child cried, 'Stop, for *I'm not dead!*
I haven't died, I'm happy, join me here!   790
   It only looks like fire, so have no fear!
The fire just blinds you to what's really there:
   God's mercy which has come out of thin air.
Enter, and witness living proof of God,
   The joy which makes His own élite applaud,
Come and see water that's like fire, it's true,
   A world of fire which seems like water too!
And Abraham's well-hidden mysteries:*
   Here he found jasmine and tall cypress trees.
When you gave birth to me I saw my tomb—   795
   How much I feared I'd fall down from your womb!
Once born I fled the confines of that cage
   To fresh air and a bigger, brighter stage.
But now that world seems like a womb to me
   For in this fire I've found serenity:
I've seen a world without a trace of death,
   All atoms here have Jesus's pure breath,*
A world that's dead in form, but lives in essence,
   While that world lives in form, the realm of transience.
Enter, for every mother has the right,   800
   You'll see it has no flames though it shines bright!
Enter, for all good fortune's found in here,
   This opportunity will disappear!
You've seen the might of tyrants who are base,
   Now come and see the power of God's grace!

His mercy is what makes me now implore,
    Since drowned in joy I think of you no more;
Come in, and call the other people too,
    A royal banquet's waiting here for you!
Come in believers! Our pure faith apart,   805
    All other things bring torment to the heart—
Enter the flames like moths which burn their wings,
    Good fortune blossoms here like endless springs.'
The child's repeated shouting was so loud
    Amazement filled the souls of all the crowd,
So, selflessly, each one of them in turn
    Jumped in believing that they wouldn't burn:
They dived through love, they didn't drag their feet,
    All for the one who makes the bitter sweet.
The king's assistants weren't long to arrive   810
    To stop them—they said, 'No one else must dive!'
That Jew turned red for he now felt ashamed,
    Regret had left his bitter heart inflamed
Because he saw the people's faith increase—
    Through self-annihilation they'd found peace.
Thank God this evil plot left him disgraced,
    For Satan even would have been red-faced,
What he'd rubbed on the faces of that crowd
    Now covered his own face just like a cloud,
That one who tore the shirts that we all wore,   815
    Saw his own ripped, ours perfect as before.

How the smirk of that man who pronounced the name of
    Mohammad mockingly remained fixed on his face

He smirked as he read out the Prophet's name,
    Then couldn't wipe it off, and so he came
To beg Mohammad, 'Prophet, pardon me,
    You have such grace and know Truth's mystery;
I made fun then because I was a fool,
    I should myself have met such ridicule.'
When God decides to show they're immature
    He makes men feel inclined to mock the pure,

He also hides men's faults, preserves their name, 820
　By stopping them from giving others blame;
When God should wish to help he first decrees
　That we must humbly beg him on our knees—
How great it is to cry for just his sake
　And for a heart, through love of him, to bake!
Your tears will end with laughter—can't you tell?
　How blest are those who know this secret well:
Wherever water's flowed some grass has grown,
　Wherever tears are wept God's mercy's shown—
Be like the water-wheel, weep endlessly 825
　So that your soul can grow its greenery!
Have mercy first if tears are what you seek,
　To gain God's mercy pity all the weak!

The fire's reproach for the king of the Jews

The king turned to the fire, 'Short-tempered one,
　What's going on, are you not meant to burn?
What happened to your special quality?
　Have your intentions changed by destiny?
Fire-worshippers you chose not to forgive
　So why let those who don't adore you live?
You're not known for your patience, so why now 830
　Will you not burn—have you forgotten how?
This world deprives us of our sense of sight,
　But how can fire not burn—this can't be right!
Have spells been cast, or is it sorcery?
　Is this unnatural outcome fate's decree?'
The fire said, 'I've not changed, idolater,
　Come in and feel my heat, you murderer!
My nature and my essence stay the same,
　As God's own sword, I slash when he takes aim!
The Turkmen's dogs all linger by his hut, 835
　Before each guest they fawn and whimper, but
If they should see a stranger pass one day,
　They'll roar like lions, and chase him away—

I'm not less than a dog in servanthood
   And God controls more than the Turkmen could!'

If the fire in your nature makes you grieve
   Remember that it's only by God's leave,
If the fire in your nature gives you bliss
   The lord of faith has filled your soul with this.
When you feel sorrow beg forgiveness, friend,   840
   He's sent grief as a means to a good end!
Your pain he'll turn to joy, and equally,
   If he should choose, from fetters you'll be free.
Earth, water, wind, and fire, his faithful slaves,
   Alive with him, to us seem dead as graves:
In front of God, flames always stand up straight
   And writhe like lovers in a passionate state,
A spark leaps out when iron's struck with stone,
   It travels out by God's command alone,
Don't strike it with the stone of tyranny—   845
   It multiplies like men relentlessly;
Though stone and iron are the cause, you can
   Attempt to look beyond them, noble man.
This cause was prompted by a prior one,
   So how can men assume that it has none?
Those causes which decide what Prophets do
   Are higher than these causes you can view,
Those ones can choose to make these take effect,
   Or make them fruitless things we all neglect;
These causes can be grasped with just your mind,   850
   But only Prophets know the other kind—
What is it? Say, '*A rope*' in Arabic,
   Hung in the well so straight it seems a stick:
The water-wheel's spin moves this rope in front,
   If you can't see this, then you're ignorant!
Don't say rope-like effects seen in this world
   From heaven's wheel directly have been hurled,
Don't be a zero, round just like this wheel,
   Hollow wood for the fire—discern what's real!

The wind can clash with fire by God's decree,   855
    Drunk through God's wine which adds ferocity:
Water is gentle, fire enraged, my son,
    Open your eyes, see both come from the One.
If the wind's soul had not been taught by God
    How could it tell apart the men of Aad?
Hud drew a line around his righteous men,
    On reaching it the wind died down again,
But all those standing on the other side
    Were flattened for wind there did not subside;
Just like Shayban the Shepherd* who would draw   860
    Around his flock a line all clearly saw,
So when he left on Fridays for the prayer
    No wolf would ever harm the sheep in there,
While wolves dared not ignore the shepherd's sign
    No sheep would ever step across this line:
The grunts of greed from both the wolves and sheep
    Were silenced by the circle of his keep.
For mystics too the wind that signals death,
    Like Joseph's scent, seems soft, refreshing breath,
And Abraham from fire felt no alarm*—   865
    God's chosen prophet bonfires couldn't harm!
The faithful can't be burnt by fires of lust
    Though it reduces men to less than dust.
On God's command, the fierce waves in the sea
    Could still tell Moses from his enemy,
When orders came the earth dragged Korah* down
    Into its depths, despite his throne and crown;
Jesus's breath made water mixed with clay*
    Grow wings, become a bird and fly away!
Your praise is now hot air, but will appear   870
    A bird of heaven if your heart's sincere;
Moses's light made Sinai dance and spin,*
    Becoming thus a dervish, free of sin:
Mountains can change to dervishes each day,
    Moses's body used to be mere clay!

*The Jewish king ridicules, denies, and refuses to accept
the advice of his own élite*

The king saw all these wonders, but did naught
　　But mock and then deny what they all taught,
Advisers warned, 'Don't push the limit, king,
　　Don't ride too far your steed of quarrelling!'
He cuffed and locked them up immediately   875
　　And then continued with his tyranny;
At this point all the people heard a shout:
　　'Stop, dog, our wrath has come to sort you out!'
A fire soared forty feet above, and then
　　It formed a ring and burnt all of his men:
Their origin was fire right from the start—
　　Back to their source they now had to depart.
That group were also born of fire, of course;
　　Particles track their universal source,
A fire to burn believers with foul deeds,   880
　　This fire consumed itself like burning weeds!

His mother's called Hawiya, which means 'hell',*
　　So she must be his everlasting cell:
A mother seeks her child each day she lives
　　As sources seek their own derivatives;
If water is confined inside a pond,
　　The wind extracts and carries it beyond,
Then sets it free by wafting drops back home
　　Gently, without creating waves or foam.
Likewise, it's breath which steals men's souls away   885
　　From this world's prison, bit by bit each day:
For thus, *From us sweet perfumed words shall rise**
　　To places known alone by God, the Wise;
Our breaths are granted leave selectively,
　　Gifts for the realm of His eternity,
Rewards for good speech come down to us then
　　Twice over, mercy from God to good men.

Then He entrusts us to exemplars, so
    His servants can receive what such men know—
These breaths ascend and grace comes down from there,   890
    May you not cease from doing your own share!
Let's speak in Persian: this attraction's pull
    Is from the source of all things spiritual;
The eyes of every group look to that side
    Where inner cravings might be satisfied,
For each one seeks another of its kind—
    The part pines for the whole you'll always find;
But maybe it can join another sort,
    Becoming one of them when they consort?
Water and bread with us you can't compare   895
    But, once they're eaten, turn to flesh in there,
Water and bread don't look compatible,
    The end-result shows that it's possible.
So if it's something different that you like
    It must at least in some way be alike;
Things that are similar only can be lent,
    A loan is never something permanent:
A hunter's whistle sounds just like a bird
    To capture those deceived by what they've heard!
Sea vapour can mislead all men who thirst,   900
    For water they mistake its form at first;
The penniless are pleased to find false gold,
    But in the mint its shameful truth is told.
Don't let false gold divert you straight to hell
    Or fickle fancies lead you down a well,
Look up this tale in *Kalila and Dimna**
    And find the page to which this part is similar:

Explanation of trust in God: the lion's prey tell it to stop self-exertion

Once in a valley all the beasts ran scared:
    A lion preyed on them and none were spared.

It used to hide, then pounce and seize its prey—   905
　　That's why they couldn't face another day;
Once, with the lion they agreed a deal:
　　'Each day we'll satisfy you with a meal,
But you must not attack us any more!
　　This means our grass won't taste bad like before.'

The lion answers its prey and explains the benefit of exerting oneself

The lion said, 'Alright, if you're sincere,
　　But I know every trick, let that be clear!
Men's schemes have ruined me, I've made mistakes,
　　Been bitten by men's scorpions and their snakes.'
One's carnal soul that's hidden from our sight   910
　　Is worse than them in scheming and in spite,
'Believers are not stung,' when I first heard
　　I followed with my heart the Prophet's word.

The lion's prey prefer full trust in fate to exerting oneself

The beasts of prey said, 'Sage who clearly sees,
　　Precautions can't *prevent what God decrees*,
To play safe just means extra bother too—
　　Have trust in destiny, that's best for you!
Don't wave your fist at fate and shake your head
　　In case fate picks a fight with you instead!
With God's decree be dead just like a pawn,   915
　　Protected from *the Lord of every dawn*.'*

The lion prefers exertion of effort to trust in fate

The lion said, 'If trust will guide, okay,
　　But effort also is the Prophet's way:
For once Mohammad firmly clarified:
　　"Trust God, but still make sure your camel's tied!"
God loves the one who earns, so I urge you:
　　Trust God but don't forget you must act too!'

The lion's prey prefer trust in God over exerting oneself

They said, 'But trying to earn means you're weak,
    Birds say such bites fill no more than one's beak,
And earning can't surpass full trust in fate,   920
    Complete surrender to the Lord's dictate.'
Many fled problems, but found more despair:
    Don't run from snakes straight to a dragon's lair!
A man's scheme backfired with his first real shot,
    It seemed the food of life, but made him rot,
He locked the door, but with his foe inside!
    Such was the plot that Pharaoh once had tried:
A hundred thousand babies he had slain,
    But let the one sought in his home remain!
Our vision has such flaws, to end your plight   925
    Annihilate your vision in God's sight:
His sight for ours—what a terrific swap!
    With His sight your fulfilment will not stop;
Until a child has learned to walk he must
    Ride father's shoulders, placing there his trust,
If he impatiently sets off alone
    He'll end up wretched, bruised, and on his own;
Men's souls, without a hand or foot, could be
    Seen flying through the realms of purity,
But when God told them, '*Go down** in your cage!'   930
    They were entrapped again by lust and rage.
We're children of the Lord who want love's milk,
    Men are God's family, though not of His ilk,
If He can drop the rain down on your head
    Through mercy He can also bring you bread!

The lion prefers exerting oneself over trust

The lion said, 'But God has caused to rise
    A ladder right before our very eyes;
We must climb rung by rung up to the top—
    It's selfish to resign to fate and stop:

When you have feet, why make out that you're lame?
   When you've a pair of hands why do the same?'
If a king puts a spade in his slave's hand
   Without a word he's given his command:
Think of your hands the same as that slave's spade—
   Mere thought of action means his judgement's made:
Act on His signs with heart, and be sincere,
   And then their truths before you shall appear;
He'll give you hints of secrets that he masks,
   Lift off your burden, give you other tasks—
If you consent, then you'll be carried through,   940
   If you accept, you'll be accepted too,
Become His spokesman—follow His command:
   The union that you seek you'll reach as planned.
Exertion's thanking God for strength to act
   While fatalism spurns it—that's a fact!
Through giving thanks our means to act increase,
   Through fatalism grace from Him will cease:
Don't doze while travelling, for if you should sleep
   You'll miss His gate and court, and then you'll weep!
Don't sleep, you lazy brat, so heedlessly,   945
   Except beneath His own fruit-laden tree,
So when the wind should make the branches sway
   Some fruit will fall to help you on your way!
Sleeping near highwaymen so trustfully
   How can you ever feel security?
Don't turn your nose up at His signals, brat,
   Spoilt women who believe they're men do that!
The little sense you have will not remain:
   A head is just a tail without a brain!
For such ingratitude is mean and low   950
   And leads you to the fiery depths below—
Trust God, but also act and not just wait:
   First sow your seeds before you count on fate!

The lion's prey say again that trust is better than exertion

The animals made a hullabaloo:
  'The greedy who have "sown" their deeds like you,
A thousand men and women who have tried,
  From fortune then why were they all denied?'
For countless centuries from creation's start,
  Like dragons who have spread their jaws apart
These clever people planned such schemes at will   955
  Which lift up mountains from their base, but still
God has described their schemes as disapproved:
  He's warned: *the tops of mountains might be moved.**
Apart from that which had been pre-ordained
  From all their scheming nothing has remained,
They fell from grace and lost the power to act
  While God's decrees have all remained intact—
Don't think that earning's more than just a name,
  Or that exertion's more than just a game!

How Azrael once stared at a man who then fled to Solomon's
palace; the demonstration of the superiority of trust over exertion,
the latter being of relatively little value

A noble man once barged in through the crowd   960
  In Solomon's famed court, and cried aloud;
His face was white with fear, his lips were blue.
  Solomon asked, 'Friend, what is wrong with you?'
'It's Azrael—he gave me such a stare
  That showed more rage than any man could bear!'
Solomon said, 'Whatever you want, just ask!'
  He pleaded, 'Please assign the wind this task:
To transfer me to India with its breath
  So, over there, I might escape my death.'
People will run away from deprivation   965
  To be devoured by greed and expectation;
His fright was like the fear of feeling need,
  His flight to India represents his greed.

Solomon told the wind to make this trip,
   To take this man to India's southern tip.
The next day at exactly the same time
   He questioned Azrael right at the chime:
'Angel of death, did you drive that good man
   From home and family—was that your plan?'
He answered, 'Now you know I wouldn't lie,   970
   I just looked on amazed as he strolled by,
For God had said today he would be dead
   Not over here, but India's tip instead—
Even with wings to take him through the air
   I thought he was too far to die down there!'
All of the world's affairs are planned this way,
   Open your eyes to see this clear as day!
Whom shall we leave? Ourselves? Impossible!
   To flee from God? That's simply laughable!

The lion again claims exertion to be superior to trust, and explains the advantages of exertion

The lion said, 'That's true, but don't forget   975
   The works of prophets and believers yet.'
All their exertions God himself made good,
   Like all the trials and torture they withstood,
Their plans succeeded—take that as a sign!
   What issues from a fine man must be fine.
Heavenly birds they captured with their traps
   New virtues made of their own handicaps—
So strive your utmost on the mystic way
   Just like the prophets and the saints, don't stray!
For striving hard does not mean fighting fate   980
   Since fate itself has served this on our plate—
Call me an infidel if men lose out
   By trying to be faithful and devout!
Your head's not broken—treatment's not required,
   Just strive a bit, then rest like those retired!
Those after this world seek a rotten place
   But seeking what's beyond is no disgrace;

All schemes to gain wealth here fail miserably
    But schemes to flee this world taste victory,
So dig a tunnel to escape your cell, 985
    Don't block it up, or you'll be stuck in hell:
This world's a prison, we're locked up inside,
    To free yourself dig all the way outside!
What is this world? Being heedless of the Lord,
    Not women and those precious goods you hoard!
But wealth you hold for your religion's health
    Is good: the Prophet called it '*righteous wealth!*'
Water that's poured inside will sink the boat
    While water underneath keeps it afloat.
Driving wealth from his heart to keep it pure 990
    King Solomon preferred the title 'Poor':
That sealed jar in the stormy sea out there
    Floats on the waves because it's full of air,
When you've the air of dervishhood inside
    You'll float above the world, and there abide;
Although the world is this man's property
    To his heart's eye it's worthless vanity—
So seal your heart's mouth shut like Solomon
    And fill it with divine breath from the One!
Like pain and cure, exertion's being's true, 995
    Denial of this is mere exertion too.

The establishment of the superiority of exertion over trust

So many proofs the lion would relate,
    The fatalists grew tired of this debate;
The fox, the deer, the hare, the jackal too
    Stopped answering back, abandoning their view;
With him they then agreed a deal, where he
    Would not lose out—they gave a guarantee:
Each day a beast would come straight to his den
    Without the need for him to hunt again:
Whoever drew the shortest of the straws 1000
    Would race just like a cheetah to his jaws!

But when the hare's turn came he screamed a lot:
  'How long must tyrants take all that we've got!'

The other animals blame the hare for his delay in going to the lion

They told him, 'Many times we've sacrificed
  Our lives to keep our pledge, and that's sufficed.
You stubborn hare, don't shame us any more,
  Now hurry up before he starts to roar!'

The hare answers them

The hare said, 'Friends, won't you give me respite,
  My scheme will save you from your sorry plight,
Life then will be secure for all of you,   1005
  The same applies for all your children too:
Each prophet called on his community
  In the same way to seek security,
A route beyond each could identify
  As narrow as the pupil of an eye—
Their people thought them, like the pupil, small,
  But who could boast their greatness—none at all!'

The other animals object to the words of the hare

'Don't be a donkey's hair, now listen well,
  Act like the hare you are, so all can tell!
You're bragging to your betters, don't ignore   1010
  The fact we might have thought of this before;
Either you're arrogant, or it's our fate,
  How can your speech fit someone in your state?'

The hare's answer to the other animals

He said, 'My friends, by God I've been inspired,
  A weakling's learned strong views, that's what's transpired.'
God taught the bee a skill that's something more
  Than what he taught the lion and the boar:

The bee can make a moist, sweet honeycomb,
　　God's opened up to it His wisdom's home,
Like when He taught the silkworm how to spin,　　1015
　　An earthworm wouldn't know where to begin!
And Adam learned such truths from God that fire
　　Blazed up to heaven as a massive pyre,
But the good name of angels was wiped out
　　By that blind one, who God's own word would doubt:*
Satan, ascetic for millennia, then
　　Was muzzled and would not be freed again,
So he could not drink wisdom's milk at all,
　　Nor walk around God's heavenly castle's hall.
Physical senses are like muzzles too　　1020
　　That keep the milk of mystic truth from you;
A jewel has dropped in your heart's deep core,
　　Which neither seas nor heaven knew before,
So why still worship form, an empty shape—
　　Your soulless spirit must learn to escape!
If humans could be men through form and name
　　The Prophet and Bu Jahl would be the same:
Paintings can look like men, but still we doubt
　　When we look closely—something's been left out:
Its form is perfect, but it lacks a soul—　　1025
　　Go, seek out that rare jewel—that's your goal!
The lions bowed their heads at what God gave
　　The dog of the Companions of the Cave:*
Despite its ugly form it reached the height
　　Of animal perfection through God's light.
The author's pen will not record your looks—
　　'Learnèd' and 'just' instead they write in books:
Such qualities are spiritual and real,
　　Not things you can locate, observe, and feel;
Rays strike your frame from God's unknown domain,　　1030
　　The Lord's divine sun heaven can't contain.

An account of the hare's knowledge and an explanation of
the virtue and benefits of knowledge

This discourse has no end—let's leave it there
    And listen to the story of the hare,
Sell those dumb ears and buy some better ones
    For donkey's ears are just for simpletons!*
Witness the hare outfox the lion with tricks,
    Come, learn about the plot he tried to fix!
In Solomon's realm knowledge was the goal,
    This world's material, knowledge for the soul,
Knowledge is what makes Man magnificent   1035
    While other creatures are all impotent:
Lions and leopards turn to mice through fear
    And crocodiles turn pale when he comes near,
Angels and demons run out to the shores,
    All seek a hiding-place or bolt their doors;
So Man has very many hidden foes,
    A cautious man is one with sense, who knows:
All kinds of creatures hidden from our sight
    Attempt to strike your heart with all their might.
If you should ever wash down by the stream   1040
    A thorn inside is bound to make you scream,
Although it's hidden down below, beware!
    Once you are pricked you'll know for sure it's there!
Some thorns inspire, some tempt you from your course,
    They come from thousands, not a single source,
Wait till your outward senses have evolved
    To see them all, and find your problems solved—
You'll see then just whom you have failed to heed
    And whom you've judged as qualified to lead.

The other animals seek from the hare the secret of his thoughts

The other beasts then said, 'Quick-thinking hare,   1045
    What is it you perceive of our affair?

You've dealt with king-size problems, so relate
   What you conclude about our present state!'
Conferral aids perception, helps one learn,
   Like minds can help their fellows to discern:
The Prophet said, '*Consult them, counsellor,*
   And trust the ones with whom you must confer!'

The hare withholds that secret from them

The hare said, 'Every secret can't be shown,
   Dice bring up odds then evens when they're thrown:
To clean a mirror first you'll want to blow   1050
   But steam will quickly dull the mirror's glow.'
Keep your lips sealed, don't mention, as a rule,
   Your path, your wealth, and your religious school,
For these three can attract so many foes,
   Each one will wait to catch you once he knows—
Don't even tell a few, have you not read:
   '*All secrets shared by more than two are spread*'?
Tie up two birds together and you'll see
   That they stay grounded, trapped, in agony,
They're actually conferring, though they're bound,   1055
   With metaphors to fool all those around.
The Prophet gave exclusive teachings too,
   Answering his men though they then had no clue;
To cloak his words he'd use a parable
   So foes could not grasp what was valuable,
And he extracted answers from each foe
   While from his questions none of them would know!

The story of the hare's plot

The hare delayed his journey for a while,
   Then started to complete that final mile,
That lion slew foes, and the hare was late,   1060
   So he would beat the ground and roar, irate:
'I knew those wretched beasts were bound to break
   Their promises—their contract was a fake!

They've tripped me up so cruelly with deceit,
    How many times will fate's tricks thus repeat!'
All feeble-minded princes feel despair
    When they can't see what's happening out there:
The road looks smooth, but traps are set below,
    When they lack meaning, names are just for show,
Both words and names are hidden pitfalls too: 1065
    Flattery is sand which saps all life from you.
The sand which gushes water is so rare,
    You'll have to search for that kind everywhere!
The man of God is like that type of sand;
    Fleeing himself he grabs God's helping hand,
Faith's waters flow from him relentlessly,
    Reviving seekers with love's gifts for free.
But other men are like the driest sand,
    They sap all life from you, please understand:
Seek wisdom from the sage now, if you can,   1070
    Gain knowledge and new vision from this man!
Seek wisdom, and then you'll become its source,
    Needless, safe from what drives men from their course;
The student's tablet turns to one 'preserved',*
    When intellect from spirit grace is served:
At first his intellect would lead the way
    But like a student now it must obey,
The intellect repeats what Gabriel said:
    'Prophet, I'll burn if I should move ahead!
But you can still proceed towards the goal,   1075
    I've reached my limit, Sultan of the Soul!'*

Each heedless and impatient, low ingrate
    Complains that he must always follow fate,
Excuses like from those who feign being ill—
    They'll suffer from a sickness that can kill:
'Saying you're sick in jest', the Prophet said
    'Will bring an illness that will leave you dead!'
Fate ties up broken bones to heal the pain
    And joins together every broken vein:

You haven't any broken bones—we know!   1080
   So who're you fooling with your bandaged toe?
One suffered so much striving on this course
   And so Boraq was sent down as his horse;
He was now borne, for faith's demands he'd faced,
   He followed orders first, then was embraced,
Before he'd have to meet the king's demands
   But now the army follows his commands,
Stars also used to influence him then
   But now he rules the stars just like his men,
If you have problems in perceiving it   1085
   You'll also doubt the fact *the moon was split*,*
Revive your faith, but not just with your tongue,
   Secretly to your lusts why have you clung?
When lusts are fresh, faith can't be any more,
   Lust is the very key that locks the door!
Now you are judging God's inviolate word—
   Examine your own soul, not truths you've heard!
Since you read through desire the Holy Verse
   You make its meaning wretched and perverse!

On the shallow interpretation of the fly

A fly in donkey's urine, perched on straw,   1090
   Just like a boatman gazing at the shore,
Said, 'Straw and urine are my boat and sea,
   I've contemplated this fact recently:
I'm in the sea, the captain of my boat,
   Following maps and methods learned by rote.'
In urine it would steer its straw-made raft
   As if in boundless seas, for it was daft:
It thought a single drop could stretch so far
   Unable to observe things as they are,
Its world stretched out as far it could view,   1095
   Small eyes count as a sea a drop or two!
Narrow interpreters are like this fly,
   With straw and urine they all falsify,

If you stop reading from your own small view,
    The phoenix will grant kingdoms then to you!
Still, those who've worked this out aren't really flies,
    Spirits don't correspond to body-size:

The lion roars loudly because the hare arrives late

Like that brave hare the lion had thought tame
    Whose soul was not restricted by his frame.
The lion roared, 'Through my own ears my foes   1100
    Have blinded me: they've dealt such vicious blows!
I've been bound by those fatalists' vile plots,
    With wooden weapons too they've taken shots!
No longer will I listen to their word,
    They're screams that from the ghouls too can be heard!
Just tear them up, O heart, don't be led on,
    And skin them for they've nothing once that's gone!'
What's skin? The specious words which lead astray!
    Like ripples on the tide they fade away.
The meaning's flesh, while speech is just the shell—   1105
    Like form in contrast to the soul as well.
The rotten kernels can't be seen through skin,
    Nor good ones, for skin hides its pride within.
When water is the pad and wind the pen
    The words you write will soon be gone again,
They're etched on waves; if you seek constancy
    You'll be dissatisfied by what you see!
Renounce lust's breath, which fills you to the brim,
    And wind will bring you messages from Him.
God's messages are always sweet and pure   1110
    Because throughout they always will endure:
All rulers' glories and their sermon-praise*
    Must pass, but not the prophets' perfect ways,
While pomp of kings comes from their own desire
    By God the prophets are admitted higher,

The names of kings are scraped off coins in days
    But Ahmad's name no coiner can erase!
His name contains the whole prophetic line
    The way that ten includes one through to nine.

Further explanation of the hare's stratagem

His journey to the lion he delayed   1115
    In order to rehearse the plan he'd made;
After a while the hare then headed near
    To whisper something in the lion's ear.
What worlds the strength of gnosis lets you see,
    More vast than oceans filled with purity!
Our forms traverse this lovely ocean fast
    Like cups which on its surface have been cast;
Until they're full like tubs they float on top
    But once they're filled they finally start to drop,
Truth's sea is hidden, land is on display,   1120
    Our forms are waves, or just the ocean spray.
Whatever means form uses to come near
    By that same means waves toss it far from here,
Until the Giver of the Truths they know,
    Until the arrows learn who's fired the bow.
The foolish think their horses have no worth
    And force them to race all across the earth:
Each places little value on his horse
    Though rapidly it bears him on the course,
Such that a foolish, simple-minded twit   1125
    Will even ask, 'Has anyone seen it—
Who stole my horse and where is he now hiding?'
    'Dear fellow, what is that on which you're riding!'
'This is a horse, I know, but where's that one?'
    'Wake up famed knight, your brain has been undone!'
The soul seems lost although it's so close by:
    Your bladder's full although your lips are dry.

How can you see bright colours with your sight
   When you've not even learned to see the light?
With colours you completely lost your mind,   1130
   Their glare became the veil which made you blind.
Did you not see when colours fade at night
   That they are all dependent on the light?
Without light, colour disappears from view,
   The same applies for inner colours too,
While outward light the sun and stars may shine
   The source of inner light is the Divine:
Vision's light comes from light inside your heart,
   This inner light's required for it to start.
Your heart's light's source is naught but God's own light   1135
   Safe from the reach of sense and reason's blight.
No colours can be seen at night unlit,
   For light, the darkness is the opposite:
You must see light to see the colours too,
   The opposite of light has proved it's true,
As God created hardship and distress
   So through them you would learn of happiness:
All hidden things by opposites are known,
   Since He has none, God's hidden on His own.
Man can discern all colours once there's light,   1140
   Each as distinct as black skin next to white:
You know of light thanks to its opposite,
   Things show their opposite through lack of it.
No opposite for God's light can exist
   Through which it might be known—this is the gist,
Our eyes can't see Him, even with our pleas,
   Moses's mountain proves to us *He sees*;*
Like lions from thought's jungle, forms have come,
   In this way, thought's where speech and sound come from;
Though speech and sound have thus emerged from thought   1145
   You have no clue where that sea should be sought,
But since you've seen the wave of speech is fine
   You know its source, that sea, must be divine.
From knowledge when there first arose thought's wave
   Through His speech then a form to you it gave:

This form was born of speech, then died again,
    The waves drew back like cattle to their pen.
From formlessness comes form originally,
    And *We return to Him** continually!
Each moment you must die and then return,   1150
    'The world is but a moment', you'll soon learn;
Our thought's an arrow He's shot from the sky,
    Can it rise up again to Him on high?
Each breath the world's renewed, though we can't tell,
    While it's renewed, the world persists as well:
Life's constantly renewed just like the stream,
    A single mass in form though it might seem,
Its swift flow makes it seem continuous
    Like sparklers twirling round—it's marvellous!
For if you spin a lit torch round and round   1155
    Its flame looks like a circle that is sound;
A stretch of time appears thus through sheer pace—
    Speed in creation covers time like space,
But scholars can't perceive beyond the looks—
    Even Hosam, who's read the loftiest books.

The hare reaches the lion

The lion in a rage first lost his patience,
    Then saw the hare approaching in the distance,
Running, bold, unafraid, self-confident,
    Angry, outraged and fierce in temperament—
Meekness would be in vain, the hare'd worked out,   1160
    While bravery wouldn't make the lion doubt.
The hare came nearer to the lion's den
    And heard it roar, 'Here comes that wretch again!
I've torn apart the limbs of elephants
    And boxed the ears of lions during hunts—
Who does this half-wit hare think that he's found
    To wrestle with and pin down on the ground?
Continue with your heedless sleep no more,
    Listen, you ass-eared beast,* to my deep roar!'

The hare's apology

The hare cried, 'Please hear my apology,   1165
   I pray that your forgiveness pardons me!'
'What kind of explanation do you bring
   As you approach the presence of the king?
For such bad timing we'll chop off your head,
   No cheap excuses do we let be said.'
A lame excuse is worse than the misdeed,
   It ruins all you might have earned, take heed!
'Hare, your excuse is bound to be absurd,
   I don't have donkeys' ears to hear a word!'
'This worthless wretch, king, count as someone true   1170
   For tyranny's what held me back from you,
My noble lord, show mercy please today—
   Don't drive from here a slave who lost his way!
That ocean which fills up each river-bed
   Bears all the flotsam happily on its head:
By being kind seas don't end up with less,
   They don't decrease in spite of their largesse.'
He said, 'I'm generous when the time is right,
   I tailor cloth to fit each person's height.'
The hare said, 'If I don't deserve your grace   1175
   Before your snake-like wrath I'll turn my face:
Since breakfast I've been on my way to you,
   A fellow traveller made the journey too—
The other beasts sent out another hare
   To come with me, it's safer as a pair—
But then a lion stopped us in our tracks:
   It pounced on us and gave us heart attacks!
"We are the slaves of a great king," I warned,
   "At court our disappearance would be mourned."
He said, "Which king makes you now feel no shame   1180
   Before me to recall another's name?
You and your king I'll tear apart like clay
   If you two hares should try to run away!"

I pleaded, "Let me see my king again
    To tell him where we've been—I'll come back then!"
He said, "But leave your friend as guarantee,
    Or you will be the sacrifice for me!"
Although we begged him, we could not succeed,
    My friend was tied up, so that I'd be freed;
My captive friend was twice as fat as me   1185
    And twice as fine in grace and dignity.
That lion's blocked the road since this event,
    This is what happened after I was sent.
Abandon hope of more allowances,
    The truth tastes bitter, but that's how it is:
If you need daily meals unblock the way—
    Come and drive off that shameless wretch today!'

The lion answers the hare and sets off with him

The lion said, 'By God, we must rush there
    If what you say is true, then show me where
So I can deal the likes of him their due,   1190
    But if you're lying I'll deal it to you!'
The hare led like a guide who has a map,
    Taking the lion straight into his trap,
Towards a well which previously the hare
    Had cleverly converted to a snare.
The pair soon reached the well they'd headed for,
    The hare's effect like water under straw:*
Water transports a blade from place to place,
    But can it move a mountain from its base?
His guile's trap was the lion's noose, my friend,   1195
    The clever hare made tyranny thus end,
As Moses killed the Pharaoh through the Nile
    With his huge army and the rank and file,
Just like the gnat with half a wing which split
    The skull of Nimrod,* disregarding it;
Watch those who listened to their enemies,
    Hear what befell those plagued by jealousies,

For Pharaoh heeded what Haman conveyed,*
    As Nimrod heard the devil and obeyed—
If foes should chat with you just like a mate   1200
    Look for the trap that comes with every bait!
For sugar he gives poison, so beware,
    He treats you cruelly, though he seems to care.
When destiny strikes, you just see the ends
    And not the means, nor enemies from friends,
Since you're like this, confess to God your shame,
    Begin to mourn and fast, and praise His name!
'*Knower of hidden things*', plead all the while,
    'Don't crush us with the rock of evil guile!'
The lion's maker, though we're a disgrace   1205
    Don't let it jump out from its hiding-place!
Don't make fire and sweet water look the same,
    Nor change to water's form a burning flame!
Your wrath's wine can intoxicate each brain,
    Let non-existents thus existence gain!
What's drunkenness? To keep your eyes shut tight
    So stones appear like jewels in your sight,
It's changing every sense round for the good
    So tamarisk should smell like sandalwood.

*The story of the Hoopoe and Solomon, explaining that
    when destiny is fulfilled open eyes are shut*

Solomon's tent was put up by his men   1210
    And all his birds came back to him again,
He spoke their tongue and knew them personally
    So one by one they flew there eagerly.
The birds stopped twittering inside his tent,
    Than brothers they became more eloquent:
Sharing a language is a bond so deep,
    With foreigners we're prisoners in their keep,
Some Turks and Indians though might speak the same
    While fellow Turks are strangers but in name—
The tongue of intimacy is set apart,   1215
    Beyond mere words, it's being one at heart;

By verbal and non-verbal intimations
   Our hearts give thousands of interpretations.
The birds talked of their secrets as plain facts
   About their skills, their knowledge, and their acts:
They shared them, one by one, with Solomon,
   To gain his gifts they talked up what they'd done!
Not out of self-assertion or sheer pride
   But so he'd let them sit with him inside:
To gain his freedom back once he is caught   1220
   The prisoner shows his skills till he is bought,
But if the buyer sickens him with shame
   He'll claim he's ill, unstable, deaf, and lame!
The hoopoe first explained his worthiness
   By speaking of his skills and thoughtfulness:
'Although this talent seems inferior
   To speak concisely is superior.'
Solomon said, 'By all means, go ahead!'
   'When from the zenith I look down,' she said,
'I see with accuracy, like my own hand,   1225
   The water lying deep beneath the land:
Its depth, its colour, where to dig a well,
   The nature of its source too I can tell—
If on a camping-place you must decide
   Keep this perceptive hoopoe by your side!'
Solomon said, 'We do need such a brain
   In vast and empty, waterless terrain,
To lead the men to water in the ground—
   So take the job of serving water round!'

The crow's attack on the claim of the hoopoe

On hearing this, the crow rose jealously   1230
   To claim the hoopoe spoke dishonestly:
'It's rude to speak to kings in such false ways,
   More so to lie absurdly in self-praise:
If she could see that from beyond the sky
   How come that snare had still escaped her eye

In which she was entrapped so easily?
　　How come she stepped inside unwittingly?'
Solomon asked, 'Well, hoopoe is this true,
　　Are dregs in the first glass I'm served by you?
You've drunk mere yoghurt, don't claim that you're high!　1235
　　The boasts you made before me were a lie!'

The hoopoe answers the criticism of the crow

She said, 'Though I'm a beggar, poor and bare,
　　Don't listen to the things my foes declare,
If you consider false the words I've said
　　Here is my neck—feel free to chop my head!
The crow who would deny that God's will rules
　　Rejects faith, though she's studied in great schools:
If you don't have an ounce of faithfulness
　　You're like the crotch of lust and filthiness!
I see all snares, while flying in the skies　　　　　　1240
　　If fate does not deny them to my eyes:
When fate decrees our brain sleeps in its spell,
　　The sun's eclipsed, the moon turns black as well;
It's not so strange that fate should thus decree,
　　Fate too wills your denial of destiny.'

The story of Adam: destiny blinded his sight, so that he failed to observe the message, and to refrain from interpreting it differently

*He taught the Names** to Adam at the start,
　　Thus knowledge filled our ancestor's pure heart,
The names of things, which showed how they'd turn out
　　Were granted to his soul to rid all doubt;
Each name that he'd assign would therefore last,　　1245
　　What he called 'slow' did not then turn out fast,
The faithful at the end of time he knew
　　And those who'd turn out unbelievers too—
So learn the names of things as He decrees,
　　He taught the Names holds all the mysteries.

Our names for things convey the way they're seen,
 Their inner natures are what God's names mean,
For Moses simply called his stick 'a rod',*
 While 'snake' was what had been assigned by God;
'Omar' meant polytheist once in the past,   1250
 Although it meant 'believer' at Alast;*
Our names are like a seed that's just been sown,
 Before God is the fruit that's finally grown;
In non-existence seeds are just a form,
 Existent with the Lord, they must transform,
And in the end our names from God dictate
 How we will truly be and what's our fate:
He names men thus according to their end
 While for their present state a name He'll lend.
When Adam gained the light of purity   1255
 He then perceived souls and reality,
God's light in him when angels could observe
 They fell prostrate and vowed that they would serve!
If I recount the virtues of this sun
 The end of time will come before I'm done,
But though he was so wise, when fate decreed
 One prohibition Adam failed to heed:
'Is this to be forbidden? That seems odd!
 Or is interpreting allowed by God?'
Since he tried to interpret on his own   1260
 He couldn't leave forbidden fruit alone,
Like when a gardener stepped upon a thorn:
 A thief snatched all his things and then was gone,
The gardener soon calmed down and found relief,
 But saw his tools were stolen by the thief.
'*O Lord, we've erred!*'* He sighed with heart aflame,
 'We lost the way as soon as darkness came!'
So destiny can block the sun's bright light,
 Turn lions into mice because of fright.

If I don't see a snare by God's decree   1265
 I'm not the first who can't see destiny;

Blest is the one who follows righteousness,
    Who gives up all his power for lowliness:
If fate should dress you up in black like night
    Still it will help you in your hardest plight;
If destiny should try to murder you
    First it makes sure that you'll be born anew;
If it waylays you, hurls you in a ditch,
    A tent for you in heaven it will pitch:
By frightening you, know that He's being kind,   1270
    In His safe kingdom space for you He'll find,
This talk remains unfinished, but it's late,
    Now listen to the tale while I narrate:

The hare steps back from the lion when it approaches the well

The lion now approached the well they'd found
    But saw the hare retreat and turn around:
'Why is it you retreat, hare? what is wrong?
    Don't stop like that, come forward and be strong!'
The hare screamed, 'Oh, my feet have fled from me!
    My soul now trembles and desires to flee!
Can you not see my face has turned so pale?   1275
    About my inner state it tells the tale.'
Since God has called the face 'a tell-tale clue'
    On this the mystic focuses his view,
Colour and scent like bells make you aware,
    The horse's neigh informs you that it's there:
The sound of each thing thus gives it away,
    A door's creak differs from a donkey's bray;
The Prophet said, in judging people's souls,
    '*A man stays hidden till his tongue unrolls.*'
Complexion also shows what's in your heart—   1280
    Have mercy on me, plant love that won't part!
A bright complexion is your thanks' applause,
    A sickly one denies love and withdraws.

I've faced the one who pulls limbs out of place
    And saps all trace of life out of your face,
The one who breaks all things He goes inside,
    Uprooting ancient trees, however wide,
That one who traps you, then declares it's mate,
    Man, beasts, and plants must follow His dictate;
Though these are small things, big things fall as well,   1285
    Becoming pale, filled with a rotten smell.
The world now holds back, then shows thankfulness:
    The blooming orchard once knew nakedness;
The sun which rises up with flames of fire
    Then sinks head-first when it can't go up higher;
The stars shine while the lofty heavens turn
    Each single moment they are caused to burn;
The beauty of the moon is cherished most,
    But when it's sick it looks more like a ghost;
The earth, as if through manners, keeps so still,   1290
    But tremors make it shake as if it's ill;
So many mountains through sheer agony
    Were crushed to piles of dust so easily;
The air which was the soul's associate,
    Turned stale and sick when fate commanded it;
Water, the spirit's kin, was sweet to taste,
    But turned so bitter, left in pools of waste;
The fire puffed up with pride its flaming head,
    But soon the wind pronounced that '*it is dead*'.
From turbulence that strikes the ocean tide   1295
    You can detect the torment that's inside;
The wheel of heaven in its search rotates
    And thus acquires its children's changing states:
First low, next in the middle, then up high,
    Armies of bright stars decorate the sky.
Of elements like these you all consist,
    To try to know their state you must persist,
Since all of these are filled with pain and grief
    Of course you're pale and thinner than a leaf,
Because of all these opposites in you   1300
    Like earth and fire, the wind and water too.

That sheep should flee the wolf should not seem strange
   But when with wolves kind greetings they exchange,
Living is reconciling opposites
   While death is when war starts because of splits;
Wild-ass and lion feel close through God's grace
   Although each seems a very different case,
The world is trapped and suffers otherwise,
   That it must die should come as no surprise.
The hare recited wisdom of this kind: 1305
   'It was because of this I lagged behind.'

The lion asks why the hare has stepped back

The lion asked, 'What makes you sick? Tell me
   The primary reason that you want to flee.'
The hare replied, 'The other lion's there,
   Out of harm's way in this well-hidden lair.'
The well's where every wise man wants his seat:
   To purify their hearts they choose retreat;
It's better than the darkness that's outside—
   The world outside can't keep men satisfied.
The lion said, 'I'll knock him to the floor!   1310
   Check whether he's inside just as before!'
'But I'm consumed by fear and want to hide!
   Would you perhaps protect me by your side,
So, generous lion, safe within your shade,
   I then can look down and not be afraid?'

The lion peers down the well and sees his own reflection and that of the hare

The lion came and held the hare so near
   That he proceeded, purged of all his fear,
They both peered down to find the enemy—
   Their own reflection was all they could see:
The lion saw cast on the water there   1315
   His own reflection next to a plump hare—

Thinking he'd found his foe, he then leapt in,
    Which meant the hare could go back to his kin!
His foe fell in the pit of his own crime—
    His sins came back to haunt him one last time!
Oppressors' crimes are wells devoid of light,
    All scholars have confirmed that this is right—
The worst oppressors dig a deeper well,
    Justice requires a fate far worse than hell!
For personal profit wickedly behave   1320
    And you'll be simply digging your own grave!
Don't spin webs round yourself like silkworms do,
    Nor dig your own grave now without a clue!
And don't imagine weak men have no friend,
    Recite: *When God's help comes** until the end!
The elephant whose enemy had fled
    Then earned the wrath of *birds in flocks** instead:
A weak man who requests security
    Will hear war cries from heaven's cavalry!
If you should bite and make him bleed, you'll earn   1325
    A painful toothache! Then where will you turn?

Being too keen when looking down the well,
    His rival from himself he could not tell,
The lion thought his image was his foe
    And swung with force to deal himself a blow!
The things you see in others which offend
    Are just your own faults shown through them, my friend:
Your being's mirror-image lets you see
    Your cruelty, baseness, and hypocrisy,
You're beating up yourself—the foe is you!   1330
    You're swearing at yourself and cursing too!
Your own bad faults if only you could see
    You'd then become your own fierce enemy!
You've pounced upon yourself, you simpleton,
    It's just as mad as what this lion's done!
On reaching your own nature's depths, you'll know
    The vileness comes from you and not your foe.

To this sad lion it was clear at last:
 The other was the image he had cast!
If you pull out a weak man's teeth, that's worse   1335
 Than this dumb beast whose eyes became his curse.
You've found a blemish on your uncle's face,
 It's not his fault, it's you who's the disgrace:
'Believers are each other's mirrors',* friend.
 The Prophet said this—won't you comprehend?
You're wearing lenses tinted funeral blue
 And so this world is dark with grief to you—
Unless you're blind, accept that you're the source,
 Then blame yourself and not an outside force!
If faithful men do not see by God's light   1340
 Then why is the unseen within their sight?
Through fire and not His light, your eyes have seen,
 That's why they can't tell good things from obscene!
So, drop by drop, pour water on the pyre
 To turn to light this all-consuming fire.
Pour cleansing light on us, O Lord, I pray,
 To change this world of fire to light this way!
The ocean's waters follow Your command,
 All water and all fire is in Your hand,
If You choose, waves will turn to flames of fire   1345
 And flames to water if that's Your desire,
The urge to seek the truth You gave us Lord,
 To flee injustice was Your kind reward,
You gave this urge to us without request
 And opened up to us Your treasure-chest.

*The hare brings the news about the lion falling in the
well to the other animals*

The hare escaped like this through his shrewd plan,
 To celebrate towards the rest he ran,
He'd seen the lion humbled now and slain
 And so he cartwheeled all across the plain.
On fleeing death the hare began to clap   1350
 And dance like leaves which in the breeze would flap;

Both branch and leaf like this escape earth's gaol—
    They lift their heads and with the wind set sail:
When leaves burst forth from branches, they ascend
    Up to the tree's most high and furthest end;
Using the words of God who said, '*It sprouts*'.
    The praise of God each leaf and fruit then shouts:
The Giver nourished every root of ours
    Until our trees *stood tall and straight** like towers.
Souls that are bound in bodies made of clay   1355
    Feel ecstasy when they can fly away,
They dance to songs of passionate, sacred love,
    Expanding like the full moon high above,
Dancing inside as well as outwardly,
    Whirling around their souls which we can't see.
He'd gaoled the lion, who now burnt with shame,
    A lion hares can slay must be so tame!
Although he was thus taken for a ride
    This lion claims the title of 'Faith's Pride'!*
He's in the empty well, abandoned there,   1360
    Slain by his carnal soul, not just the hare.
Your donkey self feeds in the open plain,
    You're down the well bound by your questioning's chain.
The lion-slayer rushed back home to sing,
    '*Rejoice, dear kin, good news is what I bring*:
It's time to celebrate and sing our songs,
    That dog from hell is back where he belongs!
Our own survival's foe has lost the bout,
    The lion's maker pulled his teeth all out;
That one who loved to bully, pounce, and bash   1365
    The broom of death has brushed away like trash!'

The beasts of prey gather round the hare to praise him

They formed a circle there immediately,
    Happy and laughing, wild with ecstasy—
He was the torch around whom they all stood
    And bowed while shouting, 'Heavens, this is good!

Are you an angel or a spirit-friend?
  Or Azrael, who tells foes it's the end?
We'd give our lives no matter who you are,
  May you stay strong and fit, victorious star!
Since God diverted water to your stream,   1370
  "Bravo!" to both your hands and arms we scream!
Please tell us how you thought up this fine trap
  And rubbed it in his face with a hard slap!
Tell us, and let the tale become our cure,
  The balm to make our souls feel quite secure,
For that cruel tyrant's constant wickedness
  Wounded our souls and caused so much distress.'
The hare said, 'Friends, it was God's loving care—
  Without that what on earth is a mere hare!
He gave me strength and made my heart shine bright,   1375
  My hands and feet were strengthened by that light;
From God come both kind favours such as these
  And wrathfulness that brings you to your knees:
In turn, God shows his sheer beneficence
  To those who ask to see some evidence.

The hare advises the other animals: 'Don't celebrate merely this!'

'Now don't rejoice in wealth that's temporary,
  Victim of time, don't eat as though you're free!
When one has wealth beyond vicissitude
  The drums of heaven make this understood;
Eternal kings by time are never bound,   1380
  Their spirits with the Saqi circle round—
Stop drinking here for just a little while,
  Sip the eternal wine, and always smile.'

*Interpretation of 'We have returned from the lesser
jihad to the greater jihad'**

Dear kings, we've killed the enemy outside,
  A worse foe still remains for us inside:

Your brain does not know how to kill this foe:
  A hare can't bring this inner lion low!
The self is hell, a dragon wishing harm,
  The sea can't cool it down or keep it calm:
I drank the seven seas, was fully drenched,   1385
  That human-burner's thirst was still not quenched!
The infidels, whose hearts are hard as stones,
  Enter this fire, ashamed, with screams and groans,
But hell's not sated by such food at all,
  At least until the Lord should finally call:
'Are you full yet?' The glutton answers, 'No!
  Can you not see from there my burning glow!'
It makes the world a morsel, swallows it,
  Then screams, *'Is there not still another bit?'**
God stamps on it from Placelessness,* before   1390
  *Be! And it was,** makes it feel full once more.
Our stubborn selfhood is a part of hell,
  Parts show the nature of the whole so well,
It's God who must deal out the fatal blow—
  Who else can pull the string to fire this bow?
Straight arrows only will God's bow admit,
  Your bow holds arrows crooked, bent, and split:
To leave the bow the arrow must be straight,
  It then won't fail to fly and penetrate.
When from the outward fight I turned around   1395
  The war inside our soul was what I found:
'The small jihad we have just left behind'
  For a jihad of a much greater kind;
The strength from God is what I long to win
  Which can uproot Mount Qaf with just a pin,
Don't overrate the lion which can kill!
  The one who breaks himself is greater still.

The emissary from Byzantium comes to Omar, the Commander of the Faithful* and sees his miracles

Now listen to this story, which spells out
    Some of the secrets you've been told about:
A man came to Omar once from the west,   1400
    Through deserts till Medina with no rest:
'The Caliph's palace—please show me the way!
    I need to ride there with my load today.'
'He doesn't have a palace,' he was told,
    'Except his soul, illumined like pure gold;
His well-earned fame as leader is secure
    Though he lives in a hut just like the poor.'
How can you see a palace of this kind
    When one stray hair has made your heart's eye blind?
Rid your heart's eye of hair to have a prayer   1405
    Of seeing this great Caliph's palace there!
Whoever's soul is free from lust has found
    Admittance to God's kingdom's hallowed ground:
Mohammad, purged of fire and smoke's last trace,
    Whichever way he turned saw just *God's face*,*
While you are still the evil whisperer's friend
    There is God's face how can you comprehend?
If you've an opening in your heart you'll see
    The sun's bright rays wherever you may be—
In everything God can be seen through love   1410
    Just like the moon among the stars above.
If you place fingertips upon each eye,
    Can you see anything at all? Don't lie!
Though you can't see things, they all still exist;
    The fault lies curled inside your self's tight fist—
Just lift the fingers from your eyes, to then
    Observe whatever you should want again.
Noah, when asked, 'Where's the reward?' replied,
    'Beyond *beneath their clothes their heads they hide*'*

You've hidden it beneath your clothes; that's why   1415
   You still can't see although you have an eye!
A man's his eye, he's mere skin otherwise
   For the beloved's only seen by eyes,
If they can't see him, then they're better blind,
   That's best for idols of a transient kind.

On hearing this, the messenger grew keen
   To reach his goal, more than he'd ever been,
Omar with his own eyes he wished to find,
   And so he left his horse and load behind
To search for this great master everywhere   1420
   Just like a madman with no other care:
'Can such a man exist—can this be true?
   He's hidden like the soul—what can we do?'
He sought to serve him like a slave in need—
   Such seekers always in the end succeed.
An Arab woman saw him come, and said,
   'Omar lies near that tree as if in bed:
Far from the people under that date-palm
   God's Shadow* sleeps in shade where it is calm.'

*The emissary from Byzantium finds the Commander of
the Faithful* sleeping under the tree*

The man approached, but wouldn't go too near,   1425
   On seeing him his body shook with fear—
Awe of a sleeping man left him undone,
   A blissful state now filled him like the sun;
Such contradictory states as love and awe
   Together in his heart the stranger saw,
Saying inside, 'A thousand kings I've seen
   Who honoured me, with sultans too I've been,
But fear had never given me such fits—
   Now awe of this man's robbed me of my wits!
Jungles of lions even I've explored   1430
   And not turned pale, however much they roared,

And on the battlefield I've earned renown
　　For acting bravely when the rest are down—
I've taken and dealt out such mighty blows
　　For I'm the bravest, everybody knows.
This man lies sound asleep and he's unarmed
　　So why do I now shake and feel alarmed?
It's awe of God, not just a human being,
　　A man dressed in a gown that I'm now seeing.'
Whoever's path is fear of God will find   1435
　　That he is feared by jinn and all mankind.
With folded hands in a submissive pose
　　He stood until Omar woke and arose,
He then saluted him and bowed his head:
　　'First say salaam, then talk!' the Prophet said.*
Omar responded, told him to come near
　　And to sit next to him and have no fear:
'*Don't fear!*'* for scared men is quite suitable,
　　But not for those who aren't afraid at all:
The scared are reassured they won't be harmed—   1440
　　By this advice, their fearful hearts are calmed;
Why say 'Don't fear!' to one who isn't scared?
　　This is a lesson brave men should be spared!
Omar thus helped a troubled heart to find
　　Abundant happiness and peace of mind,
With subtleties that few can comprehend
　　About God's attributes, our greatest friend!
He spoke of God's love for his true élite
　　And of the states and stations one could meet:
The state is the unveiling of the bride,   1445
　　The station's being alone with her inside,*
For her unveiling's seen by every guest
　　But with the groom alone the bride will rest—
The bride unveils for every onlooker
　　But afterwards he lies alone with her!
So many Sufis have enjoyed a state
　　But few know of the stations that await.
Omar taught him the journey of the soul,
　　Spiritual travelling to the furthest goal,

And of the time which stands beyond all time,   1450
   That lofty station, sacred and sublime,
And of the realm in which the spirit flew—
   Before this life both flight and grace it knew,
Seeing beyond horizons coast to coast,
   The utmost faith and zeal it then could boast.
Thus, when Omar saw that he was a friend,
   He knew this man desired to comprehend:
The shaikh was perfect and the student keen,
   The rider fast, the thoroughbred so lean.
The guide saw he would suit the brotherhood,   1455
   Then sowed good seed in soil he knew was good.

The emissary from Byzantium questions the Commander of the Faithful

'Commander of the Faithful,* please expound
   For me how spirit came down to the ground:
How did that bird become caged in a cell?'
   He said, 'God chanted to the soul a spell;
The non-existents have no ear nor eye,
   But when God chants a spell they stir and fly,
His spells give non-existents such a jolt
   That to existence they all somersault!
And when existents hear God's formula   1460
   To non-existence their route's similar.'
The rose smiled once He'd chanted to its stem,
   His spell has made a stone turn to a gem,
Bodies transformed to souls by just one line,
   His words have also caused the sun to shine,
But dark words whispered sometimes to its ear
   Have made eclipses of the sun appear;
He also made the clouds perform the task
   Of weeping tears just like a water-flask—
What spells He must have whispered to the ground   1465
   To make it think, but not make any sound!
Whoever is perplexed by doubt and fear—
   The Lord will chant a riddle in his ear

To hold him captive with this thought a bit,
  'Shall I obey or do the opposite?'
God's preference is implicit for one side;
  This factor helps the doubter to decide.
You don't want to be plagued by doubts and fears?
  Then put less cotton wool inside your ears
To hear those riddles that the Lord will tell,   1470
  The secret hints he gives, the clear as well—
Your spirit's ear will hear His revelation.
  What's that? It's speech that's far beyond sensation!

Spiritual ears and eyes transcend mere sense,
  While rational ones can only claim pretence.
The word '*compulsion*'* spurs my heart ahead
  While those who lack love feel ensnared instead,
It's not compulsion but divine communion,
  Not clouds, but the full moon in total union;
If it's compulsion it's a special kind,   1475
  Not that commanding self's* type which is blind:
Compulsion like this few identify,
  God's given these men's hearts an inner eye—
Hidden things and the future they can see,
  Mentioning the past near them is blasphemy!
For them compulsion's different as well:
  Drops turn to pearls inside an oyster shell,
However big each drop looks to your eyes
  It forms a pearl exactly the same size;
This group are like the gland of the musk deer: 1480
  Inside there's musk though this may not be clear:
'There's only blood around this gland,' men claim,
  'How can it turn to musk scent all the same?'
They say, 'This copper's hideous; I don't see,
  How it can turn to gold through alchemy.'
You found compulsion and free will in form,
  For them, to God's own light it can transform:
Bread on the table is inanimate
  But forms a living part inside your gut,

Unchanging on the table where you dine,   1485
    The soul transmutes it with some heavenly wine—
The soul has strength to carry out this role;
    What then the power of God, who rules the soul!
Man would be merely flesh but for his heart,
    Both seas and mountains he can split apart:
The heart splits rocks, lifts mountains through the sky,
    God's verse *He split the moon** proves I don't lie—
Just lift the cover of this mystery,
    Your soul will seek God's Throne then eagerly.

How Adam attributed that error to himself, saying 'O Lord, we
have wronged ourselves!' And how Satan attributed his own sin to*
*God Almighty, saying 'Since you have sent me astray!'**

Let us compare our acts with God's now here,   1490
    Consider our acts real—this much is clear:
If acts aren't by creation, there's no need
    To ask, 'Why did you do that awful deed?'
God gives acts being for they're His creation.
    Each act of ours is God's manifestation.*
In words men see the meaning or its form,
    They can't see both at once, this is the norm:
Choosing its meaning, form he throws away,
    No one can look both ways at once, can they?
When you are looking straight in front of you   1495
    How can you see what's there behind you too?
Meaning and form aren't both in its control
    So how can their creator be your soul?
The Lord encompasses all things, my son,
    For Him one act won't stop another one.
'*You led astray*', though Satan claimed, he lied:
    His own deeds that vile devil tried to hide.
'*We've wronged ourselves*': when Adam thus confessed
    He still knew acts are God's—he spoke the best:
Out of respect he said it was his sin,   1500
    Through bearing this, more favour he would win;

He then repented. God said, 'Didn't I
   Create that crime in you—Why did you lie?
Wasn't it all because of my decree?
   Why did you take responsibility?'
He said, 'Through fear I kept respect for you.'
   God said, 'I've kept in mind your actions too.'
Whoever shows respect, respect will meet:
   Bring halva and you'll eat an almond sweet.
For whose sake are *good women*? *For good men*!*   1505
   Spread joy! Hurt friends and see what they do then!
Produce a fitting parable, O heart,
   Compulsion from free will to tell apart:
The hands of sick men which shake constantly
   And those hands which you shake deliberately,
Both movements God creates, in that they share,
   But these two pairs of hands you can't compare:
You may regret you forced their hands to shake,
   But sick men can't be blamed, for heaven's sake!
The intellect explores these words I speak   1510
   For it's a fox which tries to lead the weak;
Though pearls may be on offer as the goal
   Its quest's unlike the journey of the soul:
Spiritual quests are on a different sphere,
   Like mystic wine and wine fermented here;
When intellectual quests were the top aim
   Omar and Bu'l-Hakam were just the same,
Omar then chose his soul before his head
   And Bu'l-Hakam became Bu Jahl instead,
In intellect as perfect as can be,   1515
   But the most ignorant man inwardly!
A secondary cause is the brain's quest,
   The mystic's quest lies far above the rest!
The soul's light shone, O seeker of God's light,
   Then logic's quarrels disappeared like night,
Because the seer on whom God's light rays shine
   Supporting proofs can't hinder nor confine.

Commentary on 'He is with you wherever you may be'*

We've come back to the tale we had in mind,
  How could we ever leave that tale behind?
If we meet ignorance, to gaol we're bound,   1520
  If knowledge then His palace we have found;
When we're asleep we're drunk, then for His sake
  We're back in His hands also when awake,
When weeping we're an ostentatious cloud,
  Then lightning when we start to laugh aloud,
We show His anger when we fight with men,
  His love when we forgive, at peace again—
Who are we, coiled and twisted like a string?
  What's straight apart from 1? Name me one thing!

The emissary asks Omar about the reason for the suffering of spirits in bodies of water and clay

He asked, 'Omar, what aim's behind this plot   1525
  To lock pure beings in a filthy spot?
Pure water's hidden when it's sprayed on ground,
  Pure souls in bodies likewise have been bound.'
He said, 'Your question seems to be quite apt—
  Pure meaning in a word you've tightly wrapped:
You've shackled what was once free like a bird
  As you have trapped the wind inside a word—
Have you done this to make a personal gain
  Though you can't see what spirits thus attain?
The one from whom all benefits arise   1530
  Can surely see what you've seen with your eyes!'
A million benefits are here, and all
  Compared with that one are extremely small,
Your speech's breath is part of what is whole,
  So don't deny pure being its true role!
Though but a part, your acts help all the same—
  Don't raise your hands and give the whole the blame!

If talking has no value, speak no more
    Or else give thanks, don't be so mean and sore;
To thank's to place a halter round your neck,   1535
    Not quarrelling about a tiny speck,
If it meant to look sour only, then
    Mere vinegar would thank God more than men!
If vinegar must penetrate the liver
    Tell it, 'Turn to a healing brew with sugar!'—
Meaning in verse is nothing but insane,
    It's like a sling which no one can restrain!

On the meaning of 'Let whoever wants to sit with God sit with the Sufis'*

This made the messenger lose self-control,
    Forgetting all about his mission's goal:
The power of God left him completely dazed,   1540
    He came, and to a higher state was raised;
On reaching it, a flood becomes the sea,
    In soil a seed may grow to form a tree,
When bread is in our gut it comes alive,
    And soaks up knowledge, which helps all things thrive,
When wax and timber both are set alight
    Their essence, which was dark, becomes so bright,
If you apply some kohl around your eye
    You'll learn to see as well as any spy:
Happy the man who from himself is free   1545
    And joins with Being in true unity,
Alas the one who mixes with the dead—
    He'll die himself because he's been misled.
So many prophets the Koran extols—
    Read it! Become familiar with their souls!
For it describes each one's biography
    As fish in the sea of divinity.
If you recite but don't accept the Book
    You've turned them down although you've had a look,
If you accept the stories on each page   1550
    You'll feel your soul's a bird trapped in a cage;

The reason that the caged bird settles there
    And doesn't flee is that it's unaware.
Spirits which have escaped from their constraints
    Are fit to guide like prophets and like saints;
Their voices speak of faith when they should say:
    'This is your one escape route—come this way!'
Through faith we have escaped the narrow cell—
    There is no other way out of this hell
Than to be seen as suffering what's worse,   1555
    In order to flee reputation's curse,
For reputation's such a heavy chain—
    Much worse than iron chains in this domain.

The story about the merchant to whom his caged parrot gave a message for the parrots of India when he was due to go there for trade

A merchant kept his parrot so confined
    Inside a cage you'd think he was unkind,
But when he planned to make a trip for trade
    To India where the finest goods were made,
To all his servants he went down to say,
    'What shall I buy for you while I'm away?'
They listed things on which their hearts were set   1560
    And he swore that he never would forget;
He asked the parrot, 'What would you prefer
    That I should bring for you from India?'
The bird said, 'When you see the parrots there
    Please tell them all about my sad affair:
Tell them a parrot pines continually
    To see you, but she's caged by fate's decree;
She sends her greetings and she asks for justice,
    She wants to learn the faith you parrots practise;
She says, "Should I stay longing here for you   1565
    In exile, and then give my life up too?
Should I stay in this cage—can this be right,
    While in the woods and meadows you take flight?

Where now is our famed solidarity?
    While I'm in gaol the rest of you are free!
My noble friends, remember this poor bird
    And drink to me tomorrow—spread the word!
If friends remember one, then one is blest,
    Majnun's love for his Layli though was best!
In fine surroundings you recline and think,   1570
    While I just have my blood left now to drink!
So down a glass of wine for my sake, friends;
    If you don't want to try to make amends,
Remembering one who's fallen in the dust
    You'll pour the dregs upon the ground, I trust.
What happened to the oath that we all swore—
    Don't promises you make count any more?
Have I deserved my fate for some offence,
    If you hurt sinners what's the difference?"'

The harm You cause in war and retribution   1575
    Delights me more than musical audition,*
Good fortune can't match torture that's from You,
    Your wrath is dearer than my own life too!
This is Your fire—how great must be Your light:
    The funeral's now, the party starts tonight!
Because of sweetness in Your wrathfulness
    None know the full depth of Your tenderness,
I moan, but fear that He might answer me
    By kindly softening his tyranny—
I'm smitten by his wrath and kindness too,   1580
    My love for opposites amazes you!
If I escape these thorns now for a rose
    A nightingale's lament I will compose—
Strange nightingale whose mouth is open wide
    To fit both thorns and roses now inside!
That's no bird but a fiery dragon there:
    Love's made all seem to him so sweet and fair!
He loves the Whole, which is here and above—
    He loves himself thus, and seeks his own love!

Description of the wings of the birds of divine intelligences

The parrot's tale now seems appropriate,   1585
    With bird-like souls find one who's intimate,
One like a weak obedient bird outside
    With Solomon and armies deep inside!
When he should wail without complaint or praise
    An uproar sets the seven spheres ablaze;
Each breath for him God's messages appear:
    He cries, 'O Lord!' God says, 'I'm always here!'*
For God, his sins excel mere blind obedience,
    Next to his unbelief, pure faith is nonsense.
Each moment privately to God he's led,   1590
    A hundred crowns God places on his head,
His form's from earth, his soul is from *No-place*,*
    Beyond the dreams that travellers can chase,
Not somewhere which the mind can comprehend
    From where a telling clue might once descend;
By him the world and *No-place* are controlled
    Like those four rivers ruled by heaven's fold;*
Cut short the explanation, turn around,
    God knows what's best, don't make another sound!
Let's now resume what started earlier   1595
    About the bird, the merchant, India:
The merchant then said 'Yes' to her request
    To give her message there at her behest.

The merchant sees the parrots of India in the countryside and delivers the message for that parrot

He entered India, travelled deep inside,
    Then saw some parrots in the countryside:
He drew his steed back, shouted to the birds,
    To keep his promise he passed on her words—
One of the birds shook violently then dropped,
    She fell just like a corpse, her breathing stopped!

He then repented that he'd brought the news: 1600
    'I've killed this creature, what is left to lose!
Was she one of my parrot's relatives,
    The same soul which in separate bodies lives?
Why did I tell them when she's out of reach?
    I've burnt the poor thing's heart with my crude speech!'

The tongue and stone on iron are the same:
    What leaps out from your tongue's tip is a flame—
Don't strike the stone on iron for you'll roast
    For telling stories or just for a boast!
We're in a field of cotton in the dark   1605
    So don't you carelessly create a spark!
In darkness tyrants choose to shut their eyes
    And with their words allow the flames to rise:
A world can be destroyed by what is said
    And foxes turn to lions thus instead.
Spirits like Christ's breath give new life to you,
    First as a wound, then as a plaster too,
If spirits were unveiled, it would be known
    Their speech is just like the Messiah's own.
If you want something sweet to say, hold on!   1610
    Don't grab them greedily before they're gone:
Through self-restraint the clever men reach higher,
    Sweets are what simple children all desire—
You can ascend to God with self-control,
    Choose sweets and you'll sink farther from the goal.

*Commentary on the saying of ʿAttar: 'You have an ego, heedless
one, drink your own blood while on earth, for if mystics drink
poison it will become an antidote'**

The mystic is not harmed one bit if he
    Should drink down deadly poison knowingly:
When you have true health why choose abstinence
    Though others suffer if they touch it once:

The Prophet said, 'Wise man, just turn aside,   1615
    Don't challenge one who's sought out as a guide!'
With Nimrod in you, don't approach the flame,
    Become first Abraham to do the same—
You don't know how to swim or sail in there,
    Don't dive in vainly just to show you dare!
He can pull out a red rose from the fire,
    From loss he can send profits soaring higher,
His touch turns earth to gold in just a flash,
    While gold imperfect men touch turns to ash:
God has accepted him, so understand   1620
    In all he does his hand is like God's hand,
The hands of others are the devil's own,
    In their abuse and lies it's clearly shown;
Ignorance turns to knowledge with pure men,
    It's ignorance with infidels again,
A sick man spreads to others pain and grief,
    A perfect man turns sin to true belief—
While standing don't fight someone on a steed,
    Step back, there is no way you can succeed!

The reverence of the magicians towards Moses, whom they asked,
'What do you wish—would you like to cast your rod first?'*

In Pharaoh's reign magicians set a date   1625
    To challenge Moses, object of their hate,
But these men still showed Moses deference,
    These vain magicians showed much reverence
By saying, 'You choose when, O Messenger,
    And throw your rod down first if you prefer.'
Moses said, 'No, magicians I implore
    That you throw down your tricks first on the floor.'
They earned God's grace by being subservient,
    This cut their power and means of argument:
When they acknowledged who he was this time,   1630
    They lost the power to carry out their crime.
Each morsel and each word is lawful too
    For the perfected, not for men like you!

While you're an ear, this man's a tongue, you see,
>   And God told all men '*Listen!*' * Didn't he?
Each baby when it's born screams out its fears
>   But then stays silent for a while, all ears;
For hours it has to keep its small lips sealed
>   Till speech's secret should become revealed,
And if it doesn't listen, but just cries   1635
>   It's the most stupid thing beneath the skies!
The one born deaf who's never heard a word
>   Is mute, how can speech move him—that's absurd!
To learn to speak, first hearing's necessary,
>   Through hearing learn how to speak properly:
'*Enter their houses by their doors!*' * He said,
>   *Seek through their cause the outcomes up ahead!*
Speech not in need of hearing is unknown
>   Apart from God's desire-free speech alone,
For the Creator follows no one's lead,   1640
>   We're helped by Him, of help He has no need.
In making things and speaking we've relied
>   On teachers or a pattern that can guide—
If these words haven't left you in a shock
>   Start weeping now and wear a dervish frock!
Adam's tears freed him from admonishment,
>   Tears are the breaths of those who're penitent,
Adam came down to earth so he could grieve,
>   To weep for what he'd done and then take leave:
He came from Eden and the seventh heaven   1645
>   To beg and plead that he might be forgiven,
So if you're really Adam's progeny
>   Then keep on striving in his company—
Blend in your tears with fire to make a sweet:
>   The orchard blooms through rain and solar heat.
What do you know about how tears might taste?
>   You just love bread like blind men—what a waste!
Empty your belly that you've filled with bread
>   Then fill it up with precious jewels instead!
It's devil's milk you've fed your infant soul,   1650
>   Take it to angels—feed it from their bowl!

When you are weary, gloomy, and depressed,
  You must be feeding from the devil's breast;
The food which can increase light and perfection
  Is paid for through a lawful occupation;
And oil which puts the lamp out we should call
  'Water', it can't be really oil at all:
Knowledge and wisdom lawful meals produce*
  And love and tenderness they can induce,
While morsels filled with envy which can snare   1655
  Are all unlawful—ignorance breeds there!
Have you sown wheat then seen just barley rise,
  A horse give birth to donkeys—don't tell lies!
Pure food is like a seed, its fruit's pure thought,
  And it's a sea, while thought's the jewel sought;
With longing, lawful food will overwhelm
  Your heart, so it can reach the highest realm.

The merchant relates to his parrot what he saw of the parrots in India

The merchant on completing all his trade
  Returned home, not prepared to be delayed,
He brought a present back for every slave   1660
  And to the slave-girls souvenirs he gave.
The parrot asked, 'Where's what I chose instead?
  Please tell me what you saw and what was said.'
He said, 'No, for all that I now repent,
  With biting fingernails my hours are spent—
Why did I say it? It was premature!
  Through ignorance, or is my judgement poor?'
'Master, what's this repentance for?' she said,
  What's brought this rage and grief inside your head?'
He said, 'I passed on your complaint once there   1665
  To birds like you, who flew without a care—
One of them felt your pain so much she cried,
  Her frail heart broke, she shuddered, fell, and died!
Why did I say this for my little pet!
  Ah, now it's done what use is my regret!'

Regard the words you utter with your tongue
 A dangerous arrow which you have just flung;
An arrow can't be brought back from its course—
 We have to block the torrent at its source;
Floods can submerge the world each time they rise,   1670
 If they destroy the world that's no surprise,
Actions bring forth effects beyond our goal,
 Unseen effects beyond our own control,
The Lord created them, let this be clear,
 Though they're attributed to us down here:
Jim once was shot at by a man named Jack;
 The arrows flew like leopards in attack;
A year passed, but Jim's suffering wouldn't end.
 The Lord creates all pain, not Man, my friend:
Even if Jack, on shooting, fell, and died,   1675
 This wouldn't have made Jim's deep pain subside,
But since this pain led to the death of Jim
 For triggering it, we say Jack murdered him—
Pin all the blame on Jack that Jim was slain
 Even though God created all the pain!*
Breath, sex, and sowing are comparable,
 They're all effects which God makes possible:

The saints have gained from God such awesome might
 That they can pull back arrows in mid-flight:
Effects which stem from the original cause   1680
 When saints repent are then compelled to pause:
By grace he makes unsaid what has been said
 So no harm comes to anybody's head,
From all the hearts which heard that harmful word
 He wipes it out, unseen now and unheard!
Dear gentlemen, if you need proof it's true
 *A verse we cause you to forget** should do,
They caused you to forget, don't be upset,
 Observe their power to make you forget:
Then they made you forget, now they remind,   1685
 And thus they rule the hearts of all mankind.

When you are blinded with forgetfulness
    You're impotent, your skills could not count less,
Though *you thought them a joke*, they have God's might,
    As far as *they made you forget* recite!*
Landlords may rule your bodies, not your soul,
    That's in the owner of the heart's control,
Deeds are derived from sight, please realize
    That men are just the pupils in their eyes—
Its explanation I am forced to hide   1690
    By barriers put up by those inside.
Since all forgetfulness and memory
    Depend on Him, He'll answer every plea:
Thousands of good and evil things each night
    He empties from men's hearts and out of sight,
By day He pours them in their hearts once more—
    Refilling shells with pearls they used to store—
Knowledge of things we used to utilize
    God's guidance helps our souls to recognize—
Your skills and talents all return to you   1695
    To let you keep on doing what you do:
The jeweller's skills don't reach mere ironmongers,
    A good man's virtue won't reach vile warmongers,
Your skills and virtues like your property
    Will be returned on Judgment Day, you'll see,
Just as they do when from your sleep you wake—
    Back to the rightful owner, no mistake,
Returning from that place that can't be seen,
    Where good and evil thoughts had also been,
Like carrier pigeons which have been abroad   1700
    They bring back to their home a wondrous horde.

*The parrot hears about the actions of those other parrots and
then dies in her cage, so the owner laments for her*

About the other birds when she was told
    His parrot trembled, fell, was knocked out cold,
On seeing her fall like the one before
    The merchant leapt, his cap fell on the floor;

When he saw her look like she'd nearly died
    He tore his jacket open, and then cried,
'O darling parrot, sweeter than a kiss,
    What's happened to you, why are you like this?
My sweet-voiced bird, please say it's not the end!   1705
    Alas, my confidante and closest friend!
My parrot had a singing voice so fine
    And smelt like basil, she was my soul's wine!
If Solomon had had a bird so rare
    He'd have forgotten all the rest, I swear!
Alas, this bird for whom I didn't pay,
    Which led me then to easily turn away.
O tongue, you hurt so many everywhere,
    Since you keep talking what can I declare!
O tongue, you're like both fire and stacks of hay;   1710
    How long will you set them alight this way?
The soul mourns secretly because of you
    Although it does the things you tell it to,
But you are treasure too which will endure
    As well as pain for which there is no cure;
Just like the hunter's whistle you deceive,
    But then console the trapped birds when they grieve—
How long will you keep offering sanctuary,
    You who, in hatred, draw your bow at me!
You've made my bird fly off due to distrust,   1715
    Stop acting like you're born to be unjust!
Please answer me or let me have redress
    Or give me reasons to feel happiness!
Alas, that light which burnt the dark away,
    Alas the dawn that brightened every day:
Alas that bird which flew so beautifully,
    From one end to the other deep in me!
Until the end, heart, sing my love-sick grief:
    "*I swear*" until "*in hardship*", for relief!*
I fled from pain through love of your kind face,   1720
    Then, in your stream, of scum I felt no trace!
I cry, imagining you in the distance
    While cut off from my blissful past existence;

God's jealousy's* the cause—what can one do!
    Which heart by His love wasn't torn in two!
Since He's alone, beyond all other things,
    Our explanations and our mutterings,
Would that my tears were waves of a vast sea
    That spray on my beloved constantly.
My parrot was a most perceptive bird,   1725
    Translator of my thoughts that were unheard:
My lot and what would be held back as well
    Right from the very start she could foretell.'

That bird's voice came from revelation's source,
    Her birth before existence took its course,
Inside one this true parrot is concealed,
    Through her reflection everything's revealed,
She takes away your joy, but you don't care,
    You even swear her tyranny is fair!
Lighting your spirit for your body's sake—   1730
    You've burnt your spirit, now the rest must bake:
I am on fire, get tinder here for free,
    So you can set your scraps alight through me!
For setting things on fire since tinder's fit
    Come, take this tinder which is easily lit!
It's such a shame that ravishing full moon
    Was clouded over by the fog so soon!
How can I speak now that my heart's ablaze:
    My exile's lion's hungry, in a daze—
When sober violent, and when drunk he's mad,   1735
    Picture him after all the wine he's had;
The drunken lion is beyond all words,
    Too big for pastures which can hold vast herds!

I think of rhymes, but the Beloved says:
    'Just for my face reserve your constant gaze!
Sit comfortably my rhyme-enthusiast,
    To me you rhyme with fortune that will last.

Words aren't for lovers to reflect upon:
    What then are words? Around vines, they're a thorn,
Word, sound, and speech I strike relentlessly   1740
    So I can talk to you without these three.
The word I kept from Adam all these years,
    My secret, I'll now whisper in your ears,
What I would not tell Abraham I'll tell
    And things that Gabriel doesn't know as well.'
The words that the Messiah couldn't say,
    Even without *maa*, here God won't convey—
What's *maa*?* It can affirm, and it negates,
    I'm not affirmed, for love annihilates!
I've found a person in a nobody,   1745
    An individual and non-entity,
For every king's subservient to his slave—
    Men die for those who for them choose their grave:
Before prostraters kings fall down prostrate,
    And sober people drunks intoxicate,
The hunter changes to the birds' own prey
    To make them his own victim in this way,
The lovesick seek their sweethearts with their soul,
    Their sweethearts are their prey, this is their role.
Regard each lover as beloved too   1750
    Since it depends on just your point of view,
For if the thirsty search for water, then
    That means the water's seeking thirsty men.
Since he's in love keep quiet, there's no harm,
    And if he grabs your ear, let him, stay calm—
No, dam the rising flood, don't let it loose
    To shame us all with damaging abuse!
If there's destruction now why should I care?
    The ruins hide a royal treasure there.
Those drowned in God want more, they want it all,   1755
    Just like the tide, their souls rise up, then fall,
The ocean's depths or surface—which is best?
    An arrow or a shield—which worthiest?
You must have been ripped up by whisperings, heart,
    If you can still tell joy and pain apart—

You lust for sugar, don't you know it's true
    Beloved God wants lack of lust from you?
For moons he puts out all the stars at night,
    To kill the whole world he has every right!
We've also earned from God a high blood-price,   1760
    By offering up our lives as sacrifice:
The lover's life is found in death: it's known
    You'll earn a heart by giving up your own.

I sought his heart, but had so many cares,
    He made excuses, weary of my airs:
I claimed, 'My soul is drowned in you, you know!'
    He said, 'Stop chanting spells at me—just go!'
I know well what you tried then to insist
    When you saw the Beloved, dualist!
You've held Him in such low regard, you fool,   1765
    Because you bought Him cheaply—heed the rule:
If you've bought cheaply, cheaply you'll resell:
    A child will swap a pearl for bread—heed well!
Inside the same pure love I now have drowned
    As that which lovers of the past have found,
I don't explain it all, but summarize,
    My tongue would burn itself up otherwise:
When I say 'lip', read: 'borders by the sea',
    When I say '*none*', read: '*but*' the Deity!*
Because of sweetness I look bitter now,   1770
    I've talked too much, now silence is my vow,
So no one sees our sweetness, not one trace
    Behind the mask of my most bitter face,
Since they're not suitable for everyone
    Of countless secrets I'll divulge just one:

Explanation of the saying of the Hakim: 'If something holds
you back on the path, what does it matter whether it is infidelity
or faith? If something leads you far from the beloved, what does
it matter whether it is ugly or beautiful?' On the meaning of the
Prophet's words: 'Saʿd is truly jealous,* and I am more jealous
than Saʿd, while God, who is even more jealous than me, has
forbidden inward as well as outward foul deeds because of
His jealousy.'

The whole world's jealous, for God's jealousy
    Surpasses that of all humanity:
He's like the soul, the world's His body-frame
    Which must accept from Him all things the same.
If someone's prayer-niche faces certainty   1775
    To turn around to faith is treachery:
If you're now waiting on the king, you'll lose
    If travelling off to trade instead you choose,
If those now with the sultan later must
    Wait at the gate, they'll scream that it's unjust!
He's brought his hands, so with your lips they'll meet—
    It's sinful now to choose to kiss his feet:
Lowering your head down humbly in this case
    Is a mistake for which you'll earn disgrace!
The king grows jealous if an onlooker   1780
    His perfume to his proud face should prefer,
God's jealousy's like wheat in metaphor,
    Man's jealousy is thus a stack of straw,
God is the root of every jealousy,
    Including envy plaguing you and me.

I'll stop explaining, so I can complain
    Of that much-worshipped beauty's gift of pain,
Because it pleases Him I wail and moan,
    The two worlds must wail too, I'm not alone;
How can I not complain when things are hard,   1785
    When from His drunkards' circle I've been barred—

Without His day I can't stop being night,
    Of His bright face I still have not caught sight!
Unpleasantness from Him my soul thinks nice,
    My spirit longs to be His sacrifice,
I am in love with all my pain and grief
    To please my peerless king who brings relief!
My grief's dust I've dabbed round my ocean eyes
    So they'll produce a pearl of massive size:
They're pearls not tears which we cry for His sake,   1790
    If people think they're tears that's their mistake!
I moaned about the essence of our soul,
    But I don't moan—transmitting is my role:
My heart says, 'The Beloved tortured me!'
    I laugh at its lack of sincerity!
'Do good, O pride of good men,' I implore,
    You're on your throne, I'm waiting at the door.
What's throne and threshold in reality,
    What meaning have such terms as 'I' and 'we'?
O You whose soul has fled these and lives free,   1795
    Each man and woman's spirit's subtlety—
When man and woman join, You are that 'one',
    And when one is effaced You are that 'none'!
You made these I's and we's so You could play
    The backgammon of worship every day,
So all these I's and we's can finally merge,
    In their Beloved totally submerge.
Bring here the order '*Be!*'* for only You
    Transcend all speech and all our wishes too.
The body thinks that You are one as well,   1800
    Your grief and laughter it thinks it can tell—
A heart that's bound by joy and misery
    Does not deserve to see You properly;
Those trapped in misery and laughter's snare
    All live dependent on such borrowed ware.
Love's blooming garden which lives evermore
    Apart from joy and grief has fruits galore—
Being a lover is beyond this pair,
    Fresh always, in both spring and autumn air.

Pay tax on Your fair face,* light of my heart,   1805
   And speak about the soul that's torn apart,
For teasing glances from this expert flirt
   Has branded this big heart inside my shirt;
I let Him shed my blood, and then I say
   'It's lawful for You', but He runs away,
Since from all men's laments You thus depart
   Why fill with grief each tired and aching heart?
While each dawn sends out from the East its light,
   You are its source, full, shimmering and bright.
Your frenzied lover how can You dismiss,   1810
   You whose sweet lips for no sum grant a kiss!
To an old world a soul You can provide,
   I therefore wail I have no soul inside—
Stop talking of the rose, describe for me
   The nightingale which must live separately:
Our fervour does not come from joy or grief,
   Our consciousness is not a false belief,
It's different, very rare and valuable—
   Don't say it can't be, God is capable!
On someone's humble state please don't decide,   1815
   With doing good do not be satisfied:
Good, evil, joy, and grief are transient states
   Which die and leave to God all their estates!

It's dawn, Our Refuge, who fills dawn with light,
   Please make Hosam forgive it took all night*—
To grant forgiveness to us is Your role,
   The coral's splendour, You're the whole world's soul!
Dawn's spread its light, now through the rays You shine
   We sit and drink Mansur's most potent wine*—
Since Your kind gift makes me experience this   1820
   What need have I for earth's wine to feel bliss!
Compared with ours, wine has no strength at all,
   Compared with our expansions heaven's small,
All wine gets drunk through us, not us through it,
   Our form lives for us, not the opposite:

We're bees, our body's like the honeycomb,
   Since through our soul we've built home after home.

Resumption of the story of the merchant

It is too long to detail in this text
   In that last narrative what happened next:
The parrot's owner pined and burnt with pain,   1825
   Muttering nonsense which now filled his brain—
Opposite states: in need, then haughtily,
   True ecstasy, then metaphorically.
A drowning man believes he's going to die,
   And grasps at straws that happen to drift by,
To see if one might save him from this strife
   He flaps his arms to hold on to dear life!
The Loved One loves to see us scream and weep,
   To struggle thus is better than to sleep;
The king is not without work, but he still   1830
   Will never moan because he isn't ill,
And so the Merciful chose to declare,
   '*Each day He's busy with a new affair.*'*
Persist in struggle till you meet your end,
   Don't even take the slightest pause, my friend,
So that your final breath may be the one
   Which wins the gift of mystic union;
Whatever men and women seek to try
   Is noticed by the soul's king's watchful eye.

The merchant flings the parrot out of the cage and the dead bird flies away

He emptied out the cage just like a cup;   1835
   The parrot fell out, but then flew straight up,
The dead bird soared just like the solar ray
   That rises in the East to start each day;
This left him dumbstruck, he could not see how:
   Amazed, he sensed the parrot's secrets now;

He looked up, asked her, 'Parrot, won't you wait!
    Like nightingales explain our present state!
Is it that Indian parrot's ways you've learned,
    To trick and roast me till my heart is burnt?'
Yes, through her actions, she showed me how to   1840
    Give up my voice and loyalty to you:
Since it's my voice for which I've been confined—
    She acted dead to bring this to my mind,
To say, 'Sweet-singing bird, pretend like me,
    Just make yourself look dead and you'll be free.'
If you're a seed, you're feed for every chick,
    If you're a bud, you're just what children pick;
So hide the seed and be a snare instead,
    Change buds to roof straw there above your head;
Whoever auctions off his own best trait   1845
    Will soon be sent the worst of luck by fate,
Evil eyes, rages, jealousies begin
    To pour on him like water from a skin,
And envious enemies tear him in two—
    Friends steal his life from him, I swear it's true!

Those unaware that spring is for rebirth
    Cannot perceive what time is really worth,
Take refuge in God's grace and you will know
    That He pours kindness down on us below,
Why seek another refuge from your plight?   1850
    For you both fire and water now will fight:
Moses and Noah's refuge was the sea
    Which showed its anger to the enemy,
And fire protected Abraham as well—
    Smoke rose from Nimrod's heart as if from hell;
The mountain beckoned John the Baptist near,*
    Its rocks made his pursuers run in fear:
It said, 'Come and escape now with your life,
    'You're safe in me from every sharpened knife.'

The parrot says farewell to the merchant and flies away

The parrot gave him words to contemplate 1855
 Then said, 'Farewell, we now must separate.'
The merchant said, 'God be with you each day
 Now that you've shown me a more worthy way!'
He said then to himself, 'I've understood
 To take the path of all the wise and good.
How can my soul be less than that mere bird's?
 The soul must follow good ways, heed her words.'

The harm in being venerated by people and standing out

Your cage-like body is the spirit's thorn
 Fed by deceit from those you come upon:
One says, 'I'll be your confidant my friend,' 1860
 Another, 'I'm your partner till the end.'
The next, 'No one can ever take your place,
 To match your beauty, virtue, and sheer grace.'
Another says, 'Both worlds belong to you,
 And all our souls feed off your great soul too.'
When he sees people drunk with him, he'll lose
 All self-control, for self-conceit he'll choose,
Not realizing thousands just like him
 Satan threw in a stream where they can't swim:
The world gives flattery which men desire— 1865
 Eat less, for it's a morsel full of fire!
It's fire's unseen, it's taste though you can tell
 And then its smoke will rise as if from hell;
Don't say, 'I'll never be so gullible'—
 Through your desire you're always vulnerable.
And should one mock you in the public's gaze,
 Your heart will burn with shame for several days,
Although you know he speaks from disappointment
 That his high hopes did not find their fulfilment;
Still its effect will linger inside you— 1870
 The same applies when you hear praises too,

And this effect will slowly take its course
　　To be your arrogance and error's source;
To praise's faults, like sweets, we all stay blind,
　　They're known through bitterness they leave behind,
Just like a potion or a pill you take,
　　Then suffer irritation for its sake:
Eat sweets, then feel their taste soon disappear—
　　Short-term effects can't last—this should be clear.
But they still take effect, though far from view—   1875
　　All things through opposites are shown to you:
Sugar's effects persist far from your eyes
　　To form boils nurses then have to excise!
The self becomes like pharaoh with such praise,
　　Be self-abased, don't choose that tyrant's ways!
So strive to be like slaves and not like kings,
　　Be struck like balls, don't be the bat which swings!
Or else, when all your beauty fades from view
　　Your sycophants will then grow tired of you;
That group who falsely praised you will be found   1880
　　Calling you 'devil' when you come around,
On seeing you arrive such men will say:
　　'A corpse has risen from the grave today!'
Just like the beardless youth whom they call 'lord'*
　　To trap him with deceit when they applaud,
But when his beard grows with his infamy
　　Vile demons will feel shame at what they see.
The devil seeks a human he can curse,
　　He doesn't come to you, for you're much worse!
While you were human he would still come up   1885
　　And offer you his evil drinking-cup,
But now you're like a devil through and through,
　　You good for nothing—Satan flees from you!
The ones who used to hold on to your hem
　　Flee from what you've become—you're worse than them!

Explanation of 'What God wills happens'

What we've said is a basis, not the end,
  But for God's favours we're worth naught, my friend!
Without God's grace and that of his élite
  Angels would earn a blotted record-sheet.
O God, whose grace fulfils our every need,   1890
  Remembering someone else is a misdeed,
For so much guidance You've bestowed on us
  It hides our flaws and utter wretchedness!
The drop of knowledge which You gave before
  Unite now with your ocean, please, once more!
The drop of knowledge in my soul please free
  From lust and from my body's tyranny,
Before the soil should soak it deep inside,
  Before the wind should spray it far and wide,
Though if they snatch it You'd be capable   1895
  To take it back, for it's redeemable:
The drop which spilled or vanished in the air
  To flee Your power how could it thus dare?
Though it should enter deepest non-existence,
  When You call, it will run back through the distance,
Opposites kill each other just like men,
  But Your decree can make them live again,
From nothing to existence, Lord, You can
  Each moment send another caravan.
Logic and thought each night, especially,   1900
  Become annihilated in Your sea,
But new true beings once again at dawn
  Raise up their heads like fish and are reborn.
Thousands of leaves are vanquished every fall
  Into the sea of death, which conquers all,
And draped in black as though he mourns, the crow
  Laments the garden's grass was forced to go,
The village-chief, however, will dictate
  To non-existence : 'Give back what you ate:

Black death give up what you ate like an ass   1905
    Of plants, medicinal herbs, the leaves, and grass!'
Collect your thoughts now, stop meandering,
    Each breath, within, your fall's replaced by spring!
Your own heart's garden is so fresh and green,
    There cypress, rose, and jasmine can be seen;
The crowd of leaves now hides the branch from view,
    The scores of roses hide the palace too.

From Universal Intellect this came,
    As rose and hyacinth it smells the same:
Without a rose can you detect rose scent?   1910
    When there's no wine can you see wine ferment?
Scent is your leader and your perfect guide
    To heaven—it will lead you deep inside,
Scent is a balm for eyes which gives them sight:
    Jacob's eyes opened, darkness turned to light;
Bad smells can blind a person instantly,
    While Joseph's scent enables one to see—
Since you're not Joseph, be like Jacob—cry!*
    Love's tumult will be seen then in your eye.
Listen to this advice from Sana'i,*   1915
    Find freshness in your withered frame like me:
'Your airs presume a face just like a rose,
    Since you don't have one, don't strike such a pose:
A face that's plain turns ugly when it's vain—
    Even blind eyes should not endure such pain!'
In front of Joseph, don't assume such airs,
    Like Jacob sigh in need and say your prayers.

The parrot's dying showed her neediness—
    Now make yourself a corpse, feel even less,
That Jesus's breath might serve as your cure   1920
    And make you like itself so blessed and pure.
Don't claim in spring on stone some verdure grows,
    Be soft like soil to raise a lovely rose—

For years you've been a stony-hearted man,
    Try being like the soil now if you can!

The story of the old harpist who in Omar's reign would play the harp in the middle of a graveyard without any food just for the sake of God

There was once in Omar's huge caliphate
    A harpist whose sweet music was so great,
His voice made nightingales fall stunned and cry
    While also making each joy multiply,
His breath graced meetings where the lords would throng,   1925
    The Resurrection* listened to his song
Like Esrafil, whose voice was heard ahead
    And brought back souls to bodies of the dead,
Or one of Esrafil's close friends, whose cry
    Could make an elephant grow wings and fly!
For Esrafil revives men totally
    Though they've been rotting for a century.
The Prophets too have special tunes inside
    From which to seekers precious life's supplied,
The sensual ear can't hear such melodies   1930
    Since it's been tainted by iniquities;
A man can't hear the angels' tunes inside,
    Their inner secrets humans are denied,
These tunes are from this world of time and death,
    The heart's tune's loftier than every breath,
Angels and men are captives equally
    In ignorance's gaol without a key:
Recite: '*Community of jinn and men*'
    And learn: '*If you can pass beyond, go then!*'*
Within the saints are soulful melodies   1935
    Which sing '*There is one God*', so listen please!
Lift up your heads from 'not'* which means negation
    And cast off fancies and imagination—
You've rotted in this planet of decay,
    Your soul could not grow up and fly away!

If I give just a hint about this song,
     Men's souls would rise from tombs before too long—
Bring your ear close, for this tune isn't hidden,
     Though to relate it now I am forbidden:

The saints take Esrafil's place from today,   1940
     They give life to the dead and show the way;
From corpses souls ascend without a choice
     Up from the body's tomb due to this voice,
Saying, 'This voice has a distinctive tone,
     To grant life is the job of God alone;
We'd died and been left there to decompose,
     Then came God's blast* and everybody rose.'
Whether God's blast is open or concealed,
     It gives that which in Mary was revealed*—
You who beneath your skin have lost it all   1945
     Return from non-existence at His call!
This call comes from the King Himself, it's true,
     Although His servant utters it to you.
God told him, 'I'm your tongue and eye, my slave,
     Your wrath and your contentment too I gave,
Go forth, because *through me you hear and see.*'*
     Though you're God's secret, don't claim mastery,
Since to *Him who is for the Lord* you turn,
     I'm yours, for '*God's for him*',* as we all learn;
Sometimes I say 'It's you', sometimes 'It's me';   1950
     Regardless, I am sunlight, can't you see?
When I emit a breath just like a ray,
     The problems of the world all fade away;
That darkness which resists all solar light
     My breath makes like the morning, clear and bright!

The names to Adam God himself explained,
     This knowledge all the rest through Adam gained;
Whether in Adam's light or God's you bask,
     You choose between the goblet and the flask,

For with the flask the goblet has a link   1955
    So potent, blessed be that fine goblet's drink!
The Prophet said, *'Those who've seen me are best,*
    But people who've seen them are just as blest.'
When lamps reflect a candle, men of course
    See it as well and know what is the source,
A hundred times like this though it is passed
    The source stays linked to those who see it last—
Either be nourished by the final flame
    Or the soul's candle, for they're all the same,
Either receive light from contemporaries   1960
    Or from the candles of past visionaries.

In explanation of the hadith: *'Your Lord sends in the days of your era special breaths, so make sure to receive them!'*

The Prophet said, 'The breaths that God exhales
    In our own present time that's what prevails,
So always be attentive with your ears
    To catch a breath before it disappears.'
A breath came, saw you, slowly travelled on,
    Gave life to whom it wanted, then was gone,
Another breath will come soon, be prepared
    So you don't miss this other one He's spared;
The mother of all fires this breath extinguished,   1965
    A dead man inner motion thus distinguished:
The flame's heart felt the loss of its existence,
    The dead then wore new garments of subsistence,
Like movements of the Prophet's heavenly tree,*
    Not like those of this world's menagerie;
If it should fall upon the earth and sky
    Then it would terrify all passers by,
From fear of breath like this that's infinite—
    Recite: *'But they refused to shoulder it!'*
Why should *'they shrank from it'** be mentioned here   1970
    Unless the mountain turns to blood through fear?
Last night I found You in a different hue,
    But then some morsels blocked the path to You,

For just a bite Loqman is held at bay,*
   It's now Loqman's time—morsel go away!
The morsel's what these pricks are set upon:
   In Loqman's sole they're looking for a thorn—
There's none at all, nor semblance of one, there:
   Your greed stops you discerning things with care!
The thorn's what you mistook to be a date   1975
   Because you're blind with lust, you low ingrate!
God's rosary is in Loqman's pure soul,
   How can a thorn have pierced this sage's sole?
This thorn-consuming realm's a dromedary
   That's ridden by Mohammad's progeny—
Camel, you're bearing roses, you should know
   That from their scent more roses soon will grow!
But you prefer to head for thorns and sand—
   What roses will you find on barren land?
You who in search have travelled here and there   1980
   For roses, why do you keep asking 'where?'
From your own foot until you first remove
   The thorn, you're in the dark and you can't move.

A man so great the world can't hold his size
   A thorn's tip still can blinker from our eyes.
The Prophet came to bring us harmony:
   '*Please speak, sweet redhead,* come and speak to me,*
And throw a horseshoe in the fire as well*
   So mountains turn to rubies by its spell!'
The redhead's feminine, it's Aisha's name,   1985
   Arabs make 'soul' in gender just the same,
It makes no difference if it's feminine:
   The soul is genderless, alone within,
It's too sublime for either gender's hold
   For it's not something which blows hot and cold;
The soul does not grow large by eating bread,
   Nor turn like this and then like that instead,
Since it's pure goodness, it does what is good.
   Without it there's no goodness—understood?

If it's through sugar that you taste sweet too,   1990
   Remember sugar may abandon you,
But when you turn to sugar through your state
   Then how can sugar ever separate!
When lovers find within themselves the wine
   They lose their intellect, dear friend of mine;
This intellect denies love, but would claim
   It's privy to love's secrets all the same—
It's just a know-all, fighting self-negation,
   Angels are devils till annihilation,
It seems a friend by what it does and says   1995
   But it is far apart from mystic ways—
It's nothing, for it won't leave self-existence,
   Unwilling, it's dissolved by our insistence.
The soul is perfect and so is its call,
   Mohammad said, '*Belal, refresh us all!*
Lift up for us your powerful voice once more
   With breath I breathed inside your big heart's core,
That breath which once left Adam so amazed,
   Made heaven's fold feel mesmerized and dazed!'*
Mohammad lost himself in that fine voice,   2000
   His prayer was not performed then by God's choice:
He didn't lift his head, asleep he lay,
   His dawn prayer thus was subject to delay,*
But with the Bride alone that previous night
   His soul kissed both her hands and saw Her Light:
Love and the soul are veiled in the unseen,
   Because I called Him 'Bride' don't scream 'obscene!'
I broke my silence not to be a bore—
   Would that He'd given me a little more!
He says, 'Speak up, it's not objectionable!   2005
   Fate thus decreed in the Invisible.'*
Fault lies with those who only see what's wrong,
   With such as these, pure spirit can't belong:
Fault lies with creatures who are ignorant
   And have no link to the Omnipotent;
For God though unbelief is wisdom too,
   It's just a curse if held by me or you,

For if impurities are mixed with gold
    It's like the candy's stick you have to hold:
They're both weighed on the scales as if one whole,   2010
    Together like the body and the soul.
The greats did not speak idly, they were sure
    'For pure-souled men, their body's just as pure.'
Their speech, their soul, their body, and their face
    Are absolute, pure soul that leaves no trace,
The soul's mere body if it thinks them foes,
    Worth naught, like backgammon dice overthrows;
That one returns to soil and turns to earth,
    While others in white salt find pure rebirth;
Salt made Mohammad the most excellent,   2015
    Than that well-formed *hadith* more eloquent:*
This salt's his permanent inheritance,
    His heirs are with you—seek them out at once!
One sits before you—which way do you face?
    Where is the soul that contemplates each trace?
If you imagine you've a front and back,
    Your body's trapped you, soul inside you lack—
Bodies have fronts and sides in all directions
    But the enlightened soul has no dimensions.
Open your eyes to vision through His light,   2020
    Avoid the search that's the short-sighted's plight!
You're trapped in joy and grief, completely blind—
    In non-existence where's front and behind?
Today it's raining, walk until it's night,
    It's special rain God sends to those with sight.

The story of Aisha's asking the Prophet: 'It rained today when you went to the graveyard, so how is it that your clothes aren't wet?'

The Prophet visited a grave one day
    Because one of his friends had passed away,
With handfuls of dry earth he filled the grave,
    Thus to a precious seed new life he gave.
Just like interred men, plants we see around   2025
    All lift their outstretched hands up from the ground,

To humans they give countless signs, so clear,
　　They speak to those of us with ears to hear,
With outstretched hands, or like a tongue that's green
　　They share earth's secrets which lie deep, unseen;
Like birds with heads in water that soon rose
　　As peacocks, though they used to be mere crows:
In winter He had locked those crows in gaol,
　　But now He's given them a gorgeous tail;
In winter He grants death, and each one grieves,　　　　2030
　　But then revives them in the spring with leaves.
'They live on by themselves,' deniers said,
　　'Why then attribute this to God instead?'
Despite their blindness, in His friends who know
　　God's planted orchards which will always grow,
Every sweet-smelling rose that you should see
　　Reveals God's mysteries so openly,
Despite the sceptics' claims, we smell their scent
　　Across the world wherever veils are rent.
Like bugs on roses, sceptics clamber off—　　　　　　2035
　　Their ears can't bear Truth's drums, so they just scoff;
They act like they're immersed in what we say
　　But when the lightning flashes, turn away—
They've turned their eyes away from what's shown here:
　　The eye seeks safety first when ruled by fear.

To his wife Aisha then Mohammad turned
　　On coming home, to share what he had learned,
But when she saw his face she felt surprise
　　And touched him, just in case it was her eyes:
His turban, face, and hair she touched and felt,　　　　2040
　　His collar and his sleeve she also smelt.
The Prophet asked, 'What do you seek this way?'
　　She said, 'I saw the rain pour down today;
I've checked your clothes in case they're wet just now,
　　But there's no trace of rain—I'm wondering how!'
He asked, 'What's that you're wearing on your head?'
　　'I made that scarf of yours a veil instead.'

He said, 'This then is why the Lord made plain
   To your pure eyes the special, hidden rain:
That rain did not come from those clouds, my love,   2045
   Other clouds float in different skies above.'

> *Commentary on the verse of Hakim Sana'i:**
> *Other skies found beyond, up with the soul,*
> *Command our own skies in their earthly role,*
> *And ups and downs obstruct the spirit's way*
> *Like mountains and deep seas to cross each day.*

Some other clouds and rain far from your view
   Exist in the unseen, and more suns too,
Just His élite see this manifestation,
   The rest *feel doubt as to a new creation.**
Rain nurtures with its fresh, reviving spray,
   But also causes ruin and decay:
The rain in spring is great, it makes things grow,
   Autumnal rain is like a fever though:
The former nurtures tenderly like breath,   2050
   The latter makes things sick and pale as death;
The wind and sun are just like this as well—
   Find the point of their differences, then tell!
In the unseen too there's variety
   While here there's barter, fraud, and usury!
From that spring comes each breath the saints emit,
   Inside one's heart a garden grows from it,
Spring rain's effect, enabling trees to live,
   Is found too in the grace their breath can give.
If there's a tree that looks as dry as sand,   2055
   Don't blame the wind which helps each soul expand:
The wind first did its work, then moved ahead,
   Those who had souls chose by it to be led.

Concerning the meaning of the hadith: *'Take advantage of the coolness of the spring'*

The Prophet told his friends once, 'Please beware,
    Don't cover up yourself against spring air,
Because your soul will gain from that pure breeze
    Which does to it what spring does to the trees,
But you must flee autumnal cold instead
    For it will leave you like these gardens—dead!'
Transmitters brought us just the form outside   2060
    And simply with that they were satisfied,
So unaware that there's a soul to win—
    They saw the mountain, not the mine within.
For God, the carnal soul's lust is autumnal,
    Wisdom and heart spring's essence, thus eternal;
Your clever reasoning hides like a cheat,
    Seek one whose intellect's divine, complete;
Through his, your intellect may end up whole,
    That intellect restrains your carnal soul.
Here's the interpretation put in brief: 2065
    Pure breaths, like spring, breathe life in every leaf.
Don't close your ears to what the saints report,
    Soft words or harsh, for they're your faith's support,
Embrace with joy warm words and cold as well
    Till you escape from fickleness and hell—
They're both life's spring, the source of all that's good,
    Knowledge, sincerity, and servanthood,
Because the spirit's garden lives through Him
    The heart's sea's filled with pearls up to the brim;
A wise man's heart is filled with endless grief   2070
    If his heart's garden misses just one leaf.

Aisha asks the Prophet, 'What was the inner meaning of today's rain?'

Aisha then asked, 'Dear Prophet, please convey
    To me the wisdom of the rain today:

Was this the cleansing rain of clemency
   Or wrathful justice from divinity,
A gift of kindness from the pure spring breeze,
   Or one of harmful autumn's qualities?'
He said, 'This was to heal the misery
   Which has afflicted Adam's progeny:
If Man were to remain inside that fire   2075
   The rate of loss and ruin would soar higher,
The world would be destroyed at once no doubt,
   Cupidity in men thus driven out.'
The pillar of this world is heedlessness,
   This world sees as a curse pure thoughtfulness:
It comes from that realm, when it dominates
   This world is brought low by what it dictates;
This wisdom's sunshine, greed is icy cold,
   Wisdom's fresh water, this world's foul and old,
From that world gentle sprinklings always pour   2080
   So lust and envy here shall live no more,
If such rains that are hidden should increase
   Both vice and virtue in this world would cease.
This topic has no limit, let's return
   The outcome of the harpist's tale to learn:

The remainder of the story of the old harpist and the explanation of it

That man through whom the world was filled with sound,
   From whose voice grew such visions that astound,
So bird-like hearts would fly in ecstasy
   While souls, perplexed, would lose stability,
As time passed, aged—his falcon soul grown weak,   2085
   More like a finch that scrapes dirt with its beak,
His back became as hunched as jugs of wine,
   His eyebrows hung down like a trailing vine,
His lovely, soul-expanding voice had turned
   Into an ugly, worthless noise men shunned:
What once made Venus green with jealousy
   Resembled now a mule's bray tragically!

Has any fine thing not turned foul before?
    Has any rooftop not become a floor?
Only the voices of saints from the past   2090
    Whose breath provides the Last Day's trumpet blast,*
A soul which makes our hearts drunk in an instant,
    A non-existent which makes us existent,
The loveliness in every voice and thought,
    The joy which inner revelation brought.
When he grew old and weak that man looked dead,
    He needed loans just for a loaf of bread:
'You've granted me long life, Lord, whom I serve,
    And countless blessings which I don't deserve,
For seventy years although I sinned each day   2095
    You never would withhold grace from my way,
Without means I'm your guest, so hear my song:
    I play for God's sake, to whom I belong.'
He picked his harp up, sought God on his own,
    Crying inside the graveyard all alone:
'I seek from God the cost of just one string,
    He'll kindly take the counterfeits I bring!'
When he had played a long time and thus wept,
    With harp as pillow, grave as bed, he slept;
His spirit fled the prison of his breast,   2100
    Abandoning the harp now for its quest:
Free from the body and this world of pain
    Into the simple world, the soul's domain;
His soul sang of what he'd now come upon:
    'If I could only stay here from now on!
I'd love to stay in vernal realms instead,
    Inside this mystic plain and tulip bed—
I'd crawl there now without a head or feet,
    Without a lip or teeth its sweets I'd eat,
With thoughts free of affliction from the brain   2105
    I'd joke with those up there in heaven's plain,
Up there, with eyes closed, a whole world I'd view,
    Without a hand I'd pick some roses too;
Like birds which in a sea of honey sink,
    Job's fount *which cleanses* and serves as a *drink:**

It cleansed Job from his head down to his toes,
　　Like dawn's first light, from all his earthly woes.'
If this book matched the sky's expansiveness
　　It still could not contain a drop of this!
The earth and sky's vast space has sliced my heart　　2110
　　With feelings of confinement, locked apart;
That dream world which I've seen with my own eye,
　　Through its expansiveness spurs me to fly—
If that world and its gate were manifest
　　Then few would stay here for a moment's rest.

Then the command came: 'Don't be greedy—no!
　　Now that the thorn's come out, step forward—go!'
The harpist's spirit lingered, reticent,
　　Clung tightly to the Most Beneficent.

While he was asleep a voice told Omar: 'Give this much gold from
the treasury to that man who is sleeping in the graveyard'

Omar was then made drowsy for God's sake　　2115
　　Until he could no longer stay awake,
He felt amazed, and said, 'This is no game—
　　It comes from the unseen, it serves an aim.'
He lay down, slept and had a dream so clear
　　That God's own voice Omar's soul then could hear;
That voice is the sole source of every sound,
　　All noise is just its echo going round,
Each Nubian, Persian, Arab, Turk, and Kurd
　　Without their ears this wondrous voice has heard—
So what if Turks and Tajiks understood—　　2120
　　That voice is heard as well by stone and wood!
Each moment '*Am I not your lord?*'* we hear
　　And essences and accidents appear,
Though all don't cry out '*Yes!*' still their emergence
　　Is like a '*Yes!*' sprung forth from non-existence.
I said that stone and wood can understand,
　　This tale will illustrate this, and expand:

The complaint of the moaning pillar when a pulpit was made for the
Prophet because the congregation had grown and they had said, 'We
can't see your blest face when you're preaching.' The Prophet and
his companions hear the pillar's complaint, and the Prophet
converses with it plainly

A pillar, cut off from the Prophet, moaned,
    Just like a living being, and it groaned;
He asked it, 'What are you reacting to?'   2125
    'My soul bleeds now that it's cut off from you:
I was your firm support, but you've moved on—
    Do pulpits have a post to lean upon?'
'Do you want to be made a palm instead,
    So everyone can pick your dates?' he said,
'Or that God should make you a cypress tree,
    So you'll stay fresh and moist eternally?'
The pillar said, 'I want what lasts forever'—
    Don't you behave worse than this piece of timber!
He buried then that pillar so it may   2130
    Be resurrected on the Final Day.

Those men whom God has called, as you should know,
    Involvement with this world choose to forgo:
Whoever gets work straight from God will find
    Admission there, and leave his job behind,
But those who've not had gifts from realms unknown
    Will not believe inanimates can moan:
He says, 'Yes!' though inside he scoffs at it,
    So you won't say that he's a hypocrite;
Unless informed about His order, '*Be!*'*   2135
    They would reject my discourse totally;
A thousand men who just obey what's told
    Were filled with doubt when one new thought took hold,
Their skills in logic, proofs, and imitation
    Are based upon their false imagination.

That wretched Satan sows doubt in each mind,
   In order to trip up the ones who're blind;
The legs of theorists are made of wood;
   A wooden leg's unstable, it's no good.

The Pole of each age* is a visionary—   2140
   Mountains feel dizzy at his constancy,
While blind men need a stick to walk around,
   To stop them tumbling over on the ground,
That horseman through whom armies won their fight—
   Who is this man? The one who has true sight;
Though with a stick the blind can walk with ease,
   Seeing through help received from visionaries,
If there were no kings of the mystic kind,
   As stiff as corpses you would see the blind:
Sowing and reaping blind men cannot do,   2145
   Nor trade, nor building, as is plain to you.
If He had not shown mercy to your heart
   Your staff of reason would have split apart—
What is this staff? Proofs and analogies.
   Who gave it? That Most Glorious One who sees;
The staff's become a weapon for your hate,
   So break it into bits, you blind ingrate!
He gave this staff that you might benefit,
   In anger has He struck you once with it?
Blind people, what's kept you preoccupied?   2150
   Look for an intermediary, a guide!
Don't disobey! He gave the staff to you!
   Remember just what Adam was put through!
The miracles of Moses and Mohammad*:
   A stick became a snake, a pillar muttered,
The pillar moaned, the stick turned to a snake:
   They strike five times a day* for their faith's sake.
But if this truth were comprehensible
   We wouldn't need a single miracle—
That which is grasped by your intelligence   2155
   Does not need miracles as evidence.

Consider this path—it's irrational,
    And yet to wise men it's acceptable,
While demons, fearing Adam, chose to flee
    To far off islands, filled with jealousy:
Likewise when prophets' miracles appear
    The sceptics hide their heads in sand through fear
So they can act like Muslims in deceit,
    Without you knowing that they only cheat;
They rub on silver, fake insignias   2160
    To make seem real their worthless replicas,
They falsely speak of laws, God's unity
    Like loaves which hide within impurity.
Philosophers don't dare to breathe a word
    Because true faith will show them they're absurd:
Their hands and feet do what their spirits say,
    Since they're inanimate and must obey—
Although they spread doubts and they falsify,
    Against them their own limbs still testify.

The manifestation of a miracle of the Prophet through the
speech of gravel in the hand of Abu Jahl, as it bears witness
to the truth of Mohammad's status

While holding gravel Abu Jahl came near   2165
    To ask the Prophet, 'What do I have here?
If you're a prophet, tell me what I've brought,
    Since heaven's secrets you must have been taught.'
'Would you prefer it if I answer you
    Or if the stones speak up to tell what's true?'
He said, 'The latter's more incredible.'
    'Of course, though of much more God's capable.'
Within his fist each stone began to say
    That it had Muslim faith: without delay
Each said, '*There is no God except Allah*,'   2170
    And joined, '*Mohammad is His Messenger*.'
On hearing this, he threw them on the floor,
    Much angrier than he had been before.

*The remainder of the story about the musician: the Commander
of the Faithful Omar conveys to him the message that the unseen
voice had uttered*

Let's go back to that old musician's tale:
　　With waiting he became so weak and pale,
Omar was then told: 'Free him from his need,
　　He's been our servant in both word and deed,
He's a much-valued slave for whom we care—
　　You'll find him in the graveyard deep in prayer;
Arise, and from the public treasury   2175
　　Take seven hundred dinars rightfully,
Tell him: "God's chosen you among us all,
　　Take this amount, forgive me that it's small;
It's for those silk harp strings we know you lack—
　　Once it is spent, if you want more, come back." '
That awesome voice thus shook Omar awake
　　To then exert himself just for God's sake—
Towards the graveyard quickly now he ran,
　　Clutching his purse and searching for that man.
He ran around it for a while, but found   2180
　　Apart from some old codger none around;
'This can't be him,' he thought, and searched again.
　　He tired and still had not seen other men;
He thought, 'God said: "A slave, immaculate,
　　A pure man, worthy, blest and fortunate"—
Can some old harpist be this venerable?
　　Mysterious secret, you're incredible!'
He went around the graveyard once again
　　Just like a lion prowling round his den,
When he knew there was no one else in sight,   2185
　　He thought, 'In darkness hearts can still burn bright!'
He sat down next to him with utmost care,
　　But then he sneezed—the man jumped in the air!
He saw Omar—confused, he scratched his head;
　　He felt like leaving, but just shook instead.

'God help me please!' the old man prayed inside,
   'It's the police for me, and I can't hide!'
Omar glanced at his face and it was clear
   The old man was ashamed and pale with fear.
He told him, 'Don't be scared, don't run away,   2190
   I've brought good news from God for you today:
God praised your nature, so that I, Omar,
   Came to admire and love you from afar—
So sit back down beside me, and stay near
   So I can whisper secrets in your ear:
God sends his greetings, and He asks you this:
   "How are you with your pain that's limitless?"
Here's cash—first buy your silk harp strings, and then
   Once you have spent it all come back again.'
The old man shook on hearing what was planned,   2195
   His heart throbbed wildly and he bit his hand,
He screamed, 'My Peerless Lord who's free from blame,
   Please stop! You make this old man burn with shame!'
Due to abundant pain he wept in fits,
   Then slammed his harp down, smashing it to bits:
'You veiled me from my Lord, you stupid thing,
   And chased me off the highway to the King!
You sucked my blood to make me a disgrace
   For my whole life before God's perfect grace!
Have mercy, God, supreme in loyalty,   2200
   Upon a life spent in iniquity:
The value of each day God's given you
   Exceeds all things, but no man has a clue—
Throughout my life I was a waste of space,
   I spent my days with treble notes and bass!
Immersed forever in my fickle art
   I thus forgot the pain of being apart,
The freshness in my minor keys instead
   Has shrivelled up my heart and left it dead!
Due to my hours spent on each melody   2205
   The caravan moved on too soon for me.
Against my self, please God, come to my aid:
   Of no one else complaints have I now made;

I can't receive such help from any source
    But God, who's closer than my self, of course—
My being comes each breath from Him to me—
    Once this declines, I'll see His Unity,
Like when near someone counting out your gold—
    Your whole attention soon this man will hold.'

*Omar turns the old man's gaze from the station of weeping, which
requires self-existence, to the station of absorption*

Omar then told him, 'Your acute distress   2210
    Points also to your own self-consciousness,
Annihilation has a difference—
    Self-consciousness is there a gross offence:
It's thinking of the past to no avail,
    From God the past and future both will veil—
Set fire to these two now, and please take heed,
    Don't stay blocked up with knots like a bad reed;
While it's blocked up it can't be intimate,
    No lips count it as an associate.
While walking, all your thoughts are wandering,   2215
    Back home about yourself you're pondering:
You've knowledge, but you're heedless of its source—
    It's worse than sin, your kind of blind remorse!
Why still repent about a state that's passed?
    Repent of your repentance now at last!
You thought then just of music in your ears,
    Now you prefer to weep your salty tears!'
Omar, discerning mirror of God's light,
    Woke up the old man's soul from its dark night:
He stopped his weeping and his laughing too,   2220
    His old soul died, but he was born anew;
Then he was filled with such bewilderment
    He rose beyond the earth and firmament:
A search beyond all searches thus began,
    Not that I understand—perhaps you can?
Such states and words beyond what's known to us,
    Drowned in the beauty of the Glorious,

A drowning, neither meaning his deliverance,
    Nor that the Sea and he still show a difference:
Your intellect can't know the Whole unless   2225
    You keep on pleading and show neediness—
When such demands are made repeatedly
    At last a wave will come from that Pure Sea.

Now that we've reached the ending of this tale,
    The old man and his states have drawn the veil;
He's shaken words off just like crumbs of bread
    Though half of this long tale is left unsaid.
For such delights, to gamble is the cost,
    A hundred thousand souls may thus be lost—
Be like a hunting falcon in your soul,   2230
    Risk your life like the sun—let the dice roll!
The sun which radiates life to all men
    Each moment empties, then fills up again,
Sun of Reality, diffuse life too!
    Make this old world shine bright as though it's new!
Spirit and life arrive here from beyond,
    Like water pouring non-stop in a pond.

Commentary on the prayer of those two angels who
call out at every market each day: 'God, give every
spender change to spare and bring every miser harm!'
with the explanation that the 'spender' refers to the
aspirant on the path to God, not the one who
squanders it for the sake of desire

The Prophet said, 'Two angels always shout
    With voices that sound sweet when they cry out:
"Please God, keep all the spenders satisfied,   2235
    Let them go home with their wealth multiplied,
But don't give misers anything, please Lord,
    But loss of income, so they'll lose their horde!"'

Yet stinginess excels a generous hand—
    Don't give what's God's except at His command!
Then, in return, you'll gain a boundless treasure
    And not an unbeliever's paltry measure—
Seek God's command from those in union's sea,
    Not every heart has this capacity.
In the Koran those who chose to forget   2240
    Found all their spending only buys regret:
The Meccans who reviled the Prophet* tried
    A sacrifice to draw God to their side,
Such camel sacrifices thus they made
    To sharpen on his neck a murderous blade,
But they were like that overgenerous slave:
    The king's wealth to his enemies he gave!
So to the king this kind of generous act
    Warranted exile—this slave was attacked!
That's why believers fearfully recite: 2245
    '*Show us the straight path!**' in their prayers each night.
The generous give coins to all those who ask,
    But offering up one's soul's the lover's task!
Give bread for God's sake, more will come to you,
    Give up your soul, receive a soul that's new:
When leaves fall off the tree, then God will give
    The leafless tree what it should need to live;
Your being generous won't leave you without,
    God's grace won't leave you ruined—never doubt!
Your barn is emptied when you sow what's there   2250
    But soon your field sprouts goodness everywhere;
What you save in your barn as capital
    Gets eaten up by mice, it's temporal.
This world is naught, look for the lasting whole,
    Your body's void, try searching in your soul!
So bring your bitter soul now to the sword,
    A soul just like the sea is the reward,
If you don't know how to find this location
    Just listen to the following narration:

The story of the caliph who surpassed Hatem Ta'i* in generosity for his own time, and was peerless then

There was a caliph once in history   2255
 Who seemed superior to Hatem Ta'i,
The flag of generosity he'd raise,
 Eradicating need through his kind ways,
His generous deeds produced pearls in the sea
 And stretched around the world repeatedly,
He was like clouds or rainfall for dry land,
 Thus representing God's own giving hand;
His gifts made deepest mines and oceans quake,
 The route to him all caravans would take.
The needy turned towards his door in prayer,   2260
 News of his generous ways spread everywhere:
Persians, Greeks, Arabs, Turks, with eyebrows raised,
 By his munificence were left amazed—
Water of Life*, and sea of kindness too,
 Through him all humans were soon born anew.

Story about the poor bedouin and his wife's altercation with him because of their want and poverty

A bedouin lived with his weary bride;
 Since they were hard up, every day she cried:
'We always have to suffer and be poor,
 The rest rejoice, while you and I endure:
We have no bread, just jealousy and pain,   2265
 We have no water—tears replaced the rain;
Just sunlight clothes us in the afternoon,
 At night our sheets are beams shone by the moon—
Imagining the moon's a wholesome pie
 We lift our hands to grab it from the sky!
Paupers, ashamed at our sad poverty,
 Just watch us starve, filled with anxiety;

Our kin as well as strangers keep away
  Like Sameri* when not allowed to stay:
If I ask for some beans to fill my cup   2270
  They shout, 'May you die painfully—shut up!
In war and charity is Arab pride,
  Among them you're a blemish that must hide!'
Fighting? We don't need that to have no life,
  Beheaded thus by poverty's cruel knife!
Charity? We must beg for our food first!
  We suck the blood of flies to slake our thirst!
And if a guest should ever come our way,
  While he's asleep I'd take his coat away!'

*The deception of needy disciples by false claimants whom they
imagine to be venerable authorities who are in union with
God, not knowing the difference between fact and fiction, between
what grows naturally and what has been grafted*

Because of this the wise have understood   2275
  'One must become the guest of someone good':
You're the disciple of a person who
  Through meanness will steal all your gains from you—
How can he help you when he has no power?
  He gives no light—you'll darken by the hour!
Since he has no light, how can people say
  By seeing him they'll gain a single ray!
Just like a half-blind doctor treating eyes
  He pulls wool over them—this man just lies!
'In poverty and wealth we are this way,   2280
  May no guest by us two be led astray!
If you've not seen a famine's face before
  Look at us bedouins now at your door!
Each false guide hides our features inwardly:
  His heart is dark though he talks cleverly.'
Of God he doesn't have a single trace
  But claims more grace than Adam to your face,
The devil won't show him a single hair,
  'I'm greater than the saints,' he'll still declare,

He's stolen terms from Sufis for his speech   2285
    So men might think he's qualified to teach,
To Bayazid he even deals out blame,
    His inner being makes Yazid* feel shame—
Without a crumb from heaven, he's alone,
    God hasn't even thrown to him a bone.
He's said, 'I've spread a feast, come everyone,
    For I'm God's deputy, the caliph's son;
Hey simple-hearted people everywhere,
    Come fill your stomachs here with my hot air!'
Some waited years for promises he made,   2290
    Tomorrow never comes, and dreams must fade.

It takes a while until one's inner soul
    Becomes revealed to others as a whole:
Is there some gold beneath the body's wall
    Or just a snake-pit where foul insects crawl?
Once it is known that this man was depraved,
    His students will be too old to be saved.

In explanation of how it happens occasionally that a disciple
sincerely believes that a false claimant is authentic, and, through
this conviction of his, reaches a station that his shaikh has never
even dreamt of, such that fire and water cannot harm him
though they do harm his shaikh. But this is very rare

Occasionally, we see the opposite:
    From falsehood some disciples benefit;
With a sincere aim they may reach their goal   2295
    Though a mere body they had thought a soul.
Guessing the qebla* in the dead of night,
    God heard their prayers though they did not guess right.

'This vain impostor lacks a soul within
    Just as we both lack food and are so thin—

Why should we hide our want like this big fake,
    And merely for our reputation's sake!'

*The bedouin tells his wife to be patient and explains the
virtue of poverty and patience*

'Why keep on seeking wealth?' her husband said,
    'Most of our life has passed—we'll soon be dead!
The wise don't think of gain and loss like you   2300
    For both are like a flood that passes through—
Whether it's clean or foul, don't waste a breath,
    Within a moment it will meet its death.
Thousands of animals live wild and free
    Without such ups and downs, so joyfully:
The dove gives thanks to God from that tall tree
    Although for food there's still no guarantee,
The nightingale sings praise of God as well:
    "We count on you, and you respond so well!"
The falcon finds her bliss on the king's hand,   2305
    Forgetting all the carrion in the sand;
From gnats to elephants the same applies:
    They're all God's family, whom He supplies.
The grief inside our breasts is worthless nonsense,
    Mere fog and dust of our wind-like existence,
Uprooting griefs are scythes which wickedly
    Keep whispering, "It's like this, can't you see?"
Each suffering is a piece of death no doubt—
    If you know how to, cast that portion out!
Since you can't flee that part of death, heed well: 2310
    All of it will be poured on you in hell!
But if this part of death tastes sweet to you
    God will make all the rest of it sweet too.
Pains are like messengers from death—don't shun
    Death's messenger, you weak, distracted one!
Those who live now in pleasure die in pain,
    The body's worshippers no soul will gain:
From pastures sheep are driven to their pen,
    The fattest ones are picked for slaughter then.

The night has passed and dawn has come, dear wife,   2315
   Will you just talk of gold for all your life?
When you were young you were more satisfied,
   Now you seek gold, then you were gold inside,
A fruitful vine once, now you can't be sold,
   Your fruit should ripen, but you're dry and old,
Your fruit ought to be sweeter now than that,
   But you've reversed the way rope-makers plait,*
Since you're my wife we should be similar,
   To make our life together easier :
Partners must match, in basics they must share,   2320
   Like gloves and shoes, together as a pair;
If one shoe of a pair does not quite fit
   The other must be thrown away with it,
Have you seen double-doors of different size,
   A wolf and lion mate before your eyes?
Two loads won't balance on the camel's back
   If one's much smaller than the other sack.
Contentment is the aim of my brave soul—
   Why do you make repulsiveness your goal?'
The man spoke with sincerity this way   2325
   To his old wife until the break of day.

*The wife advises her husband, 'Don't talk any more about your own
merit and spiritual station. "Why preach what you don't practise",
for even though these words are true, still you haven't reached the
station of trust in God, and to speak like this above your own station
and affairs is harmful and "more abhorred by God"'*

His wife screamed, 'Image is what you adore,
   I won't endure your stories any more!
Don't spout pretentious gibberish to me,
   Don't speak with arrogance presumptuously!
You have such airs as if you've earned much fame—
   Look at your own state now and feel some shame!
Pride's ugly and for beggars doubly so,
   Like wearing wet clothes when it's bound to snow!

Although you like to show off with hot air   2330
  Your home's a spider's web—it's hardly there!
When did you fill your soul with satisfaction?
  You've only just looked up its definition!
Although the Prophet said "Contentment's treasure",
  You can't tell it from pain though it brings pleasure!
Contentment is the spirit's treasure-chest,
  But only grief is found inside your breast!
Don't call me "wife" or try to cuddle me,
  My husband's justice, not depravity!
How can you walk with lords when you eat mud   2335
  And, for your drink, you suck a locust's blood!
You fight with dogs for bones, you're so in need,
  And mourn just like an empty-bellied reed!
Don't look at me with eyes full of disdain
  Or I'll tell what you hide inside each vein!
You think you're more intelligent than me,
  You've credited me with stupidity;
Don't jump on me like reckless wolves would do—
  Better to lack a brain than be like you!
Because your brain just shackles everyone   2340
  It seems more like a snake or scorpion!
May God oppose your lies and cruelty
  And stop your meddling brain from touching me!
Both snake and charmer lurk behind your face,
  You're both amazingly—you're a disgrace!
If you could see you're ugly like the crow
  From pain and grief you'd melt just like the snow!
The charmer chants spells like an enemy,
  The snake casts spells back though he cannot see,
If his trap for the snake were not a spell,   2345
  How could he be the snake's prey then as well?
The charmer, counting all the wealth he'd make
  Can't recognize the spell from his own snake;
The snake says, "Charmer, you think you're so fine—
  You see your own spell, but now look at mine!
You tricked me with the name of God for fun
  To make me seem possessed to everyone—

I wasn't trapped by your tricks but God's name,
   You've made God's name a trap, you should feel shame!"
The name of God will make you pay for it,   2350
   To His name soul and body I commit,
For it will slit the veins of your sad life
   Or throw you into gaol like me, your wife!'
The wife gave lectures to him of this sort
   Just like a never-ending bad report.

The man advises his wife, 'Don't look upon the poor with contempt,
but look at the work of God as perfect. Don't revile the poor with
their poverty through your own vain fancy and opinion'

He said, 'Are you a wife? You always moan!
   Poverty's pride*, so leave my ears alone!
Wealth is just like a hat that people wear
   To warm their heads if they have lost their hair;
But those with lovely, glossy curls prefer   2355
   Not to wear hats—without they're happier.'
The man of God is like the eye, and sight
   Is better than to be veiled from God's light:
The dealer at the time of the inspection
   Strips slaves of clothes that might hide imperfection,
But he can't strip them of their blemishes—
   He'll clothe them so that no one witnesses,
Claiming, 'This one's just shy through modesty;
   If I undress him, he is bound to flee!'
Up to his neck the dealer's filled with vice,   2360
   To cover this, his money pays the price—
The slaves of lust can't see his faults within
   For lust unites hearts which are filled with sin,
But if a beggar utters words of gold
   His wares still won't be put in shops and sold.
The Sufi's business is beyond your brain,
   Don't treat their poverty with such disdain
For they transcend mere outward poverty,
   Their daily bread comes from God's majesty.

Since God is just, how can He then mistreat   2365
　　Lovers whose hearts for Him alone still beat,
Or give some people all that they desire
　　While ushering the rest straight to the fire?
So may His fire burn those who hold that view
　　For He created earth and heaven too!
Was *poverty's my pride** then said in vain?
　　No, there are hidden glories to attain;
'In anger, you have sworn at me a lot,
　　"Snake-charmer" you have called me, though I'm not:
If I catch one, first I'll pull its fangs out   2370
　　So that it's safe to bash its head about,
Because those fangs are its own enemy
　　I'll pull them out with knowledge God gave me.
I don't chant spells for my own benefit,
　　I've turned desire around and shackled it;
Of this world, God knows, I don't seek a part,
　　Contentment's brought a new world to my heart:
Upon the pear tree you see things pear-shaped,
　　Those who came down from such vile thoughts escaped:
You feel so giddy when you spin and whirl—   2375
　　You see the house spin but it's you, my girl!'

*In explanation of how everyone's movement proceeds from
where he is, he sees everyone from the limited perspective of his
own existence: blue glass shows the sun as blue, and red glass as
red; when the glass is free of colour, it becomes transparent,
and is more truthful than all other glass as a leader to emulate*

Abu Jahl saw Mohammad once and said:
　　'An ugly thing the Hashemites* have bred!'
Mohammad said to him, 'Your words are true
　　Although there's none impertinent as you.'
Abu Bakr then exclaimed, 'My sun of light,
　　Not from the east nor west, may you shine bright!'
Mohammad said, 'Correct, companion,
　　You've fled this world worth less than carrion.'

Those present asked, 'Pure chief of the elect,
    How can two opposites be both correct?'
'I'm like a mirror God's cleaned to perfection,
    Indians and Turks both see here their reflection.'

The man said, 'Don't see me as covetous,
    Transcend this womanish suspiciousness:
It looks like lust but is in fact God's grace—
    When there is grace, for lust there is no space!
Try being poor a day or two, you'll see
    Twice as much richness in this poverty,
Have patience with it, don't grow so uptight,   2385
    In poverty lies God's most glorious might!'
Avoid being sour and many souls you'll see,
    Through satisfaction, drowned in the Sweet Sea,
Thousands of bitter souls too can be found
    Like roses which in syrup have been drowned.
If only you had the capacity,
    Then my heart's state could be shown candidly,
Milk from the soul's breast is what I now share,
    It won't flow out if no one suckles there:
When listeners feel a thirst and start to seek   2390
    Preachers, though they be dead, will start to speak!
When listeners aren't tired, but fresh as dew,
    The mute find tongues with which to lecture too!
If strangers enter my house, women wear
    A headscarf that can cover all their hair,*
If relatives should enter in their place,
    Then they would lift their veils back off their face.
Whatever people try to beautify
    They just embellish for the seeing eye:
How can the harp's sweet music that you hear   2395
    Have been made just to please a tone deaf ear!
God didn't make musk fragrant just for fun—
    It's for those who can smell, not everyone!
God has set up the land and sky you view
    And put both fire and light between the two;

The earth is made just for terrestrials,
     The sky's the home of all celestials,
The base man is the lofty's bitter foe,
     The customer for each place we all know.

'Veiled girl,' he said, 'Have you now lost your mind?   2400
     Would you put make-up on just for the blind?
The world with precious pearls if I should strew,
     If they're not your share, what good will it do?
No longer fight or try to lead astray,
     Or give me up instead, dear wife, today!
I do not wish to fight with enemies,
     From righteous actions even my heart flees—
Stay silent or I'll take this seriously
     And leave behind our home immediately!'

The wife takes notice of her husband and seeks
forgiveness for her words

And when his wife saw him wild as a bear   2405
     She started crying—tears are woman's snare:
She sobbed, 'I'd never guessed what you might do,
     I'd hoped for something different from you!'
With self-negation she came to his side:
     'I'm more your dust than your beloved bride;
I'm yours in soul and body, totally,
     You now possess the power to order me;
If I lost patience with being poor, it was
     On your account, my pain is not the cause:
You are my medicine for every ache,   2410
     I don't want you in need, it's for your sake,
It's not about my own wants that I care,
     I scream and moan for your sake, this I swear—
By God, for your sake you will find that I
     Would sacrifice myself, for you I'd die!
Would that your soul, which mine's devoted to,
     Could know what my soul thinks, my honest view!

Since you thought very badly then of me,
    Of soul and body I long to be free,
And gold and silver I would throw away   2415
    For you to not react like this today!
You occupy my heart and soul throughout—
    For this small slip of mine would you walk out?
You have the power to just walk away
    Although my soul pleads that you'll choose to stay.
Remember me, your idol from before,
    The one you used to worship and adore?
I've lit my heart now to agree with you,
    If you say "cooked" I'll say "All the way through!"
For I'm your spinach, one small dish you eat,   2420
    You're worth it, whether with sour sauce or sweet!
I blasphemed then, but now I understand,
    With all my heart I follow your command,
I didn't recognize your royal traits,
    I interrupted but a good wife waits.
I've fashioned now a torch from your compassion,
    Repenting, I've abandoned opposition,
I've placed before you both a sword and shroud
    To chop my head off which has been too proud!
You speak of separation's agonies—   2425
    Do what you wish to do, but not that please!
Your spirit pleads within you now for me,
    It intercedes like this perpetually,
Your loving nature pleads my case within,
    Relying on it, my heart sought out sin—
Stop feeling angry now, be merciful,
    Sweeter than honey by the bucketful!'

She spoke thus kindly and with some success
    And she would pause to shed tears in distress,
Her tears and sobbing soon became excessive,   2430
    Though she already was for him impressive—
That pain produced a lightning bolt, which lit
    A spark inside his heart and made it split:

That pretty face which turns you to her slave,
  When she acts servile, how must you behave!
That one whose arrogance astonished you
  Now cries in front of you—what can you do?
That one whose proud rebuffs made your heart bleed
  Can do more damage now she comes in need!
We've all been trapped once in her tyranny—   2435
  Now she is begging, what are we to plea?
*It's beautified for men,** God gave it shape;
  So how can men know where they can escape?
So *he's consoled by her** she was created:
  Can Adam then from Eve be separated?
A Hamza and Rostam in bravery—
  His wife still keeps him bound in slavery,
Although his words could make the whole world sway,
  '*Please redhead, speak to me!**' he still would say;
Water puts out the flames which winds just fan   2440
  But boils away when heated in a pan,
For if a pan should separate the two
  It will evaporate in front of you.
Though outwardly above her you may tower,
  You want her, so within she has the power.
This love's the special human quality;
  Beasts lack it—that's their inferiority.

In explanation of the saying 'Women prevail over intelligent men, while ignorant men prevail over them'

The Prophet once said, 'Women all control
  Intelligent men, those who have a soul,
But stupid men rule women, for they're crude   2445
  And hold a simple, bullish attitude.'
They lack all tenderness and can't be kind—
  Their animal soul still controls their mind:
Tenderness is a human quality,
  While lust and rage show animality,
A ray from God is that one whom you love,
  Creative, uncreated, from above.

The man submits to his wife's request that he should seek a
livelihood, regarding her opposition as a sign from God:

> To those who have the knowledge to discern
>> What spins you round's the thing that makes you turn

The things his wife said made the man feel shame
 Like dying officers who don't want blame:
'I have become my lover's foe,' he said,   2450
 'How did I kick my own soul in the head!'
Our sight is veiled whenever fate decrees,
 Our mind can't tell our elbows from our knees,
But once it's passed, our mind then starts to mourn:
 It rips our shirt now that the veil's been torn!
He said, 'I feel ashamed, my darling wife,
 I've strayed, but now I seek a righteous life:
I've sinned against you, please act mercifully,
 Please don't uproot my heart immediately!
If an old infidel feels as I do   2455
 Once he repents he's then a Muslim too.'
Through love of God, who's kind and generous,
 All of existence feels delirious—
He's loved by faith and infidelity:
 Copper and gold both serve in alchemy.

In explanation of why Moses and Pharaoh were both
compelled by God's decree like poison and antidote,
darkness and light, and of Pharaoh's prayers in solitude
to God that He would not shatter his reputation

Moses and Pharaoh both served God this way,
 Moses seemed guided, Pharaoh led astray;
Moses would weep for God when it was light,
 Pharaoh would do that in the dark at night:
'What is this halter on my neck?' he'd pray,   2460
 'Without it, "I am I" how could I say!'

While you've illumined Moses like a spark
   By that same power you've made this servant dark:
You've lit just like the moon his radiant face,
   My moon-like soul you've turned black with disgrace;
My star's dependent on this moon for light—
   Now it's eclipsed how can I still shine bright?
Saying I am "the lord", slaves start drum rolls
   But it's for the eclipse men beat their bowls:*
They all raise such a clamour for one aim—   2465
   So that this moon may thus be put to shame.
Although I'm Pharaoh, I'm a desperate soul,
   Each calls me "highest lord", then beats his bowl!
We're fellow servants, but your axe still chops
   The branches that it chooses in this copse,
Then joins a branch back to its trunk once more
   While other branches it will just ignore:
But over your axe power each branch lacks,
   No branch has yet escaped this ruthless axe—
Since your axe has the power to dictate,   2470
   Would you please make all crooked things now straight!'
Pharaoh said to himself once more, 'How odd!
   Do I not pray throughout the night to God?
I'm meek in secret, and in harmony—
   When I reach Moses what becomes of me?'
The gilt of false gold has ten coats, but turns
   Pitch black when it is brought near flames, and burns.

My body follows Him, my heart as well,
   One moment I'm the kernel, then the shell:
He tells me 'Be a field!' and I turn green,   2475
   'Be ugly!'—I turn paler than you've seen,
A moon that's bright then black, deprived of light:
   This is the way God works—am I not right?
Before '*Be! And it was*'* brings His decree
   We run in place and placelessness, so free,
Once colour has hemmed colourlessness in
   Two Moseses their warring then begin,

When colourlessness is acquired again
    Moses and Pharaoh even make peace then.
If doubts come to you still about this state,   2480
    How can this point be free from all debate?
Colourlessness to colour—that's the wonder,
    And how they should begin to fight each other:
Oil is made up of water, isn't it?
    So why then is oil water's opposite?
If you should try to mix them, you will see
    That they will keep apart so stubbornly.
Since rose and thorn belong together too,
    Why then is constant fighting all they do?
Is it real war, or wisdom in disguise   2485
    Like donkey-sellers' fights*—just for our eyes?
Or neither—just confusion for our mind:
    The treasure in this ruin one might find.
Your treasure with real treasure you confuse,
    Such thoughts mean that real treasure you will lose,
Such fancies are like populated land—
    Treasure is not found there, you understand;
Such settlements are filled with life and war—
    Non-being felt such shame at what it saw!
Being did not try fleeing Non-existence   2490
    But It sent being home despite resistance:
'I'm fleeing Non-existence' don't you claim!
    It runs away from you, but you've no shame!
It calls you to itself just outwardly,
    But drives you off with cudgels inwardly,
Like changing footprints so you can't be tracked:*
    Pharaoh's distaste is Moses's in fact.

*The reason for the disappointment of the wretched with both worlds, for 'He has lost this world and the hereafter'**

Once a philosopher claimed this, I've heard:
    'The sky's an egg, its yolk earth'—how absurd!
So someone asked, 'How does the earth then stay   2495
    Surrounded totally by sky this way,

Just like a lantern hanging in the air,
   Not moving even slightly while it's there?'
Then the logician said, 'It's the sky's pull
   From all the six directions to the full,
Like a magnetic vault, continually,
   It holds it like some iron centrally.'
He then said, 'You are claiming it's the sky
   Which draws this dark earth, but I can't see why:
Perhaps it just repels from every side   2500
   With heavy winds that keep the earth inside.'
The perfect with their minds repel this way
   So Pharaoh's wayward soul is kept at bay—
Due to repulsion from both worlds, my friend,
   The lost are left with neither in the end.

Even if you should shun God's slaves today,
   They're sick of your existence anyway;
They've amber which affects you just like straw,
   Inducing frenzy in you and sheer awe,
But when they hide their amber, your submission   2505
   You quickly change again to fierce sedition:
Your rank becomes mere animality—
   This is bound by and needs humanity,
While this humanity the saints control—
   Like animals we need them in this role:
The Prophet called 'my servants' all mankind,
   Recite then, *'O my servants!'** for the blind.
Your brain's the camel-driver driving you!
   It drags you everywhere and whips you too!
The saint rules all your intellects, so they   2510
   Are just like camels in their driver's sway—
Look carefully, and keep this fact in mind:
   There's one guide with a thousand souls behind.
You ask me, 'Who's the driver? Who's the guide?'
   Find eyes which see the sun and then decide!
The world has been nailed down throughout the night,
   Waiting just for the sun to spread its light:

Here in an atom is a hidden sun,
    A lion in a lamb's skin—he's the one!
A sea that's hidden under straw—take care   2515
    Not to step by mistake now over there!
Doubts and mistakes about guides may be part
    Of grace, though this may seem strange at the start.
Each prophet came alone down here below,
    His sole guide was unseen, so none could know:
He charmed the world in its entirety
    And hid in a small form, so none could see:
The stupid thought him weak and all alone—
    How can the king's companion be so prone!
They said 'He's just a man and nothing more,'   2520
    But sadly didn't know what lay in store.

*The senses' eyes see Saleh and his she-camel as wretched
and without a friend. When God wishes to destroy an army, he
makes their foes seem wretched and few, even though that foe
may be superior: 'He belittled you in their eyes so that God
could bring to pass something that needed to be done'**

Saleh's she-camel seemed no different,
    So wretches maimed her who were ignorant:
With water these vile wretches were so mean,
    For God's bestowal of water they'd not seen;
God's camel then drank from some distant pools,
    God's water they'd refused to God—what fools!
The camel, like the bodies of good men,
    Brought the destruction of the evil then,
God's she-camel, her share* thus you can see   2525
    Caused death and pain to this community.
The officer of God's wrath then laid down
    Her blood-price as the people of that town.
Spirit is Saleh, body his maimed steed,
    Spirit's in union, body's filled with need,
Saleh's pure soul can't be a sufferer,
    The essence wasn't maimed, they harmed just her,

And Saleh's spirit doesn't suffer grief—
　God's light is not harmed by men's unbelief.
God joined it with the body in one place   2530
　So grief and trials Man would have to face,
Not knowing they are God's essentially,
　That his own jarful comes from the deep sea.
God joined the body with an aim in mind:
　To serve as a safe refuge for mankind—
So serve the bodies of the saints who save,
　With Saleh's spirit be a fellow slave.
Saleh said, 'You have shown your jealous ways
　So punishment will come down in three days;
After three days, the One who can take life   2535
　Will send these signs of your impending strife:
Your face will change its hue repeatedly,
　A range of colours which all men will see:
Your skin will turn to saffron straight away,
　Then red just like a rose on the next day;
The third day every face will turn pitch black
　And after that God's wrath will soon attack.
You want a sign of this threat? Can't you see
　Her foal run to the mountains desperately?
There's hope still if you stop him reaching there,   2540
　If not, the bird of hope will flee its snare.'
No one could catch that foal as it raced on;
　It reached the mountains, and then it was gone:
Spirits flee bodies, their main source of shame,
　The Lord of Mercy being their sole aim.
Saleh said, 'His decree has not been read,
　Hope was pinned down, and now they've chopped its head!'
What is the camel's foal? One's lofty mind
　Which you can bring back home by being kind:
If it returns, you've then escaped all harm,   2545
　If not, in sheer despair you'll bite your arm.
They thus heard all about their gloomy fate,
　And stared down, for all they could do was wait;
On the first day, they saw that they'd turned pale
　And in despair they all began to wail.

Then on the second day, they turned bright red—
    All hope they'd had was now replaced with dread;
The third day, they all turned black in the face,
    Saleh's claims all proved true—they had no case.
When they became filled with the worst despair,   2550
    They knelt like birds just landed from the air;
In revelation Gabriel would dictate
    With '*jathemin*'* that men must fall prostrate—
Prostrate when you're taught how to fall this way
    And when you're told to on that dreaded day!
They waited for his wrath's blows to descend;
    It came and wiped them out—that was their end.
Saleh left his seclusion for that place,
    A smoke cloud was the last remaining trace.
He could hear body parts scream mournfully   2555
    Though when he looked no mourners could he see:
He heard some moaning from their scattered bones—
    Their souls, instead of tears, shed solid stones;
Saleh screamed, this was more than he could take,
    He started mourning for these mourners' sake:
'You've made me weep for you, community,
    You wasted all your lives on vanity!
God told me, "Suffer their abuse and give
    Advice to them—they haven't long to live."
I said, "Advice gets blocked by cruelty,   2560
    Its milk flows out with love and purity—
They've forced me to endure such awful pains
    Advice's milk has clotted in my veins!"
God said, "My grace and kindness I will send
    And place a plaster on your wounds, my friend."
He made my heart clear as a sunny day,
    From my thoughts sweeping your abuse away,
I then returned to counselling again,
    Shared parables like sugar with all men:
Fresh milk from sugar in this way I made,   2565
    Mixed milk with honey in what I conveyed—
Those words became like poison in your heart
    Since you were filled with poison from the start!

Why should I grieve that grief has now been slain?
    You stubborn people were my grief and pain!
Who mourns that grief through dying has been stopped,
    Or that a painful boil has finally popped?'
'You mourner,' to himself he turned and said,
    'That corpse does not deserve the prayers you've read.
Reciter, don't you now make a mistake: 2570
    Why should I feel bad for the wicked's sake.'*
To weeping with his heart he now returned;
    An undeserved compassion in him burned.
He shed tears in distress increasingly,
    Drops from the sea of generosity.
His intellect asked him, 'Why weep, you fool?
    Or mourn those who preferred to ridicule?
What are you crying for? Their deeds? Tell me!
    For that malicious, wicked company?
For their dark, rusty hearts, your heart now breaks?   2575
    Their tongues were venomous just like a snake's!
Or for their dog-breath do you breathe such sighs,
    Or for their scorpion's nest of mouths and eyes?
Or for their squabbling, sneering and abuse?
    Give thanks that God will never let them loose!
Their hands and feet and eyes were out of place,
    Their love and peace and anger a disgrace;
To follow the traditions of their sect
    They stamped upon the guiding intellect:
They've turned to donkeys, they don't want a guide,   2580
    They choose to show off and to worship pride;
From heaven God brought down his slaves to see
    How they're prepared for hell so perfectly!'

*Concerning the meaning of 'He lets the seas meet each other with a gap which they don't encroach upon'**

The source of hell and heaven's guests is one,
    Though there's *a gap they don't encroach upon*:
The men of fire and those of light He's mixed
    Although Mount Qaf between them He has fixed,

Like in a mine He's mixed plain soil with gold
    Though for such different prices they'll be sold,
Like necklaces of pearl and cheap black stone: 2585
    Strange fellow guests who'll soon depart alone.
Half of the sea tastes sweet and sugary,
    Bright like the moon, as clear as it can be,
The other half's like bitter venom, which
    As well as tasting foul is black as pitch;
They crash against each other as waves do,
    As if one sea not forced apart as two:
Confinement makes forms clash within its cell,
    Souls thus are mixed in peace and war as well:
The waves of peace collide with wondrous might,   2590
    Uprooting from men's breasts all hate and spite.
The waves of war though take a different form,
    Inverting our loves like a thunder storm:
Love draws the bitter to the sweet by force
    For love is rightly guided by its source.
Wrath drags the sweet to bitterness, but how
    Can bitterness suit sweetness—tell me now!
Bitter and sweet are not seen by your sight,
    Only the furthest window sheds such light.
The eye that sees the end sees properly,   2595
    While seeing just this world's delusory;
Many things look like sugar but are not,
    Like poison hidden in the sugar pot!
The wiser ones detect it by its smell,
    Some after they have tasted it as well:
Their lips reject it thus before their throats
    Although the devil bellows, 'Eat!' and gloats!
Another through his throat knows he'll be ill,
    The next once it has travelled further still,
Another feels it burning when he shits—   2600
    The pain will crush his liver now to bits!
The next one after several months perceives,
    Another, after dying, finally grieves—
If in the grave he finds respite, then he
    On Resurrection Day will finally see.

Each sugar cube in this world too receives
   Its own allotted time before it leaves,
Rubies need years beneath the sun's pure light
   To purify their hue and shine so bright;
In just two months though garden herbs may grow,   2605
   To bloom a red rose needs a year or so—
This is why God explained in the Koran
   He's given an appointed time to Man—
If you have heard your hairs will all stick up,
   Water of Life* He's poured into your cup:
Call this the Draught of Life* and not mere speech—
   In an old word new spirit is in reach.

Now listen to a further point, my friend,
   Clear as the soul but hard to comprehend:
At one stage on this path snake venom changes   2610
   To wholesome food—it's God that rearranges:
Poison can be a drug that brings relief
   And lawful things there are here unbelief,
Things harmful to the soul in that pure sphere
   Can be a remedy when they're down here:
Unripe grapes are too sour for us to eat
   But when those same grapes ripen, they taste sweet:
As wine it's bitter and prohibited
   But vinegar's use is unlimited.

*Concerning the fact that the disciple should not be arrogant and do
the same thing as the saint does, for halva does not harm the doctor
but does harm the sick patient, and the snow and the cold does not
harm ripe grapes but does harm unripe grapes, for they are still on
the way to 'That God may forgive you your past and future sins'**

If saints drink poison it becomes a cure,   2615
   If novices drink they become impure.
'*Lord grant me!*' was the plea of Solomon:
   He meant 'Give me alone dominion,

To others don't be kind and generous',
   He wasn't being simply envious:
With heart '*It is not suitable*' now read,
   '*After me*'* wasn't avarice or greed:
In kingship he'd faced danger and much strife
   Enough to make one fear for one's own life,
For head and soul and faith it makes one scared—   2620
   We've not faced trials that can be compared!
Solomon's aspiration you require
   To shun cheap vanities and aim much higher.
Despite his strength he couldn't conquer death:
   His kingdom's waves eventually blocked his breath,
Dust settled on him from this agony,
   For other kings he thus felt sympathy.
He spoke for them: 'This royalty of mine—
   Give it completely, just as strong and fine,
To whomsoever you should smile upon,   2625
   For I am he and he is Solomon.
He isn't *after me* but *with me* here
   But what's *with me* when I've no claimants near?'
You'll need an explanation first to learn
   But to the couple's tale I'll now return.

Conclusion of the incident between the bedouin and his wife

The altercation in this tale we've heard
   Requires a moral not to be absurd,
Their tale's been told, but let's now recollect
   That parable on self and intellect,
Or carnal soul and wisdom—understood?   2630
   Both are required to make the bad and good,
On earth these two essentials night and day
   Are fighting and disputing every way:
The wife wants all the household needs supplied,
   Food on the table, social rank, and pride;
The carnal soul, like her, serves its own need,
   So now it's humble, now it wants to lead;

The higher intellect has no concerns—
  It only thinks of God with pain that burns.

Although its inner meaning is the bait,   2635
  First listen to this story's form, then wait:
If inner things are all that count, explain
  The world's creation—was it all in vain?
If love were just in thought and spirit, there
  Would be no need for forms like fasts and prayer;
The gifts exchanged by lovers would be naught
  But form compared with love, if that's just thought.
For lovers, gifts serve as their evidence
  Of inner love concealed from outward sense,
Since outward acts of kindness testify   2640
  To secret loves, my friend, when they don't lie;
Your witness tells the truth then falsifies,
  Now drunk with wine, now yoghurt—truth and lies:
One drunk on yoghurt acts drunk, that is all,
  He hollers and pretends he's lost control;
In prayer and fasting hypocrites pretend
  They're drunken saints who've reached the journey's end—
In short, our outward actions are distinct—
  They serve to show what's hidden, thus they're linked.
Grant us discernment, God, we pray to you,   2645
  So we can recognize the false from true!
Do you know how our senses can discern?
  When they *see by the light of God** they'll learn:
Without effects the cause still shows what's found,
  Relationships reveal love that's profound,
The one whose leader is God's light is not
  Cause and effect's slave, victim of their plot;
From flickers love's flame grows so tall inside,
  No longer to effects is this man tied—
He has no need now for the signs of love   2650
  For love has shone its light straight from above.
This discourse needs more space to be complete:
  Reflect on this until we next should meet.

Though meaning in this form is visible
    And form seems close, they're incomparable,
Just like a tree and sap—although they're linked,
    In substance they are clearly quite distinct—
Abandon substance and particulars,
    Explain the state of those two characters!

The bedouin sets his heart on fulfilling his beloved's request and
swears 'This surrender of mine is not for show or as a test'

The man said, 'I no longer will persist,   2655
    You have control—I'll do what you insist!
At your command I won't make you wait long
    Nor try to judge if it is right or wrong.
In your existence, mine I'll leave behind:
    I love, and *Love makes men turn deaf and blind.'**
The wife asked, 'Do you sing to win my heart
    Or to find out my secret through your art?'
He said, '*The world of secrets is obscure.*'
    Adam was made from earth but still was pure,
And in his frame God placed for all to view   2660
    The Tablet's contents* and the spirit too—
Until the end whatever is in store
    He taught the names* to Adam long before.
The angels lost their wits at what was shown;
    They gained more holiness than they had known,
And this growth which from Adam entered them
    Came from beyond their own transcendent realm;
Compared with his expansive soul and mind
    The seven heavens all seem too confined:
The Prophet said: God's said, 'Naught can hold me   2665
    However deep or tall that it may be;
On earth and in the highest heavens I
    Can't be contained, to this I testify,
But I'm contained in the believer's heart—
    If you seek me look in that precious part!'
God said, '*Come here among my slaves and see*
    A paradise of images of me.'*

The highest heaven, though it has much light,
　Fell down in shock when it was shown this sight;
Although the highest heaven is so vast,   2670
　What's form worth when pure meaning comes at last?
Each angel then would say, 'Before we knew
　A friendship on the earth with all of you,
We sowed the seeds of service on that land
　Though our role there we could not understand:
"What is the link between us and that place
　When we are heavenly and that seems base?
Why do we mix with darkness when we're light,
　Can light live with the dark? This can't be right!"
Adam, our friendship was due to your scent,   2675
　The earth's your body's weft—that's what we meant,
Since it was woven from the earth, it's clear,
　Your pure light too must be located here—
From your soul what ours gained has so much worth,
　It radiated beams out from the earth.
We were on earth, but of earth unaware,
　Heedless of all the treasure buried there;
God told us to move from our previous station,
　We grew embittered by our relocation
And so we kept on arguing our case,   2680
　Saying, "But Lord, who now will take our place?
The light of all your praises that we tell
　Just for the sake of chatter would you sell?"
We were received so well by God's decree:
　He said, "Feel free to say with liberty
Whatever's on your mind without a fear
　Just like an only child whose words are dear,
No matter if they're inappropriate—
　Much more than wrathful I'm compassionate.*
Angels, in order to spell this truth out   2685
　I'll fill you with uncertainty and doubt,
And still not take offence when you should speak—
　Deniers of My mercy wouldn't squeak!
So many fathers in My clemency
　Are drowned, effaced like drops inside the sea;

Their clemency's the foam from My sea's tides—
    It passes but its ocean source abides." '

Before that pearl this shell you see is dumb,
    It's nothing but a worthless piece of scum,
By both the foam and that pure sea, it's plain   2690
    This speech is not a trial and not in vain—
It comes from love, humility, and grace,
    I swear by Him to whom I turn my face!
If this desire seems like a trial to you
    Then test the trial now for a moment too!
Don't hide your secret, so mine you might view,
    Command then anything that I can do—
Don't hide your heart, so mine might be disclosed
    And then accept whatever is imposed.
What shall I do, and where may I begin?   2695
    Look what a mess my troubled soul is in!

*The wife specifies to her husband the way to seek
daily sustenance, and he accepts*

The wife replied, 'A sun has shone its light
    From which a universe has now turned bright:
The Maker's caliph, God's own deputy,
    Through him Baghdad's like spring eternally—
Join with this king then you'll be one as well,
    Why keep on heading to misfortune's hell?
It's alchemy, these great kings' company,
    Compared with their glance what's mere alchemy!
Mohammad glanced on Abu Bakr's face   2700
    He then became *veracious** through his grace.'
The husband said, 'How can I meet a king
    Without a pretext for my visiting?
I have to have a link or stratagem:
    Things can't be made without the tools for them.
Majnun when he heard somebody once say
    That Layli had been slightly ill that day,

Said, "How can I go there without excuse?
　　If I can't visit her bring me a noose!
　　If I were a physician I could go,　　　　　　2705
　　　I would have visited a while ago."
For God said, "*Say, come!*"* freeing us from stress,
　　To signal we should end our bashfulness;
If bats had vision and ability
　　By day they'd fly around so happily.'
The wife said, 'When the king should join the fray
　　Impotence turns to power straight away,
So when your means is vile pretentiousness
　　You must choose impotence and helplessness.'
He said, 'How can I trade without the tools　　　2710
　　Unless I show I'm helpless and he rules?
I must have evidence I'm penniless
　　For any king to pity my distress.
Other than words and looks show evidence
　　To gain the pity of his eminence,
For this proof based on talk and how you look
　　Is immaterial in the judge's book—
To prove your worth he wants sincerity
　　Free from words, then his light shines perfectly.'

*The bedouin takes a jug of rainwater from the middle of the
desert to Baghdad as a present for the Commander of the
Faithful,* imagining that water is scarce there as well*

She said, 'Sincerity's to strive hard, love,　　　2715
　　Cleansed of existence then to rise above—
We've stored rain in this jug and now it's full:
　　It's your possession, means and capital,
So take this jug and journey to the king
　　To give it to him as an offering;
Tell him we've nothing more, he'll understand
　　There's nothing finer in our desert land;
His storehouses may have the finest fare
　　But they won't have such water that's so rare.'

This jug's our body so it must contain   2720
  All of our outward senses' bitter rain:
O Lord, accept this water that we've brought
  By the grace of their lives *the Lord has bought!**
This jug has five spouts, for each sense, you see,
  Preserve its water from impurity,
So to the sea the jug might find a way
  And thus take on its nature too one day,
So to the sultan when you carry it
  He'll see it's pure and we might benefit,
Then it will be a limitless fresh store—   2725
  Our jug will fill a hundred worlds and more!
Now block the spouts and fill it to the brim,
  Lower your lustful gaze!* Stay close to him!

'What a great gift!' he thought, so satisfied,
  'This water would give any king such pride!'
The bedouin's wife then was not aware
  The Tigris, sweet as syrup, flows past there
Towards Baghdad just like an ocean's tide,
  With countless boats and fishing nets inside.
Head for the sultan, see this action—go!   2730
  Perceive this way *beneath them rivers flow;**
Our sense perceptions are a drop, that's all,
  Compared with that pure river, they're so small.

The bedouin's wife sews a felt cover around the jug of rainwater and puts a seal on it because of the strength of her husband's conviction

The man said, 'Yes, let's cork the jug with care,
  This offering will bring wealth beyond compare;
Sew felt around it, so the sultan might
  Decide to break his fast with it at night,
For nowhere else is water found so fine,
  Which tastes delicious like a vintage wine;
From drinking salty water you will find   2735
  That people there fall sick and end up blind.'

A bird that lives in briny brooks can't know
   The places where the cleanest waters flow:
Those whose abode is in the briny spring
   About the Tigris don't know anything.
You who have not escaped your transiency
   Can't know effacement, bliss and ecstasy—
Such things are passed from father down to son
   For whom they're like the alphabet to learn:
It's clear for every child and not so arduous   2740
   Although the meaning may not be so obvious.

He picked the jug up and went on his way,
   Holding it next to him all night and day,
Shaking with fear it might be harmed by fate
   As he walked on towards the city's gate.
Meanwhile, his wife unrolled a rug for prayer,
   '*Lord help us!*' she appealed as she knelt there,
'Protect our water from calamity,
   Please let that pearl reach the majestic sea!
Although my husband has much sense and skill,   2745
   The pearl has enemies that wish it ill.'
Pearls were all Kawsar's waters to begin,
   A drop of that is each pearl's origin.
Through his wife's supplications during prayer
   And his determination to take care,
Safe from both theft and damage on the way
   He took it to the court without delay.
A court filled with the best of things he found
   Where needy men had spread their nets around:
Their needs are met each moment in that place,   2750
   Through gifts, and robes of honour they find grace,
The Muslims, infidels, the fair, the hideous,
   Like sun and rain, for all not just the virtuous.
He saw some being honoured, standing straight,
   And then the next in line who had to wait,
From Solomon to ants, the first and last,
   Revived as though they'd heard the final blast,*

Those who seek form bedecked with jewellery,
  Truth-seekers in Reality's pure sea,
Those previously deficient gained endeavour   2755
  While those who had it now received much favour.

In explanation of the fact that, just as the beggar loves the wealth of
the donor, the wealth of the donor also loves the beggar; if the beggar
had more patience the donor would come to him. However, whereas
patience is perfection for the beggar, for the donor it is a defect

The shout 'Come, seeker!' startled like a bell
  'Munificence needs to be begged as well.'
It seeks itself the beggars and the weak
  Just as clear mirrors are what fair girls seek:
A fair face by a mirror can be shown,
  As beggars make beneficence well known,
And so in *By the morning** God decrees
  'Don't shout, Mohammad, when the beggar pleas!'
Since beggars mirror your own generous grace   2760
  Don't speak too close—you'll blur the mirror's face.
Beggars reveal men's generosity,
  And which one has bestowed abundantly;
Thus beggars mirror God's munificence,
  With God they turn to pure beneficence,
While all the rest are corpses, nothing more,
  And they can't enter through the king's court door.

The difference between one who is needy of God with thirst for Him
and one who is destitute of God and thirsts for other things

He looks a dervish but the truth is known—
  Don't throw this image of a dog a bone!
It isn't God he seeks but food instead,   2765
  Don't serve a plateful to a man who's dead!
The dervish who seeks food is like a newt,
  He flees the sea which he appears to suit—
A housebird not the phoenix in the sky,
  She eats sweet treats not food sent from on high,

She loves God simply for what He bestows,
　　Her soul does not love beauty, heaven knows!
She may think that she truly loves the essence
　　But for His attributes she dreams up nonsense;
Imaginings are formed and they were born　　　　　2770
　　But *He was not begotten,** so read on:
The one who loves his own conception's face
　　Can't love the Generous One who has such grace,
But if that kind of lover is sincere
　　Through metaphor to him truth might appear;
An explanation of this is required
　　But I fear worn-out minds are much too tired:
Worn-out, short-sighted minds continually
　　Feed fancies to end our tranquillity,
And not by everyone is fine speech heard:　　　　　2775
　　Figs are not suitable for every bird,
Especially the dead and putrid kind,
　　Heads full of fancies, eyes completely blind,
Since for a fish's portrait sea and land
　　Are one, like soap and coal for a black hand:
Though you should paint a portrait that looks sad,
　　Feelings of grief and joy it's never had!
Its form is sad but it is unaware;
　　When its form smiles it also has no share.
This grief and joy etched in your heart are naught　　　2780
　　But a mere image next to what He's brought,
The image's form smiles still for your sake
　　So through it truth's expressed with no mistake;
The pictures painted on a bathhouse wall
　　Are just like clothes outside the changing hall:
You see just clothes so long as you're outside,
　　Take off your clothes, my friend, and step inside!
With clothes on you can never enter there
　　As body is from soul veiled, unaware.

*The caliph's chamberlains and guards step forward to honour the
bedouin and accept his gift*

Thus from the furthest desert this man came 2785
    Up through the court's gates, reaching thus his aim,
Some chamberlains approached him then to spray
    Rose water of pure grace on him this way;
They knew without words what he'd come to ask:
    To give before they're asked was their main task.
'*Chief of the bedouins*,' they then enquired,
    'Where are you from, are you not feeling tired?'
He said, 'I'm just a chief if you decree
    But helpless if you turn your backs to me;
Your faces have the mark of eminence, 2790
    Than Ja'far's gold* you've more magnificence;
One glimpse of you, to me, is worth much more,
    Your pure faith flings such coins across the floor,
You who can *see by God's light** everything,
    Who've come now to grant favours from the king,
To glance and thus perform his alchemy
    On copper heads of humans just like me.
A stranger, from the desert I've arrived
    In hope of royal grace, to be revived:
His grace's scent fills deserts like small holes, 2795
    Thus even grains of sand gain their own souls!
I came here for some gold originally
    But I've become drunk with what I now see.'
A man rushed to the bakery for bread,
    But saw the baker's beauty and dropped dead!
He went just to admire the roses, but
    He found the gardener more immaculate;
And at the village well in water's place
    One drew the Draught of Life from Joseph's face;*
To watch a fire when Moses went one day— 2800
    He managed to escape from hell this way;*
Jesus jumped up to flee the enemy—
    That jump took him to heaven instantly!*

Forbidden fruit trapped Adam, as decreed,
 His being turned then to Mankind's first seed;
For food the falcon stepped into a snare
 And found the king's wrist and good fortune there;
A boy agreed to go to school to learn,
 His father's promised gift this way to earn—
There he became so clever very soon   2805
 By working hard, just like a bright full moon;
A war of vengeance Abbas came to wage
 Against the true religion of the age,
But he and his descendants then became
 The prop of faith for centuries all the same.*
'I came here for some profit and relief,
 Inside the gates I then became a chief,
Water I brought in order to gain bread,
 To paradise this search for food has led.'
Bread led to Adam's fall—what a huge price!   2810
 But food has settled me in paradise!
From food and drink, release I now have found,
 Like heavens, at this court I whirl around;
In this world nothing moves but through desire
 Except such lovers whose hearts are on fire.

The lover of this world is like someone who loves a wall on which
sunlight shines and makes no effort to understand that this
radiance and splendour do not come from the wall but from
the sun in the fourth heaven. Consequently, he sets his
heart on the wall completely, and, when the rays
of sunshine move with the sun he is left deprived
forever: 'A gulf is fixed between them and
*what they desire'**

Some love the Whole and some love just a part,
 The latter from the Whole are kept apart;
The one who loves a part soon also learns
 That his beloved to the Whole returns:
Another's slave has made him look a clown— 2815
 He's clung to someone weak for fear he'd drown!

He has no power with which he can help you,
  His lord and master's business he must do.

*The Arabic proverb: 'If you fornicate, do it with a free
woman; if you steal, steal a pearl!'* *

They say: '*With a free woman fornicate!*'
  And '*Steal a pearl!*' the Arabs too relate:
A slave went home and he was left to mourn,
  Scent blew back to the rose, he kept the thorn—
He was left far off from the one he'd sought,
  His feet were sore, his efforts were for naught;
If hunters catch the shadow of a bird   2820
  Is this worth anything? Don't be absurd!
One grabs the shadow, waves, victorious,
  A bird perched on the tree grows curious:
'Why does he laugh when he's a stupid fool?
  He's so deluded, duller than a mule!'
'The part's joined with the Whole,' I hear you say.
  Eat thorns then! They're joined to the rose, aren't they!
There's only one way to join with the Whole
  Or else His messengers would have no role:
Since messengers are sent to join as one   2825
  What can join them when they're in union?
This discourse could go on for long, my friend,
  It's getting late, it's time this tale should end:

The bedouin presents the gift, that is the jug, to the caliph's servants

He held that jug of water in the air,
  Thus sowed the seed of service over there:
'Now take this present to the sultan, please,
  Then free from need this beggar on his knees;
Here's a new jug containing water which
  Had gathered when it rained into a ditch.'
Although this made the servants smile a bit   2830
  As a most precious gift they handled it,

Because the king's informed munificence
    On all the court exerted influence:
In subjects their king's nature can be seen,
    The sky's what makes the earth turn bright and green,
His slaves are pipes, the king's the reservoir,
    Water flows through the pipes to fill each jar.
When all the water's from a source that's pure
    Each one has water which tastes sweet, for sure,
But if it's bitter and polluted too   2835
    Each pipe delivers filth this way to you,
For every pipe's connected to its source—
    Ponder the meaning of this fine resource!
The grace of each man's exiled royal soul
    Affects so much his body as a whole:
Intelligence that's of pure origin
    Has brought the body under discipline,
Love which brings victims instability
    Drives the whole body to insanity;
The ocean like Kawsar* holds so much grace   2840
    That pearls and jewels take its pebbles' place;
The art for which a teacher is renowned,
    Among his students too that art is found:
With learned theologians students read
    Theology if they're wise and take heed,
The law professor's students learn his science—
    That's not theology but jurisprudence,
And through the grammar teacher at all schools
    The students learn by heart our grammar's rules,
Through one effaced on this path students learn   2845
    Effacement in the king who makes hearts burn—
Of all these types of knowledge you will see
    The best is knowledge of our poverty.

The story of the encounter between a grammarian and a boatman

Once a grammarian stepped into a boat
    And turned towards the oarsman just to gloat:

'Have you learned any grammar?' He said, 'No.'
　'Then half your life's been wasted just to row!'
Although this made the oarsman burn with pain
　From answering back he opted to refrain.
Wind steered the boat towards a whirlpool there—　　2850
　The oarsman shouted to him, once aware,
'Have you learned how to swim and keep afloat?'
　'I've never learned, skilled captain of my boat.'
'Grammarian, your whole life has been in vain:
　We're sinking fast—what good now is your brain!'
Not grammar but effacement's needed here—
　If self-effaced dive in and have no fear!
While corpses can float on a stormy sea,
　How can the living find security?
When you have died to human qualities　　　2855
　You'll be borne by the sea of mysteries.
He who called others 'donkey' pays the price—
　He's now left skidding like an ass on ice!
Even if you're the scholar of the age,
　Observe the passing of this world, deep sage!
We've silenced the grammarian in narration
　To teach the grammar of annihilation,
The law of law and grammar that's most pure
　You'll find through being less, of this be sure.
The jug of water is our knowledge, while　　　2860
　The caliph's is the Tigris and the Nile.
We're taking our own jugs of water there—
　We're donkeys, even if we're unaware!
The bedouin had an excuse and cause,
　Not knowing back home what the Tigris was:
If he had known the Tigris like those near
　He wouldn't then have carried his jug here—
If of the River Tigris he had known,
　He would have slammed the jug upon a stone!

The caliph accepts the present and orders gifts to be bestowed even
though he is completely without need of that present

The caliph saw this man and heard of him,   2865
   Then filled his jug with gold up to the brim,
He saved that bedouin from poverty,
   Gave gifts and robes of honour generously,
Then to his servants he gave this command,
   That world-bestower with this generous hand:
'Hand him this jug that I've filled up with gold;
   Show him the Tigris too!' his men were told.
'By land he slowly journeyed here in need
   But on the Tigris he'll return with speed.'
He reached the Tigris on a boat, and bowed,   2870
   Prostrated, blushed with shame and cried aloud:
'That generous king was unbelievable—
   His taking my gift was incredible!
How did that sea of generosity
   Accept my worthless present readily!'
The whole world is a jug which you can stop,
   Knowledge and beauty fills it to the top,
But near the Tigris that's a drop of rain—
   The boundless Tigris no jug can contain.

A hidden treasure* opened when too full   2875
   And made the world so bright and bountiful:
Its fullness made it boil and spill like milk,
   Making the earth a sultan dressed in silk.
Of God's great Tigris if he'd seen a bit
   He would have smashed the jug, effacing it—
On viewing it, men always lose control,
   Through jealousy they throw stones at their bowl:
You've thrown stones at your jug through jealousy,
   It smashed, becoming perfect totally!
The jug has shattered, but now water's poured,   2880
   Perfection's what this shattering has restored,

The jug's parts now all dance delirious—
  To intellects that sounds ridiculous!
Now neither jug nor water's manifest,
  Look at it and enjoy—*God knows what's best*.
Knock on reality's inviting door,
  Let thought take wing, like falcons you will soar!
Your thought's wing's mud-stained and weighs more than lead
  Because you now eat mud instead of bread—
Eat less of meat with bread since they form clay,   2885
  Then you won't stick like mud to earth this way:
When hungry you're a dog in temperament,
  So fierce, aggressive, and malevolent;
When full you're like a carcass in the dirt,
  Just like a wall you're ignorant, inert:
A rotting carcass then, a wild dog now,
  You claim the path of lions anyhow!
The dog's your only help in hunting prey:
  Feed it much less, so it will then obey!
If it grows proud and disobedient   2890
  It won't race happily towards the hunt.
Want drove that bedouin along the road
  Towards the court, where fortune was bestowed;
Of the great king's beneficence we've told,
  His generous granting of a jug of gold.

When lovers speak love's scent is smelt on them,
  It comes out of their mouths in love's pure realm;
If he talks law, then poverty is heard—
  Poverty's whiff spreads from his every word;
If unbelief, then we smell true faith's scent,   2895
  Certainty's perfume from his argument:
The crooked wave that's risen in the sea
  Is sound—its origin's sincerity;
Consider that wave pure and worthy too
  Like the beloved's mouth reproaching you:
That harsh expression which you didn't seek
  Became so sweet because it showed his cheek.

His words are true though faults you first detect—
  What crookedness which can make things correct!
If you bake sugar in the shape of bread,   2900
  It won't taste like a loaf, but sweet instead:
A golden idol's found by a believer—
  He'll keep it from the heathen unbeliever,
He'll burn it in a bonfire straight away
  To break its transient, borrowed form this way,
So that the idol's form won't last in gold
  And thus mislead men from truths they've been told.
Gold's essence has come from divinity:
  The idol's form in gold is temporary.
Because of one flea don't burn the whole rug,   2905
  Don't be distracted by a fly or bug!
You worship idols when fixed in form's realm,
  Leave form behind, find meaning inside them!
To make the Hajj* seek a companion
  Though he be Arab, Turk, or Indian;
Don't judge him by his figure, form, or name,
  But look at his intention and true aim;
Though he is black he's in accord with you,
  He shares your hue within—call him white too!
This story has been told the wrong way round   2910
  Like thoughts of helpless lovers that astound:
Headless, predating pre-eternity,
  Tailless, for it's like post-eternity,
But it's like water: every single drop
  Is head and tail and neither—I should stop,
For God knows this is not a tale to share
  But the pure substance of our state—beware!
The Sufi has achieved true mastery,
  Of past things this man has no memory.
We are all three: jug, king, and bedouin!   2915
  *They've turned away from it**—they're vile within!
Reason's the husband, greed the wife, that's right,
  Both dark deniers of true wisdom's light.
Now listen to how such denial starts
  Because the world consists of various parts,

For parts aren't separate from the whole: your nose
    Breathes in the scent which is part of the rose;
Leaves to the rose's beauty too belong,
    The dove's coo to the nightingale's sweet song.

If I put problems and their answers first,   2920
    I can't give water to those who have thirst;
If problems make you feel much stress and grief,
    Be patient—*patience is what brings relief*!
Abstain from thoughts though they tempt and harass—
    The heart's the forest, thought a crazed wild-ass!
The best of medicines is abstinence,
    Scratching increases itches, even once,
For this is medicine's key principle—
    Abstain and watch your soul grow powerful.
Prick up your ears to hear what I have told   2925
    And I'll make you an earring of pure gold
To mark you as a servant of the moon,
    So you will soar up to the heavens soon.
Created things are so diverse, it's said
    They differ like the letters A to Z;
The different letters may need sorting out
    Although from one view they're the same throughout:
From one view opposites, from one the same,
    From one view serious, from one a game!
On Resurrection we face scrutiny,   2930
    The beautiful wait for it eagerly,
But if you're like an Indian cheat that day
    You'll be disgraced, your cover blown away!
Since his face isn't sun-like, clear, and bright,
    He wants to hide beneath the veil of night;
He's just a thorn without one petal, so
    Spring is the secret of this rose's foe,
For one who's like a rose all over, spring
    Is a reunion that he's welcoming;
Autumn is what the soulless thorns prefer,   2935
    Rose gardens then are not superior:

Their beauty's covered like the thorn's own shame:
 You can't tell them apart, they look the same,
So autumn gives it life instead of spring—
 Then stones and rubies look like the same thing;
God's gardener spots it in the autumn too,
 His glance sees more than the whole world can view:
That person has the whole world in his soul:
 Celestial stars are part of the moon's whole,
And thus each image is now beckoning,   2940
 'Glad tidings everyone, here comes the spring!'
When blossom's radiant like a coat of mail,
 How then can fruits their charming form unveil?
When blossom falls, that's when fruit takes its place,
 When bodies are destroyed souls lift their face—
Fruit is the spirit, blossom is its form,
 Blossom's good news, fruit ripens when it's warm:
When blossom's shed, fruit then begins to show,
 When one's decreased, the other starts to grow;
How can bread nourish till it's broken up?   2945
 Can uncrushed grapes become wine in your cup?
Unless some healing herbs are ground with it
 How can a medicine give benefit!

On the nature of the Sufi guide and obedience to him

Hosamoddin, please fetch a sheet or two
 And write about the guide what I tell you;
Although you're frail, lack strength and energy,
 Without the sun there is no light for me,
Though you've become *the lamp and glass,** my friend,
 You lead the hearts which follow the thread's end:
You hold the thread's end, from which you won't part; 2950
 Your bounty gave the pearls strung round my heart!
Write down about the guide what I now say
 And choose him—he's the essence of the way,
The guide's the summer, others autumn's blight,
 He's like the moon, while they're the dark at night.

I've called young fortune, my Hosam, 'old sage'
  For he's mature with God, though not in age:
Without beginning he's extremely old,
  A rare pearl whose description can't be told:
He grows more potent just like vintage wine,   2955
  Especially the drink *that is divine.**
Don't try this path alone, first choose a guide!
  Its dangerous trials will leave you petrified!
Even on routes which numerous times you've used
  Without a guide you're hopelessly confused—
Beware then of this new, uncharted way,
  Keep focused on your guide, don't turn away!
If you're not safe in his protective shade,
  The monster's wails will leave you stunned, afraid,
Diverting you straight into further harm—   2960
  Much shrewder men than you could not keep calm.
Heed the Koran on those who went astray*
  And how the wicked Satan made them pay:
He lured them all a thousand miles from here,
  Reducing them to nakedness and fear—
Look at their bones and hair, and now take heed!
  Don't be an ass, don't let your passions lead!
Grab hold of its thick neck and pull it back
  Towards the knowing guide's specific track,
If left alone this donkey's bound to stray   2965
  Across the field towards the mounds of hay;
Don't you forget to hold with force its leash
  Or it will bolt for miles to find hashish!
A donkey drugged—what greater enemy!
  That donkey's ruined countless—can't you see?
If you don't know the proper path, just do
  The opposite of what it wants you to:
Consult them, then do just the opposite!
  *Or else you'll always be regretting it.**
A friendship with desire you can't afford,   2970
  *It leads you off the path towards the Lord,**
But nothing conquers passion better than
  The company of fellow travellers can:

The messenger of God advises Ali, 'Since everyone seeks proximity
to God by means of an act of worship, seek proximity through
companionship with the special sage and servant of God, so
that you can excel all the rest'

The Prophet called Ali once to his side,
   'Lion of God,* brave hero of my pride!
Don't count on courage on its own to cope,
   Take refuge too beneath the tree of hope:
Enter the realm of that pure intellect
   Whom no opponent can from truth deflect.'
His shadow is just like Mount Qaf* in size,   2975
   His spirit like the phoenix soars the skies,
We could continue with this man's applause
   Until the end of time without a pause,
He is the sun, though human in our sight,
   Please understand that *God knows best what's right*.
'Of all the good deeds on the path, Ali,
   You choose God's special slave as sanctuary,
Others perform each single righteous deed
   So from their carnal souls they might be freed.
Instead step in the shade of this true sage   2980
   To flee that hidden enemy's tight cage;
Of all the acts of worship it's the best,
   It makes you that much better than the rest.'
If he accepts, surrender to the guide
   Like Moses with his master Khezr* once tried,
Stay calm, don't question what he should commit,
   So he won't say, *'Enough! Here's where we split!'**
If he destroys their boat, don't you go wild,
   Don't tear your hair out if he kills a child!
Since God has said, 'His hand is as my own',   2985
   And *'Up above their hands rests God's alone,'**
With God's own hand he slays the helpless boy,
   To let him live with pure, eternal joy.

Whoever tried this journey on his own
    The guides still helped—he didn't walk alone;
The guide's hand is for all across the land,
    It has to be then naught but God's own hand;
If absent people can gain gifts galore
    Those present with the guide must gain much more,
If absent men receive such gifts for naught   2990
    Imagine what his personal guests are brought;
You can't compare his faithful followers
    With those who choose to be mere onlookers.
Don't be too squeamish when your guide's around,
    As weak as water, crumbly like soft ground,
When each blow leaves you bitter, don't expect
    Without pain like a mirror to reflect.

A man from Qazvin* gets tattooed with the image of a lion on his shoulder but regrets it because of the pain caused by the needle

Now listen to this tale on what I've seen
    And heard about the people of Qazvin:
Their shoulders, arms, and bodies they tattoo   2995
    With needles and a special ink that's blue.
One of them asked a barber casually,
    'Please draw a beautiful tattoo on me.'
He asked, 'What image do you have your eye on?'
    He said, 'Tattoo the figure of a lion;
Leo is my ascendant, so I think
    A roaring lion's best—use lots of ink!'
He said, 'Now all I need to know is where?'
    'Across my shoulder-blades—you'll find space there.'
But when the barber stuck the needle in   3000
    The man felt pain he couldn't bear begin:
Our fearless hero screamed, 'Aargh! Stop it, sir!
    What are you stabbing like a murderer!'
'You did ask for a lion, didn't you?'
    He wailed, 'What part was it that you just drew?'

'I started the tattoo back with the tail.'
  'Leave that bit out, for it's of no avail.
I've just been strangled by its tail and rear,
  They blocked my windpipe, which before was clear!
So draw a tailless lion now instead,   3005
  That needle of yours fills my heart with dread!'
He started then to draw another bit,
  Not showing mercy or restraint in it.
The man then screamed, 'Which part have you drawn here?'
  He said, 'Its ears, dear fellow, have no fear.'
'Let it be earless, nobody will see,
  Leave out the ears, and finish rapidly!'
He now pricked somewhere else just as before,
  The hero from Qazvin complained once more:
'Which part is this? I'm sure I must have bled!'   3010
  'It's just the lion's stomach, friend,' he said.
'I beg you, leave the stomach out as well!
  Don't prick so deeply, please, this hurts like hell!'
The barber grew confused and so perplexed,
  He bit his finger, wondering what's next,
Then finally flung his needle on the ground,
  And shouted, 'Where is such a lion found
Without a tail and ears, and stomach too?
  No lion like this lives, I swear to you!'
Brother, you have to bear the needle's pain   3015
  To flee your infidel self's poisonous reign;
Sky, sun, and moon bow down and show obeisance
  To that group who've escaped their own existence:
The sun and clouds obey what's specified
  By those whose self-love has completely died;
Their hearts have learned to light their lamps, and so
  The sun can't burn them with its fiery glow:
The sun moved strangely, far apart it kept,
  *Turning thus from the cave** where that group slept;
The thorn too turned completely to the rose: 3020
  Towards the universal each part goes.
How can a man praise God, the lord of all?
  Be like mere dust, contemptible and small!

What can men learn about God's being one?
    To burn themselves in Him just like the sun!
If like the day you wish to shine so bright,
    Burn up your being, for that's like the night—
Like copper burn yourself with alchemy
    In that One who gives being generously!
You've clung fast to the self of 'I' and 'you'   3025
    Although all wretchedness stems from these two.

The wolf and the fox go to the hunt in attendance on the lion

Attended by the wolf and fox, one day
    The lion climbed the mountain to find prey,
With mutual support this group of three
    Thought they might hunt them more effectively,
Combining forces in that vast terrain
    More catches thus they hoped that they would gain.
The lion, though embarrassed by this pair,
    Still honoured them by letting them come there,
For such kings feel they're burdened by their troops,   3030
    But he agreed, for blessings come from groups:
The moon is shamed by stars, in honesty,
    It lets them near through generosity.
Was not the Prophet told, '*Consult them too!*'*
    Though no one had as good a point of view,
On scales we pair mere iron weights with gold
    Though for a fraction of gold's worth they're sold;
The body is the spirit's travelling mate,
    The guard dog serves the king at his court's gate.
Towards the mountain then they made their way,   3035
    Accompanying the lion on that day;
They caught an ox, a goat, and a fat hare,
    Thus had a most successful hunt out there:
Whoever backs a lion in the fight
    Will never lack his meat by day or night.

When they took back their catch across the plain,
    Their victims, wounded, drenched in blood, and slain,
The wolf and fox then waited eagerly,
    Hoping to see the catch shared equally.
The lion sensed that they'd grown covetous   3040
    And knew the basis of their lustfulness:
Know that the lion of the mysteries—
    Whatever thoughts you have he clearly sees,
Refrain distracted heart when he is near
    From bad thoughts, for to him they all are clear!
He knows, but doesn't give you any clue,
    He wears a smile as mask and laughs with you.
About their whisperings once he was aware;
    He thought he'd better guard against the pair:
'I'll show you what you two have truly earned,   3045
    Beggarly misers, then you will have learned!
For you, will my opinion then not do?
    Is this your measure of what I've shown you?
Your own minds and opinions come from mine,
    My world-adorning gifts which are divine;
The painting thanks its painter, as is fit,
    For thought and knowledge which he's granted it—
Is your opinion of me then so low?
    Disgraces of the epoch, now I know!
*Those who think ill of God,** if I don't break   3050
    And chop their heads, then that is my mistake!
I'll free the heavens from your vile disgrace
    So that your tale remains in this low place.'
While thinking this he would smile all the while—
    Don't feel assured on seeing lions smile!
Material wealth is like the smiles of God—
    It's made us drunk, conceited, prone to fraud;
Becoming poor is best for you who're sure
    About wealth's worth—it soon sheds its allure.

The lion tests the wolf saying, 'Come forward, wolf, divide
the prey among us!'

The lion said, 'Decide each hunter's share   3055
    So we can see, wolf, if you're truly fair;
In distribution be my deputy
    Until your essence is made clear to me.'
He said, 'Dear king, the wild ox is for you
    Since you are big, well-built, and powerful too;
The goat's mine, for its size is moderate;
    Fox, take the hare and don't be obstinate!'
The lion said, 'What talk I've listened to!
    How dare you speak near me of "I" and "you"!
That wolf insulted me when it came near   3060
    And saw itself still, though I have no peer.'
The lion roared, 'Come here, conceited ass!'
    Then punched him down and slew him on the grass;
Not hearing true words in the things he'd said,
    He flayed his skin and then chopped off his head!
'You saw me, but your self you failed to leave,
    Your soul must die abased and none will grieve!
You failed to pass away before my face—
    Breaking your neck was thus an act of grace!'
*All perishes** except His face, submit,   3065
    Don't claim existence—you've no part of it!
To whomsoever in My face should die
    The rule *All perishes* does not apply:
'*There is no*' for '*except*' he's left aside,*
    Whoever's in '*except's*' realm has not died,
And those who talk near him of 'I' and 'we'
    Are not let in, thus drowned in vanity.

*Story about the person who knocked on the door of his beloved, who
asked him from inside, 'Who is it?' He replied 'It is I!' She
responded, 'Since you are you, I won't open the door: I don't know
any friend who is "I"—go away!'*

A man knocked on his lover's door one day,
    'Who is it?' he heard his beloved say.
He said, 'It's me.' She answered, 'Leave at once!   3070
    There isn't room for such raw arrogance.'
Raw meat's cooked just by separation's flame—
    What else can cure hypocrisy's deep shame?
He wandered off in pain as his heart burnt,
    In exile from the one for whom he yearned,
Matured before then going back once more
    And walking to and fro outside her door.
He tapped the door, now suffering nerves inside,
    Not to let slip a wrong word how he tried!
His sweetheart then responded, asking who   3075
    Was at the door—he said, 'None, love, but you.'
'Now you are I, please enter in this place
    Because for two I's here there isn't space.'
A needle can't accommodate split thread,
    To enter thread must have a single head.
To fit a needle thread is suitable,
    For camels, needle eyes are much too small!*
A camel's being must be cut to size
    With scissors of religious exercise—
For that to work God's hand is necessary—   3080
    His '*Be!*'* solves each impossibility.
With His hand everything is possible—
    Fear of Him tames each stubborn animal;
He doesn't heal just lepers and the blind
    But he can raise the dead too you will find,
And non-existents, more dead than the dead,
    Towards existence by His will are led.
Recite, '*He works on something new each day*'*
    And never think He idles time away.

His least achievement daily is to send 3085
    Three armies, each to a specific end:
One from men's loins to mothers has to go
    So in their wombs they'll form an embryo;
One from the wombs towards the world outside—
    Thus males and females have been multiplied;
One army's sent above straight from the earth
    So all can see good actions have much worth—
This talk is endless, so come quickly here
    To friends and followers who are sincere!

His sweetheart said, 'Come in, all of my heart, 3090
    Not like the rose and thorn that are apart.'
Make fewer errors now there's just one thread—
    If you see two, know there's just one ahead.
Just like a noose, '*Be!*'* draws you from a distance
    And thus brings non-existence to existence,
Although in form the noose may look like two
    There's just one rope and one thing it will do!
With pairs of legs all men must cross the street,
    Two scissor-blades together cut one sheet;
Look at this pair of laundry-men, for instance, 3095
    Between them there is obviously a difference:
One washed your clothes in water with some soap,
    To dry the other hangs them on a rope,
But then the first one rinses them again
    As though there is a fight between these men!
But these two who may seem to be apart
    Both act and think as one—they're one at heart;
Each prophet and each saint has his own way,
    But all lead to the One to whom they pray.
Sleep overcame the audience for a while, 3100
    Water then bore their millstones for a mile—
This water comes from up beyond the mill,
    For your sake it flows down here by God's will,
When you don't need to have mills any more
    It then will flow above you as before.

To teach, this truthful speech comes to your tongue
  Or else to its own course it could have clung;
It smoothly travels, so one wouldn't know,
  To gardens *under which the rivers flow.**
That place to my soul, God, won't you disclose   3105
  Where speech without a word is born and grows,
So that the pure soul headlong then will race
  To non-existence's vast open space!
A wide and vast realm of magnificence
  From which this false world gains its sustenance.
Tighter than non-existence is thought's realm,
  That's why it causes griefs that overwhelm.
Temporal existence is more cramped than thought,
  That's why the moon shrinks almost to a dot;
The sensual world's more cramped than this as well,   3110
  It is the most restrictive prison cell.
What makes it narrow? Multiplicity:
  Our senses drag us to plurality.
Unity's not what senses can perceive—
  If that's your goal, then this realm you must leave;
Though 'B' and 'e' formed it, '*Be!*'* was one act—
  The meaning was still pure and kept intact.
Let's now return, though this is incomplete,
  To see what fate that old wolf had to meet.

The lion teaches a lesson to the wolf who had shown disrespect in his division

That lion pulled apart the old wolf's head   3115
  To leave its wretched dualism dead—
So we took vengeance on them,* to be brief,
  When they were not effaced near their own chief—
Then, to the fox the lion turned to say,
  'Divide this food up for us straight away!'
The fox replied, 'This fat ox seems just right
  To be your breakfast, king—you have such might;
And so the goat should be preserved till lunch—
  Something, victorious king, for you to munch;

Your supper's then the hare that's left behind—   3120
    An evening snack, king, since you are so kind.'
He said, 'Fox, justice is what you display,
    Who taught you how to share the spoils this way?
Where did you learn this, excellent dear friend?'
    'From witnessing the wolf's most tragic end!'
The lion said, 'You gambled all for me
    So you can go and take with you all three!
Since you've behaved entirely for my sake,
    If I harm you that would be my mistake.
I'm yours, and all the prey can be your prize,   3125
    Step on the seventh heaven as you rise!
You took heed from that base wolf that I slew,
    So, fox, you're now a lion in my view!'
The wise take heed from deaths of friends, so they
    Can sidestep tribulation in their way.
The fox gave thanks that he had been asked last,
    After the wolf's test had already passed:
'If he had summoned me here first and said,
    "Divide this up!" How could I then have fled!'
Praise be to God who made us too appear   3130
    After our predecessors have been here,
To hear of punishments that He'd decreed
    To those of them who failed then to take heed,
So trials of past wolves may cause alarm
    And like the fox we may escape from harm.
That's why the Prophet spoke so truthfully
    When calling us '*the blest community*'.
Look at the dead wolves' bones and fur, and then
    Consider this a warning, worthy men!
Existence and pretence the wise forget   3135
    On learning what the Aad and Pharaoh met,
If not their fates for other men one day
    Will be a warning not to go astray.

Noah threatens his people, 'Don't argue with me, for you'll be
disobeying God by doing this, you abandoned men!'

'Stubborn fools, I am not I,' Noah said,
   'Through God I live, through my own soul I'm dead:
I've died to human senses like the night
   So God is now my hearing, food, and sight.
Since I'm not I, this breath's from Him as well,
   He who himself breathes is an infidel!'
A lion's in the fox's form you see—   3140
   Don't walk up to him so audaciously!
If you're not fooled by how he looks outside
   You might then hear the lion's roar inside.
If Noah never had God's light within
   How could he then have caused their world to spin?
A thousand lions in one frame of clay—
   He was a fire, the world a stack of hay,
And since the stack did not give its tithe-share
   A flame to burn the stack he lit in there.
Whoever like the wolf should dare to speak   3145
   Before the hidden lion has a cheek—
Just like the wolf he'll be gulped with one bite,
   *'We took revenge,'** the lion will recite;
The lion's blows will thus make him succumb,
   The one who's bold before him must be dumb!
If only just his body was attacked
   So that his faith and heart could stay intact.

On reaching here, my strength has sapped away
   So how can I reveal such truths today?
Think of your stomach as a worthless thing,   3150
   In front of Him don't try such bargaining!
Submit in front of Him your 'I' and 'we'—
   Give it to Him, for it's His property!
On this path, once you are a poor fakir
   The lion and his prey are yours—it's clear!

That's all because He's pure and glorious
  And has no need for what's superfluous;
So all the prey and every grace that's found
  Straight to the servants of this King are bound—
He made all things, though He has no desire,   3155
  Those who see this feel joy and may rise higher!
He made the two worlds, everything you see,
  But still what use to Him is property!

So guard your hearts from every evil thought
  When near Him, so to shame you won't be brought:
He can detect your thoughts and inner soul
  Like hair which floats on milk inside your bowl;
The one whose breast from images is clean
  Becomes a mirror too for what's unseen:
Without the need to think he reads your mind—   3160
  *A mirror for believers** of this kind;
If he should test us, he would soon find out
  Who's filled with certainty and who with doubt:
His soul's the touchstone for the coins we hold,
  So he sees what's a heart and what's false gold.

Kings seat Sufis in front of themselves so that their eyes may become illumined by them

The custom of the kings is as below,
  You've heard of this, so really you should know:
Their warriors all stand on the left-hand side
  Since their brave hearts are found that way inside;
The treasurer and scribes sit on the right   3165
  Because that hand's the one they use to write;
Sufis are seated straight in front—their role
  Is serving as the mirror of the soul:
They've cleansed their hearts through mystic meditation,
  Pure forms now fill their mirror-hearts' reflection.

With righteous natures those who have been graced
  In front of them want mirrors to be placed:
Beautiful faces want a mirror near—
  It shows *their hearts have goodness,** scrapes them clear.

A guest came to Joseph, and Joseph demanded a gift from him

To truthful Joseph came from the world's end   3170
  To be his guest, a generous loving friend;
They were so close in childhood that the pair
  Would often share the seat of one small chair.
The friend asked of his brothers' jealousy,
  Joseph said, 'They were like a chain round me:
The lion's not ashamed bound in a chain—
  About the Lord's decree I don't complain.'
Although the lion's neck with chains is bound
  He rules all chain-makers that can be found.
'In gaol and in the well, how were those days?'   3175
  'Just like the moon when in its waning phase.'
Though when it wanes, it's seen to shrink and bend,
  Still it becomes a full moon in the end;
In mortars, pearls are ground and mixed with kohl
  To grant sight to the eye inside the soul;
If seeds are planted firmly in the ground,
  Wheat will eventually grow all around;
Then in the mill they grind it to make bread—
  Its value soars now with it men are fed;
Next by men's teeth the bread is ground again,   3180
  Life, wisdom, and intelligence they gain,
And when in love that life becomes effaced
  *Farmers rejoice** the seed's not gone to waste!
This discourse could go on, so let's find out
  What that good friend and Joseph talked about.

Joseph, on telling his biography,
    Asked, 'Friend, what present have you brought for me?'
Going empty-handed to a friend's worse still
    Than setting off without wheat to the mill,
For at *the Gathering* God then will say,   3185
    'So where's your gift for *Resurrection Day*?*
Are you alone, without a present too,
    In the same shape as I created you?*
Or have you brought with you a souvenir,
    Knowing that you'd be resurrected here?
Perhaps you thought you'd not reach home again,
    That promises about today were vain?'
Deniers of this day have brains so numb
    That from His kitchen they won't gain a crumb!
If you don't disbelieve, how can you go   3190
    To your friend empty-handed like a foe!
Sleep less, reduce too the amount you eat,
    Take then a present when you're due to meet—
Be of those who *sleep little when they sleep*,
    At dawn *seek his forgiveness,** truly weep!
Move just a little like a foetus, so
    The sense which sees the light He'll then bestow;
And when you step outside this womb-like place
    You'll leave the world for a much wider space:
They said, '*God's land is vast,*'* and thus they meant   3195
    The lofty realm of prophets He has sent;
Hearts don't become depressed there, since they're free;
    You won't see shrivel up a fresh, young tree.
The burden of your senses you now bear,
    You're weary, tired, and falling everywhere,
But when you sleep you're carried off instead,
    Free then of tiredness, injury, and dread—
Consider sleep's state just a little taste
    Of how the saints are borne when they're effaced:
They are Companions of the Cave—you'll learn   3200
    That *they're asleep* although they stand and turn;
Without them seeking it, He draws them there
    First right, then left though they are unaware:

What is that *right side*? Proper and good action,
   The left?* The body's own source of distraction;
From all the prophets these two both flow out,
   Though they don't sense the echo of their shout:
Echoes bring good and evil sounds to you
   Though mountains stay oblivious to these two.

*The guest says to Joseph, 'I've brought you a mirror, so that
each time you look in it you'll see your own handsome
face and remember me'*

Joseph asked, 'Where's the gift with which you came?'   3205
   This question made his guest then moan with shame,
He said, 'How many gifts I sought for you,
   But none seemed worthy in my humble view:
How could I bring a nugget to the mine,
   A single drop to a vast sea of wine?
I'm taking cumin to Kerman,* it's true,
   By bringing here my heart and soul for you.
No seed is missing from the storehouse here
   Except your perfect form which has no peer—
To bring a mirror thus appeared just right,   3210
   One that's as radiant as your pure breast's light,
So you can see in it the face I love,
   Just like the sun, that candle up above—
I've brought a mirror, so that when you see
   Your handsome face you'll then remember me.'
He showed the mirror he'd kept by his side,
   With mirrors good men are preoccupied;
Non-being serves as Being's mirror, friend,
   So choose non-being if you comprehend:
In this way, Being will be clear to see,   3215
   Like in the poor, when men give generously:
Food is the mirror of the hungry and
   The tinder's mirror is the flame that's fanned;
Emptiness and non-being serve to show
   The virtue of the crafts that skilled men know:

When garments are already so well sewn
   How can they let the mender's skill be shown?
Tree trunks must be left for the carpenter
   Untouched, so he can make some furniture;
The doctor who mends broken bones heads straight   3220
   For that place where the injured men all wait:
If there's no casualty, who needs your aid?
   Medicine's virtue can't then be displayed!
If copper's faults aren't plain for all to see
   How can one tell the worth of alchemy?
Defects reflect perfection's purest light,
   They mirror God's own glory and His might;
All things thus make their opposites appear—
   In vinegar the taste of honey's clear.

Whoever recognizes his own faults   3225
   Towards perfection rapidly then vaults,
But if you think you're perfect as you are,
   You won't reach God for you have strayed too far—
Imagining you're perfect is the worst
   Of faults, you show-off—learn this lesson first!
Much blood will flow out from your heart and eyes
   Before your self-conceit completely dies;
Claiming, '*I'm better*'* was cursed Satan's error
   And this same defect lies in every creature:
Although they like to show themselves as meek,   3230
   There's dung beneath the surface—smell the reek!
When, as a test, the Lord should stir them round,
   Their water then immediately is browned:
There's dung in your stream's bed that you've not seen,
   And to your eyes the stream looks pure and clean!

The guide who's knowing has a special role—
   To join streams to the Universal Soul,
The streams can't clean themselves—the point's been made
   That from God's knowledge man receives much aid;

How can a sword carve its own hilt? You show   3235
   The surgeon wounds you've suffered from your foe;
Flies gather on men's wounds, so none can see
   His own wound's putrid foulness normally—
Such flies are fancies and possessions too,
   The wounds the dark states that emerge in you.
The guide puts on your wound a salve to heal
   The pain and misery that you now feel—
Don't think the pain's forever gone away,
   The salve has been sent down as just one ray!
Don't turn away, fool, from this salve again,   3240
   Not you but that guide's ray has soothed the pain!

The one who wrote down the Prophet's revelation became an apostate because one ray of revelation came down to him; and he recited the verse before the Prophet, and then said, 'So I too am a recipient of revelation'

There was a scribe before Osman who'd write
   With care the words the Prophet would recite:*
When holy revelation he'd dictate,
   This scribe would write it on a leaf or slate;
A ray of revelation shone his way
   So he found wisdom in himself that day,
The Prophet was that piece of wisdom's source
   But this scrap led that meddling fool off course:
'The truths God's messenger likes to impart   3245
   I now hold in the depths of my own heart.'
The Prophet sensed what this misled scribe thought
   And so God's wrath to this man's soul was brought;
His job and faith he then chose to forgo
   And out of spite became the Prophet's foe.
The Prophet said, 'You stubborn infidel,
   You're dark—how can you be light's source as well!
If you were a sweet fountain that's divine,
   You wouldn't have produced such filthy brine.'

His reputation to preserve from harm   3250
    He kept his mouth shut, though he wasn't calm—
He burnt inside because of this event
    Though still he felt unable to repent.
He sighed, but this did not help him—instead
    The sword was drawn to sever off his head.
God's made your reputation a huge weight,
    Too many find this out once it's too late!
For unbelief and pride have blocked the way—
    No one can even sigh once in dismay:
'*Shackled, they must keep their heads up*,' God said,   3255
    Not outer shackles, but inside instead;
'*Behind a barrier, and above a screen*,'*
    So obstacles around them can't be seen;
This barrier looks like space that's vast and free—
    Men cannot tell the dam of destiny!
You're your own obstacle to His fine face
    And to speech filled with the divine guide's grace.
Though many infidels desired religion
    They were still trapped by pride and reputation—
This chain's much harder than those men have made;   3260
    Those chains are broken by an axe's blade
And they can be released quite easily,
    While from this hidden chain no man gets free.
If men fall victim to a wasp's sting, then
    Their natural defence heals them again,
But since this sting is from your being, friend,
    The pain's much more intense and it won't end!

The explanation's bursting from my breast,
    I fear though that it might leave you depressed—
Don't you despair! Learn to live joyfully,   3265
    And cry for help—He answers every plea!
Pray: 'O Forgiving Lord, forgive us please,
    Doctor who treats the pain of our disease!'
Wisdom's reflection ruined one who knew—
    Don't let such vile conceit destroy you too!

Brother, true wisdom to you has been sent
  From God's élite saints, but it's only lent:
Inside, a house may look so warm and bright,
  The neigbouring house though has bestowed this light—
Give thanks, don't raise your nose in arrogance!   3270
  Shun self-conceit, don't live in ignorance!
It's sad this borrowed state we have today
  Has led men so far from the proper way;
I'm the slave of the one who at each stage
  Does not claim he's enlightened as a sage:
From many stages travellers must ascend
  Until one day they reach the journey's end.
Iron's not red, in fire though red it turns
  Due to the heat of flames in which it burns;
A window may fill up your house with light,   3275
  That's not the light's source though—adjust your sight!
Each door and wall may say, 'I am the source;
  I don't bear others' light—it's mine of course!'
The sun will counter, 'Errant fool, wait here,
  And when I set, the truth will then be clear!'
Plants say, 'We by ourselves turn fresh and green,
  As beautiful and joyful thus we're seen.'
But summer answers, 'Listen everyone—
  Just take a look in autumn when I'm done!'
The body shows off its own handsome face,   3280
  While spirit, which is blessed with wings of grace,
Shouts, 'Cesspool, you live just one or two days
  All thanks to my life-giving, pure light rays!
This huge world can't contain your vanity,
  Just wait until from you I finally flee!
Your mourners will then dig a grave for you
  So you can feed the worms and insects too!
That one who in your presence swooned and fell
  Will hold his nose because of your foul smell!'
The spirit's rays give hearing, speech, and sight   3285
  As water boils due to the fire we light;
Just as the body's fed rays from the soul
  Your soul's fed by God's friends who play this role.

When from the soul His spirit should depart
    It's like a soulless body, stripped of heart.
I lay my head down on the ground this way
    So earth will vouch for me on Judgment Day,
On that day when *it will be forced to quake*
    The role of witness then the earth will take,
For what it knows *it will say publicly,**   3290
    And earth and rocks will talk miraculously.
Philosophers doubt, for they're logical—
    Tell them to slam their heads on a brick wall!
For water, earth, and clay speak, and each word
    By Sufi mystics is quite clearly heard;
Philosophers doubt moaning pillars too—
    About the saints' perception they've no clue,
Saying, 'These men must be moved by emotions
    To have such fantasies and foolish notions.'
Their infidelity and vile corruption   3295
    Has filled them with vain thoughts—they choose rejection;
When they deny that demons can exist,
    They're mocked by those same demons they've dismissed!
You've not seen one? Look at yourself instead!
    Only a madman boasts a swollen head!
Each man whose heart is filled with stress and doubt
    Is a philosopher who's not come out:
He utters true belief, but all the same
    This man's philosophy still earns him shame;
Take care, believers, it's inside of you,   3300
    And there are many endless worlds there too.
The warring sects are also there within,
    Woe to you, friend, if one day they should win!
Those having the essentials of belief
    In fear of this are shaking like a leaf.

You laughed at Satan and the demons then,
    Judging yourselves, in contrast, virtuous men;
When men's souls turn their jackets inside out,
    How many Muslims in distress will shout:

The store's gold-plated things all feel delight   3305
    Because the touchstone is now far from sight,
'Don't lift the veil, don't make faults manifest,
    Concealing Lord, when we're put to the test!'
False gold can lie with real gold through the night,
    Though real gold's waiting for the dawn's first light;
Gold says by means of its own inner state:
    'Daybreak will show the truth, fake, you just wait!'
Accursed Satan for millennia
    Led faithful saints as their superior,
But then he fought with Adam out of pride   3310
    And was disgraced like dung that's thrown aside.

*Bal'am, son of Ba'ur, prayed, 'Make Moses and his people turn
back from this town which they have besieged without
achieving their goal!' It was answered*

To Bal'am men were subject at one stage
    For he was then the Jesus of his age,
To no one else would they bow down, his spell
    Could make those terminally ill get well;
He fought with Moses out of self-conceit,
    You've heard, I'm sure, the fate that he would meet,
For Bal'am, Satan, and the others too,
    Met such sad ends, unseen and in plain view.
God made these two notorious as a test,   3315
    As an example to warn off the rest:
He hanged these two thieves in the public square,
    So thieves who earn such wrath might then be rare.
He brought their banners back, victorious—
    Those slaughtered by His wrath are numerous!
When you keep in your bounds, to God you're dear;
    Don't overstep the mark! Is that quite clear!
For if you strike one whom God loves still more,
    You'll be sent to the earth's most rotten core.
What have you learned from Thamud and from Aad*?   3320
    Their tales show prophets are all loved by God:

Quakes, thunderbolts, and stones all played a role
    To show the strength of the prophetic soul.

For men's sake kill all animals, and then
    For intellect's come back and kill all men!
What's intellect here? Wisdom's perfect source,
    Not wretched human intellect, of course;
All animals are thus inferior
    To Man who is through this superior,
Thus for mankind to take their lives is lawful   3325
    Since beasts lack intellect that's universal.
Wild men were dealt a massive fall from grace
    Because they dared oppose the human race.
What honour will remain for you my friend—
    When you're *wild, frightened asses** in the end?
Don't kill an ass if it's of benefit
    But if it's wild you're free to slaughter it:
Though ignorance is what the ass might plead
    God won't forgive its failure to take heed.
When someone shuns truth's breath, don't say he can   3330
    Be still excused unlike the ass, good man:
It's lawful to take unbelievers' lives
    Like beasts, with arrows, spears, and hunting knives!
The same goes for their families, you know,
    For they lack wisdom and they're mean and low—
From truth the ones who turn away and flee
    Are soon reduced to animality.

*The angels Harut and Marut relied on their own immaculateness
and wanted to lead the people of the world, but they fell
into temptation*

Harut and Marut, angels up on high,
    Pride's poisoned arrow also caused to die,
Because they had become self-satisfied: 3335
    Two beasts defied a lion and then died—

Even if they had used their horns with skill,
   He would have ripped them up in pieces still,
With horns all over, just like porcupines,
   He would have killed them, still unharmed by spines.
Although strong winds uproot the tallest trees,
   They beautify moist grass just like a breeze;
That fierce wind pities weak grass mercifully—
   Don't show off all your strength conceitedly!
An axe does not fear branches of the tree   3340
   But chops them up in bits quite easily;
Still at a flimsy leaf it never swings—
   The axe's blade chops only solid things.
Do flames care that the firewood's layered so deep?
   Do butchers ever run away from sheep?
What's form next to Reality? So small!
   What makes the heavens hang above us all?
In water-wheels the answer can be found—
   What is the force that makes them spin around?
Your shield-like bodies' motions all begin   3345
   Deep in the hidden spirit that's within;
The motion of the wind when it should blow
   Is like this wheel moved by the water's flow:
Where is each breath, each ebb and flow, then from?
   Straight from the soul full of desire they've come;
It makes the letters: J, I, H, A, D.
   Now it makes peace, then war and enmity;
It drags things right, then pulls them left in tow,
   Now rose bushes, then thorns, are made to grow.
In this way wind was once transformed by God   3350
   Into a dragon to confront the Aad,
Then for believers wind was forced to be
   Their peace, protection, and security.
'*Reality is God*,' said one who knew,
   '*Lord of the worlds*, sea of all meaning too.'
All levels up in heaven and on earth
   Are flotsam on the sea—they have no worth;
The twigs there dance and jiggle with the tide
   Whenever there is turbulence inside,

So then to make the twigs stay still once more   3355
    The sea will throw them all out on the shore,
Though when its surge absorbs them, in a flash
    It does what fire does to turn wood to ash—
This topic's endless so let's now return,
    Harut and Marut's bitter fate to learn.

The remainder of the story of Harut and Marut; their punishment in this world inside the pit of Babylon

Since the depravity of people here
    To both of them had started to be clear,
They waved their fists in anger at mankind
    While to their own shortcomings they were blind;
One saw his ugly features in the mirror,   3360
    Then turned away from it, enraged and bitter:
Conceited men see other people's sin,
    A fire from hell then flares up deep within.
'Protection of the faith' they call this pride,
    Their infidel self-love dictates inside!
The true protector of the faith I've seen,
    He's different, he makes things fresh and green.
'If you're enlightened,' God then told the pair,
    'At heedless evildoers' deeds don't stare!
Give thanks, my angel-servants, that you're free   3365
    From bonds of lust and sexuality—
If I had given you those kinds of states,
    The heavens wouldn't let you in their gates,
The chastity that your forms both possess
    Shows my affection and immaculateness—
Consider me and not yourself the source,
    Don't you succumb to that cursed devil's force!'

That one who for the Prophet used to write
    Saw in himself God's wisdom and His light,
He thought he must himself be God's apostle,   3370
    But was a fake just like a hunter's whistle.

The songs of birds you cleverly can name,
  But do you know the songbirds' actual aim?
You've heard the singing of the nightingale,
  Not knowing love, its form's of no avail;
If you do know, it's guesswork anyway—
  The way the deaf must lip-read what men say.

A deaf man went to visit his sick neighbour

A partially deaf man heard someone say
  That his own neighbour had got sick that day,
He thought, 'I'm deaf—what will I comprehend   3375
  Of sentiments expressed by my sick friend,
For he's now ill and might have lost his voice?
  But I'm obliged to go, I have no choice.
When I see this friend's lips move, then I'll guess
  The sentiments he's trying to express:
When I ask him, 'How are you, dearest friend?'
  He'll say, 'Alright', or 'I am on the mend.'
I'll ask, 'What have you had for lunch today?'
  'Some bean soup and some tonic,' he will say,
'To health!' I'll say. 'To whom do you now go   3380
  For treatment?' He'll say, 'Doctor so-and-so',
I'll say, 'He's very talented and blessed
  So everything will turn out for the best;
I've seen myself his power and skilfulness,
  Whatever he's tried he has met success.'
He thus rehearsed such comments in his head,
  Then went to see his sick friend in his bed:
'How are you?'—'Almost dead!'—'The Lord be praised!'
  The sick friend grew offended and amazed,
Thinking, 'Praise God? Does this man want a fight?'   3385
  The deaf man's guesses hadn't turned out right!
He asked, 'What have you had?'—'A poisonous drink!'
  He said, 'To health!'—The sick man reached the brink.
The deaf man asked 'Which doctor's coming then
  To treat you so that you'll feel well again?'

'The Angel of Death—so just go away!'
    The deaf man said, 'Rejoice! He'll save the day!'
His visitor left, thinking this inside:
    'Thank God I came!' He was self-satisfied.
The sick man thought, 'He's my worst enemy;   3390
    I never knew he could act spitefully!'
He then thought of expletives in his mind
    To write to him swear words of every kind!
When someone swallows soup that has turned bad,
    He soon feels ill and vomits what he's had:
*Suppress your rage,** don't spew it out like this!
    You'll be rewarded with the sweetest bliss.
He had no patience, so he grew irate,
    Saying, 'Where are you, bastard? You just wait!
I'll ram your words back down your throat again,   3395
    My lion-like consciousness was sleeping then.
Visiting sick men is to bring relief,
    Not to antagonize and pile on grief;
You wanted just to see your foe distressed
    So that your filthy mind could find some rest.'
In acts of worship many go astray
    With thoughts of their rewards on Judgment Day.
Truly, their worship's just sin in disguise
    Although their vileness seems pure to your eyes.
The deaf man thought he'd done a righteous act   3400
    But it led to the opposite in fact,
Content, he thought, 'I did well, I feel thrilled!
    My duty to my neighbour I've fulfilled.'
But as we've seen a fire was made to start—
    He burnt himself thus in his sick friend's heart:
Beware of ever kindling such a fire,
    The sum of all your sins will just rise higher!
The Prophet told pretentious men one day,
    '*Repeat your prayers—you didn't truly pray!*'
Our remedy for such pretentiousness   3405
    Is begging Him in every prayer '*Guide us!**
Dear God, don't mix this prayer of ours today
    With those of show-offs who have gone astray!'

Due to the reasoning this deaf man applied
    His ten-year friendship with his neighbour died.
Your temporal reasoning's powers are unfit
    For revelation, which is infinite,
For if your ears still savour every word,
    This means your inner ear has still not heard.

The first person to apply analogical reasoning to revelation was Satan

Analogy and logic was used first   3410
    Before God's light by Satan, who was cursed:
'Mere clay's not worth as much as fire,' he'd say,
    'I'm made of fire while Man's just made of clay;
And judging just by origins, it's right
    To say he's darkness while I'm radiant light.'
'*There shall be no more kinship then*'* God said;
    Struggle and piety earns grace instead—
Since it's beyond the world that's temporal,
    Kinship can't win you what is spiritual;
This heritage is from God's messengers,   3415
    Souls of the pure are sole inheritors,
Bu Jahl's son found true faith a later day
    While Noah's son joined up with those astray:*
The earthling turns just like a moon, so bright,
    You're made of fire and dark with shame like night.
At night, by reasoning and by calculation
    Scholars work out the qebla's* right location,
But when by day the Kaaba is in sight
    To make such calculations isn't right—
Don't claim you still can't see, or turn away   3420
    Due to your reasoning—*God knows best the way*!
If you should hear a message from God's bird,*
    As an example you would learn that word,
Then you'd apply to it your reasoning
    To make from just one thought a concrete thing.
But those expressions God's élite saints say
    Are far beyond what language can convey:

Although you learn *the bird's tongue* through one sound
   And through analogies that can be found,
You injure saints' hearts like that poor sick friend   3425
   And, like the deaf man, think you comprehend.
The Prophet's scribe, on hearing from that bird,
   Thought he was that bird's equal since he'd heard,
The bird then blinded him and flapped a wing
   To shove him down death's well of suffering.

By thoughts or what reflects from revelations
   Don't fall back down from heaven's lofty stations,
Harut and Marut though you be, or more
   Than *those who stand in ranks** outside His door.
Have mercy on bad people's wickedness,   3430
   And curse instead your own self-centredness!
Beware lest God's possessiveness should hit
   And make you fall head-first inside earth's pit!
Both said, 'God, Yours is the command, for sure,
   Without your care how can one feel secure?'
This pair of angels hadn't understood:
   'How can our deeds be bad when we are good?'
The pair's distracting itch would not subside
   Until it sowed the seed of selfish pride.
They then said, 'Foolish, base humanity   3435
   Knows not of spiritual kings' purity;
We'll draw the curtains over all the sky
   Then land on earth and raise a screen so high,
To grant all justice and bring worship's light,
   While flying home to heaven every night,
So that as wonders of the age we'll be
   Renowned for bringing earth security.'
This view of earth and heaven isn't right,
   There's something missing here that's kept from sight.

An explanation of why one must keep one's own mystical state and intoxication hidden from the ignorant

Listen to what Hakim Sana'i said: 3440
   'Rest where you drank the wine your drunken head!'
For from the tavern if a drunk should stray
   He'll seem a clown with whom the children play:
He'll tumble into puddles everywhere
   And all the wretches will laugh, point, and stare;
They'll follow him because he's strange and new
   Although of drunkenness they have no clue.
Except those drunk in God, men are just boys,
   Mature men flee their passions and their toys:
God said, 'The world is just a toy, and you   3445
   Are merely children'*—what God says is true!
You keep on bringing toys down from the shelf—
   You won't gain wisdom till you slay your self!
Lust here's like infants having sex, my friend,
   Compared with what's there at the other end:
What's infant sex? Play-acting that brings laughter
   Compared with sex by Rostam or a martyr;
The wars of men are like an infant's fight
   Meaningless, senseless, base, without real might:
They brandish wooden swords and then take aim,   3450
   But there's no point or meaning to their game:
They ride a length of wood just like at school,
   Saying, 'Here's Boraq, and here's the Prophet's mule!'
They carry it themselves, but stupidly
   They think they're being borne majestically—
Wait till the day those borne by God should race
   Beyond the nine-tiered heavens at great pace:
Spirits and angels to Him will ascend—
   And make the heavens shake from end to end.
Children, you ride your skirts and run the course,   3455
   Clutching the hem to make it seem a horse,

Opinion does not free you from all need*—
　　You won't reach heaven on your reasoning's steed:
Relying on the stronger point of view
　　Don't doubt the sun when it's in front of you!
It's time now to look down at your own steed—
　　You've made it from your own two feet, take heed!
Your every feeling, fancy, sense, and care
　　Is like the children's wooden horse, beware!
Knowledge of mystics was the steed they rode,   3460
　　Knowledge of sensual men an extra load.
Heart knowledge helps you when it fills you there,
　　But other knowledge is a cross to bear:
'*Like asses carrying their books,*'* God said,
　　Knowledge that's not from Him wears down your head!
It has no meaning—shell without a core,
　　It doesn't last, like make-up on a whore!
But when you bear the burden well, it will
　　Be taken off and you'll feel such a thrill,
So don't bear knowledge for your own sake, friend,   3465
　　And you'll find inner knowledge in the end—
Then you may ride on knowledge's fast steed
　　And watch the load fall off and your soul freed.

If you don't chant 'He' how can you then flee
　　Your own desire? Transcend the mere name 'He'!*
A thought's produced by attribute and name,
　　This thought's a guide with union as its aim;
A guide without an aim does not exist,
　　If there were no path, ghouls would not persist:
Do names not tell of a reality?   3470
　　Can roses grow from R, O, S, and E?
You've said the name, to find the named now try—
　　The moon's not on the lake but in the sky!
Mere names and words if you wish to transcend
　　Then purify yourself of self, my friend!
Like iron give up your original colour,
　　Through discipline become the clearest mirror!

Thus purge yourself of attributes to view
Your own pure essence lying inside you!
Within your heart you'll find the Prophet's knowledge   3475
Without a book or teachers from the college:
The Prophet said, 'There are some in my nation
Who share my essence and my aspiration;
The same as me; they see me by that light
With which I also see them day and night,
Without *hadiths* and their transmitters too
Water of Life* they drink to know it's true.'
So understand '*Last night I was a Kurd,*
Now I'm an Arab though'*—it's not absurd!
A parable which shows the mysteries   3480
Is this about the Greeks and the Chinese:

The story about the competition between the Greeks and the Chinese in the art of painting and portraiture

Once the Chinese said, 'At art we're the best!'
The Greeks said, 'With more talent we've been blessed!'
The sultan said, 'I'll set a test for you
To see which of your claims is really true.'
They all prepared to paint a room's interior,
In knowledge though the Greeks were far superior.
'Come, show us to a room,' said the Chinese,
'And give the Greeks one similar to it, please.'
They found adjoining rooms which formed a pair,   3485
One half for each group, thus completely fair;
Then the Chinese requested lots of paint,
The king supplied them, generous as a saint:
Each dawn from his own storehouse men would bring
More paint for them as gifts from this kind king.
The Greeks said, 'Colourful paints will not prove
Successful—colour's what we must remove!'
They closed their space off, polished every wall
Clear as the heavens up above us all;

Colour to colourlessness can change quite soon, 3490
    Colour's a cloud, colourlessness the moon;
If in the clouds some radiance should appear,
    It's from the sun and moon that it shines here.
Once the Chinese felt their work was complete
    They banged their drums to celebrate this feat,
The king arrived and saw such paintings there
    That stunned him, for their beauty was so rare;
Then he went to the Greeks, who quickly raised
    The screen in front and left him more amazed:
The image of that work which was so fine 3495
    Reflected on the walls that they'd made shine—
Whatever he'd seen there shone on each wall,
    Out of their sockets eyes began to fall!
The Greeks stand for the Sufis clearly:
    Without techniques from books of theory,
They've cleansed their breasts so well that they shine bright
    Free from all stinginess, desire, and spite.
The heart's a mirror with such purity
    It can reflect forms from eternity:
Such a pure image, boundless, unlike art, 3500
    Shone through the hand of Moses* from his heart;
These forms the heavens even can't contain,
    Nor throne, nor ocean, nor an open plain,
For they're all numbered and delimited,
    While hearts are one and they're unlimited—
The brain falls silent here or goes astray:
    The heart's with God, or is God in some way.
No form's reflection shines eternally
    But through the heart, home of infinity,
For every image which should reach this place 3505
    Appears without a veil across its face.

Polishers fled all colours, so they could
    Each breath see what is beautiful and good:
Beyond the husk of knowledge they can see,
    They've raised the banner of true certainty,

All thought has left them, for they've seen the light,
    The sea's depths and their breasts they keep in sight.
Of death all other men are running scared,
    To mock and laugh at it these men have dared,
To conquer their hearts there's no hope in hell—   3510
    The pearl is not harmed, only its mere shell;
Transcending grammar, law, theology,
    They've chosen self-effacement, poverty,
When images from heaven shone to earth
    Their hearts received them, and they knew their worth;
Their place is loftier even than God's Throne,
    God's *Seat of Certainty** they've made their own.

The Prophet asks Zayd, 'How are you today, how have you risen from bed?' He answers, 'I've woken up a believer, Messenger of God'*

One dawn the Prophet turned to Zayd to say,
    'My friend, how have you woken up today?'
'Like a believing slave who knows what's true.'   3515
    'Then where's faith's garden's sign displayed on you?'
'I thirst,' said Zayd 'And wander in the day,
    At night I can't sleep—love burns me away:
I've passed beyond both day and nighttime's sphere—
    They're shields I've penetrated like a spear.'
Beyond there's just one army with one name,
    A thousand years and one hour are the same,
There pre- and post-eternity have merged,
    The brain can't reach there, it soon gets submerged.
The Prophet asked Zayd, 'Where's your souvenir?   3520
    Present some knowledge suitable for here.'
Zayd said, 'While other people see the sky,
    I see God's throne with those who live on high,
The seven hells and the eight heavens too
    Are visible to me—I swear it's true!
I recognize each individual
    Like wheat and barley piled up at the mill:

Who's heaven-bound and who in hell will bake
 I see just like a fish next to a snake.'

It has now been revealed like dawn's first light   3525
 *The day their faces will turn black or white.**
However many faults the soul then had,
 Inside its womb* none knew that it was bad:
The damned are damned inside the womb, that's why
 *Their states some outwardly identify.**
The body's pregnant with the soul till death,
 When birth pains make her writhe and gasp for breath,
The souls of all the dead now watch and wait
 To see the way it's born and its new state:
The Africans will claim, 'This soul is ours!'   3530
 The Greeks, 'No, he looks glorious, with great powers!'
It's now born in the realm of souls and grace,
 The blacks and whites are equal in this place;
If he's been bad, by bad men he'll be led,
 If good, he'll join the good up there instead;
Until it's born it's hidden from men's eyes,
 Unborn souls so few men can recognize—
It's *by the Light of God** that such men see
 Straight through a person's skin so easily.
Sperm's essence is pure goodness like the light,   3535
 Beyond the realm of what is black or white;
Of *those of highest stature** He'll bestow
 Colour to half, to banish them below.
This topic's incomplete, but it's now late,
 If we're not back the caravan won't wait.
The day they will turn black or white we'll learn,
 The Turks from Indians then we can discern;*
Inside the womb no man can separate
 The two, but once they're born one's vile, one great.

'As if it is already Judgment Day,   3540
 I see through men and women here today—

Shall I stay silent or share one more sign?'
  The Prophet bit his lips, 'This much is fine.'
'O Messenger of God, shall I now mention
  To all the secret of the Resurrection?*
Let me tear open this last veil of mine
  And like the sun let my true essence shine,
Such that the sun will be eclipsed by me,
  Marking the date-palm from the fruitless tree,
For Resurrection's secret I'll disclose—   3545
  Real gold from false, so everybody knows.
With hands cut off, the damned all men will see
  Distant from our pure Muslim family,
I'll make hypocrisy's worst failings plain
  In moonlight, which won't be eclipsed or wane,
The ragged clothes of damned men I'll display
  And make the Prophet's drums be heard today,
Heaven and hell, the realm between as well,
  I'll show so clearly to each infidel,
A turbulent Kawsar* I'll make appear   3550
  To splash their faces and ring in each ear,
The thirsty who keep circling it I'll show
  This very moment, so all men will know;
Their shoulders rub against mine and their screams
  Keep ringing in my ears, or so it seems,
While willingly in heaven filled with grace
  They pull each other close in an embrace—
They take each other's hands with gentle grips
  And snatch some kisses from each other's lips;
This ear of mine's been deafened by their sighs   3555
  And all the damned ones' bitter grieving cries—
From hidden depths mere hints I now relate,
  For fear, dear Prophet, you might grow irate.'
He spoke thus—drunken, wasted, almost dead,
  The Prophet curled his collar up and said,
'Your horse has grown excited, pull the reins!
  God feels no shame, in you now none remains.
Your mirror has slipped out of its own cover,
  But with Truth's weighing-scales can it now differ?

How can they both keep silent out of tact,
    So as to not shame someone with a fact?
They are both touchstones which speak truthfully:
    Though you should serve them for a century
And say, "Conceal truth for my benefit:
    Display the profit, hide the deficit!"
"Don't make yourself look stupid!" they will cry,
    "Just for your sake can scales and mirrors lie?
Since God has made us for this aim alone:
    That through us both the truth can be made known,
If we don't do exactly as we should,   3565
    We won't be worthy for the fair and good."
So put the mirror back, Zayd, in its case,
    Your breast's been split like Sinai by God's face!'
'The sun of truth and pre-eternity
    Can't be stuffed in one's arms so none can see:
It would tear off that arm which tries to hide,
    Wisdom and madness would be nullified.'
The Prophet said, 'Place fingers on your eyes
    And you won't see the sun begin to rise,
One fingertip can veil the moon at night—   3570
    This is a sign God can conceal from sight:
The world gets covered by a single tip,
    The sun can be eclipsed by just one slip.'

Keep quiet, watch the sea's depths if you can,
    God's made that subject to the will of man
Like Salsabil and Zanjabil*—both springs
    Are ruled in heaven by the King of Kings;
And heaven's streams are ruled by you and me,
    Not forcefully but through the Lord's decree:
We make them flow where we want them to go   3575
    Like magic at a good magician's show,
And, like my eyes' streams, they're in firm control
    Of what sends out the tears—my heart and soul;
If the heart wants, they'll flow towards a snake,
    Or a much better route instead they'll take,

Or if it wants—to what's perceivable,
　Or to veiled things that are invisible,
Or if it wants—towards the Universal,
　Or to contingents that are only temporal.
All outward senses are in flow this way,   3580
　The heart's decree these five pipes must obey:
When your heart tells them what it has in mind
　All five set off and drag their skirts behind,
Your hands and feet obey your heart's command
　Like Moses's rod, held in his right hand:
If it's the heart's wish, legs will dance for it
　Or flee from loss to greater benefit,
And hands will bend their fingers to hold tight
　A pen with which a book you then can write—
Hands are controlled by one unseen inside,   3585
　Which has arranged the body's form outside—
You'll be a snake against your enemy
　Or help your friend, if that's the heart's decree;
Or to a spoon with which to eat you'll turn,
　Or to a massive mace that weighs a ton.
How does the heart instruct them? How amazing!
　This marvellous, hidden link we're contemplating!
Perhaps King Solomon's ring* it can gain,
　The outward senses' yearning to restrain?
The outward senses it controls with ease,   3590
　The inward ones too follow its decrees;
There are ten senses, seven organs too—
　Try counting what no words can show to you!
Since you're like Solomon, heart, come and fling
　On angels and the demons your famed ring;
If you're free from deceit here in this land,
　No demon then can steal it from your hand;
The universe will be ruled by your name
　The way you rule your body, just the same.
But if a demon steals the seal from you,   3595
　Your kingdom will be gone, your fortune too,
Then misery will be your destiny
　Till *Judgment Day* as part of God's decree—

Though you deny your own deceit, my brother,
　　Your soul won't be saved from the scales and mirror.

His fellow servants accuse Loqman of eating the fresh fruit
that they were supposed to bring home

Loqman used to be in his master's eyes,
　　In outward form, the servant he'd despise;
The master sent some servants out one day
　　To gather fruit for him from far away.
The others thought Loqman embarrassing—　　　　3600
　　He was dark-skinned though mystically a king—
And so they ate the fruit with such delight,
　　Led by their greed, although they had no right;
When they returned they gave Loqman the blame;
　　Their master cursed him with his eyes aflame!
To make him check the cause he answered back,
　　Loqman turned to him after his attack:
'Dear master, God has often made it clear
　　The faithless slave is not one He holds dear;
Examine who is faithful and who's not:　　　　3605
　　Make everyone drink water that is hot,
Then make us run out in the countryside
　　On foot, while you are riding at our side—
You'll witness who has acted wickedly,
　　This will reveal the hidden mystery.'
The master poured hot water in each cup
　　And made each servant drink his last drop up,
He sent them out then to the yard, where they
　　Were forced to run this way and then that way;
They vomited once they had run about:　　　　3610
　　Hot water made them spew their food all out,
But when Loqman's turn came, since he'd not lied,
　　Water is all he brought up from inside—
He'd shown such wisdom though a simple man,
　　Imagine what *the Lord of Being* can:
*That day when all the secrets are revealed**
　　What you would like to hide can't be concealed;

Draughts of hot water that for each are poured*
    Will tear all veils away from what's abhorred;
Vile infidels fire's torture suits the best,   3615
    Since for hard stones fire is the perfect test:
When to the stony-hearted we've been good
    And gently talked, they've shunned our brotherhood;
A heavy wound needs treatment that is strong—
    To hungry dogs the donkey's bones belong:
*Bad women to the bad men** now dictate—
    An ugly woman is a vile man's mate;
Whichever mate fulfils your fantasies—
    Become effaced in that one's qualities:
If you want light, reflect it like a star,   3620
    If distance, be self-centred and stray far;
If from this vile gaol you long to be free
    *Prostrate before him, move near constantly!**

The remainder of the story of Zayd answering the
Messenger of God

'Zayd, none can venture to its furthest reach—
    Now shackle the Boraq* which brings your speech!
Such talk can tear apart the veil between
    This world, with all its faults, and the unseen;
God's wish is to stay hidden still today,
    So drive the drummer off and bar the way!
He's best left veiled, so draw the reins, sit tight!   3625
    In mental images let men delight.'
The Lord wants even those who're in despair
    To worship Him and never turn from there,
With just the hope that they may gain His grace
    Their goal for several days these men will chase.
On all of us He wants his grace to shine:
    The good and bad receive grace that's divine;
God wants each prince and prisoner in his cell
    To hope and fear and to beware as well;
This hope and fear are just component parts   3630
    Of the thick veil that's covering their hearts—

Where's hope and fear when you're beyond the screen,
  Might and strong rule await in the unseen.
A youth sat by a stream once with this thought:
  'That fisherman is Solomon, is he not?
If so, why's he alone and in disguise?
  If not, why does he seem so to my eyes?'
Like this, in two minds, he was wondering
  Till Solomon emerged as their own king;
From his great kingdom then the devil fled,   3635
  Solomon's fortune's sword left him for dead,
For he wore on his finger the famed ring;
  Devils and fairies were seen gathering,
Men came as well in order just to see,
  Including that youth with the fantasy—
Once he had seen the ring that his king wore,
  This wiped out what he'd thought about before.
We have such doubts when something is not here,
  We guess the qebla* when it is unclear,
Thoughts of the one who's absent fill one's breast,   3640
  But when he's present they are laid to rest;
And if the radiant sky does not lack rain,
  Plants keep on growing in the fertile plain.
*Believers in what is unseen** to be,
  Shutter the windows of the world you see.
If I should split the sky now in plain view,
  How can I ask, '*Does it look cracked to you?*'*
To find the qebla in the dark men face
  All angles, each from his own starting-place.
Things seem reversed like this for a short time: 3645
  The thief will try the judge now for a crime,
The sultans and high-ranking men as well
  Are slaves of their own servants for a spell.
Serving in absence is so laudable
  Like keeping faith in what's invisible,
For those who praise the king while in his presence
  Fall short still of those humble in his absence:
The governor at the empire's furthest end,
  Far from the capital, will still not bend;

He guards his garrison from enemies   3650
    And won't sell out for treasures vast as seas—
Out on the furthest frontier, far away,
    He's loyal like those with the king today;
He's better in the king's own eyes than those
    Who sacrifice themselves just when he knows:
Fulfilling one small duty thus in absence
    Is better than a thousand in his presence:
Faith and obedience, though now praiseworthy,
    Become void after death when truth you'll see.
Since absent and veiled things thus seem the best,   3655
    Seal up your lips—don't make things manifest!
Brother, refrain from talking! Don't you know
    Much hidden knowledge God will soon bestow;
The sun's best witness is its own bright face:
    Who's the best witness? God, in every case!
No! I will speak, since God, the angels too,
    And others who know are all telling you—
God, angels, and those who have certainty,
God is the one who lives eternally.
But who are angels when God's testified   3660
    To also now bear witness on his side!
Weak eyes and hearts don't have the strength to bear
    The radiant presence of the sun up there,
They're just like bats that cannot bear the sun
    And so they give up hope it can be done;
The angels help us, so please realize
    They manifest the sun's rays in the skies;
We've gained this radiance from the sun, so we
    Share it with weak men like a deputy.
Like different phases of the moon at night   3665
    Each angel has its own true worth and might
And different wings of light—some four, some three*—
    Each angel to a different degree,
Just like the human intellect's own wings,
    From those of fools to those of learned kings.
Each has an angel as associate,
    The one that is the most appropriate,

The blind can't bear a single solar ray,
  So stars serve as the lamps to show the way.

The Prophet tells Zayd, 'Don't divulge this secret further than this—be sure to comply!'

'*My followers are stars,*'* the Prophet said,   3670
  'Lamps for the faithful, stones for Satan's head.'
If everyone possessed such powerful sight
  That sees directly heaven's sun's pure light,
What need would men have for the stars should they
  Be guided by the sun along the way?
He told the earth and clouds what had transpired:
  'I'm just a man, but *I have been inspired.*'*
I used to be in nature like the rest
  Till revelation's light filled up my breast;
I'm dark still when compared with the Supreme   3675
  Though next to men's souls like pure light I seem:
My light is faint, so you can cope with it,
  Since to behold the sun's rays you're unfit;
I'm honey mixed with vinegar, to heal
  Your heart of the affliction that you feel—
When you're completely healthy once again
  Throw out the vinegar—eat honey then!
When your heart's passion-free for God alone,
  Witness *The Merciful sits on the throne,*
Once the heart gains this link, then God's decree   3680
  Rules him without an intermediary;
This discourse could go on, but there's no space—
  I must advise Zayd not to seek disgrace.

Resumption of the story about Zayd

You won't find Zayd now, for this man has fled
  Like horses from the shoeing-line they dread,
Who're you? Zayd cannot find himself—he's gone
  Just like a star on which the sun has shone!

You won't find hide nor hair of him today,
   Not even one star, nor the Milky Way!
The speech and senses of our fathers are   3685
   Effaced in this king's knowledge like a star,
Their senses and their reasoning in turn,
   Like waves to *stand before us** will return.
The dawn brings back the burdens of all men,
   Stars which were hidden go to work again:
God gives the witless back their wits at dawn,
   Group after group with slavery's earrings on,*
Stamping their feet and waving arms in praise,
   'O Lord, you have revived us!'* each now says.
That crumpled skin and bones is now a knight   3690
   Who raises dust on racing out of sight:
The grateful and ungrateful non-existents
   At Resurrection thus change to existents.
Why turn your face and not look? Didn't you
   Do that at first in non-existence too?
Later you dug your heels deep in the sand,
   Saying, 'Who can remove me from my land?'
Do you not see God's actions are so clear:
   He dragged you by your ears all the way here
To various different states that lay in store   3695
   Which you had not believed were real before;
That non-existence is his slave, so strive
   To work hard, devil! Solomon's alive!
A demon makes *large bowls like troughs** for him
   Scared to rebuff him or refuse his whim.
Look at yourself now, trembling fearfully
   Like non-existence, which shakes constantly,
If you are holding on to status here,
   That too is from your soul-consuming fear,
For everything will hurt and wound your heart   3700
   Though it tastes sweet, the love of God apart.
Approaching death gives such heart-wrenching strife
   If you lack Water of Eternal Life:*
People just think of death when they're on earth,
   And doubt the Water of Life's actual worth—

Try to reduce these doubts of yours, my friend,
    Go! If you sleep the night will quickly end!
Seek out that day within the depths of night,
    The dark's consumed by that pure wisdom's light;
There is much gloom in its gloom, though it's stark—   3705
    Water of Life is found close to the dark.
From slumber how can one lift up his head
    While sowing seeds of heedlessness in bed?
Eating what's dead supports a sleep death-deep,
    The burglar breaks in when the guard's asleep,
You don't know who your foes are in this instance,
    Those made of fire are foes of your existence;
For water and its family fire's the foe,
    Even though it can put it out, it's so:
Water can end fire's life if necessary   3710
    Because it's water's children's enemy;
Also, there is the fire of lust, wherein
    You'll find the root of error and all sin—
The outward fire though water deals with well,
    The fire of lust can take you straight to hell—
This fire of lust is not controlled by water
    Because it shares its nature with hell's torture.
The light of faith is lust's fire's only cure,
    It puts out infidels' fires, that's for sure;
Who puts them out? God's Light, for it's superior,   3715
    So make the Light of Abraham your teacher,
That from your Nimrod-like self's fire there may
    Be for your incense-form a route away;
Indulging it won't cool your fiery lust,
    Denial works—in this now put your trust!
How can the fire go out once it is lit
    And you keep placing planks of wood on it?
This fire dies out if you deny it wood,
    For water's poured on it through being good—
How can fire blacken faces that now shine   3720
    Rosy with rouge from *fear of the Divine?**

The fire in the city of Medina under Omar

Omar's reign saw a fire blaze up that could
   Consume huge rocks as if they were dry wood,
It spread to buildings, then soared heavenwards
   And reached the highest nests of all the birds;
Half of Medina was in days burnt down,
   Water, afraid of this, then fled the town!
Some clever men tried putting out the fire
   With vinegar and water—it rose higher:
The flames spread further still in spite of this—   3725
   They gained support straight from the Limitless.
The people hurried to Omar to cry:
   'Water can't put it out—we're bound to die!'
He said 'This is a sign from God no less,
   It's due to your own flame-filled stinginess.
What use is water now—distribute bread!
   Stop being stingy, if by me you're led!'
The people said, 'We've opened every door,
   We're generous to a fault—does He want more?'
He said, 'You gave bread then because of rules   3730
   And out of habit, not for God, you fools,
Just to show off about your piety,
   Not out of fear and inner poverty!'
Don't sow the seed of wealth on rotten land,
   Don't place a dagger in a robber's hand,
Discern the faithful from the enemy—
   With those who know the Lord keep company:
All men put first their own kind—that's a fact,
   Just fools think a good deed is their own act.

An enemy spits in the face of the Commander of the Faithful Ali, who drops his sword*

Learn how to act sincerely from Ali, 3735
    God's lion, free from all impurity:
During a battle, he subdued a foe
    Then drew his sword to deal the final blow.
That man spat in Ali's pure face, the pride
    Of every saint and prophet far and wide:
The moon prostrates itself before this face
    At which he spat—this act was a disgrace!
Ali put down his sabre straight away
    And, though he was on top, he stopped the fray.
The fighter was astonished by this act, 3740
    That he showed mercy though he'd been attacked:
'You pointed your sharp blade at me before,
    But then you simply dropped it on the floor—
Greater than fighting me what did you see
    That you eased up in your attack on me?
What did you see to end your vehemence,
    For lightning to flash bright then dim at once?
What did you see that was reflected here
    Deep in my heart, and made a flame appear?
What did you see beyond both being and place 3745
    That you spared me though I spat in your face?
You are God's lion through your bravery
    And who knows your high rank in chivalry!
You're Moses's cloud in the desert heat
    Which brought a feast beyond compare to eat.'
The clouds bring wheat which men can grind and bake
    To make some sweet and wholesome bread and cake:
The wings of mercy Moses's cloud spread
    To give him ready-made hot cakes and bread;
For those who ate this bounty he unfurled, 3750
    Through such kind grace, their banner in the world,

For forty years that wonderful largesse
  Fed those with hope without becoming less,
Until they asked, because they'd grown so base,
  Why herbs and onions weren't sent in its place!*
Mohammad's people, noble men, can see
  Such food from God will last eternally:
He said, '*I was with God the night before,*
  Who fed me'—this was not a metaphor!
Accept this reading, make no argument,   3755
  Such milk and honey you too might be sent;
Interpreting throws back what you've received,
  Due to a fault in it that you've perceived.
Seeing faults shows your mind is weak as well,
  Wisdom's the kernel, reason's just the shell.
Judge critically your own vile self instead,
  Don't criticize the rose bush but your head!

'You are completely intellect and sight,
  Ali, what did you see to stop the fight?
Our soul's been split by your most gentle sword,   3760
  Our earth's been washed by knowledge you have poured.
I know these are His secrets, but tell me!
  Slaying without a sword's His mystery.'
That Craftsman with no tools or hands still knows
  How to create the gifts that He bestows:
He'll make you taste a hundred wines and more
  Which ears and eyes have never known before.
'O heaven's hunting falcon, please tell me,
  Through the Creator what did you just see?
Your eyes have learned to see the hidden sphere   3765
  Unlike those stitched-up eyes of others here;
One sees the moon above as clear as day,
  "The whole world's dark," another man will say;
Another sees three moons in the same space,
  Though each observes the sky from the same place—
Their outward eyes are sharp, their ears are too,
  And yet they flee me but hold on to you!

Is this illusion or His marvellous grace—
  You looking wolf-like, while I've Joseph's face?
If there were eighteen thousand worlds, not all   3770
  Would find each one of them perceptible—
The secret, great Ali, won't you relate,
  You who *brought good fate after evil fate*?
Either tell what your mind's seen candidly
  Or I'll divulge what trickled down to me:
It shone on me through you, but still was bright.
  Thus, like the moon, you silently spread light;
But if the moon should speak to us one day
  It would lead men more quickly on their way—
They're safe from errors of neglectful fools   3775
  Because the moon subdues the shrieks of ghouls,
Though silently the moon can serve as guide
  A talking moon's light would be multiplied.
Since you're "the gate to where God's knowledge is"*
  A ray from the bright sun of grace that's His,
Open up gate! To seekers you're eternal,
  And, through you, every husk can reach its kernel,
So open up forever, mercy's gate
  To *There is none like Him*—don't make us wait!'
Each atom is a place where He'll appear   3780
  But if it's closed who'll say: 'the door is here!'
Unless the guard should swing it open wide
  Belief in this will not be roused inside,
But when it's opened it can vivify
  Your bird of hope, which then will start to fly.
If treasure's found in ruins by a man
  He'll then search every ruin that he can;
If from a dervish pearls you fail to find
  Why should you try the others of his kind?
Opinion, if for years itself runs on,   3785
  It can't pass its own nose, where it was born—
If you've not caught a scent from the unseen,
  Can you claim that beyond your nose you've seen?

The infidel asks Ali, 'After defeating someone like me, why did you drop your sword?'

That friendly infidel then asked Ali
    Through drunkenness and savour, thoughtfully:
'Commander, please inform me, go ahead!
    Make my soul like a foetus bow its head!'
The seven planets play in turn a role
    In nurturing the foetus, O dear soul,
But when it needs a spirit, then the sun   3790
    Provides the help required to get this done:
The foetus is stirred by the sun a bit
    When quickly it provides a soul for it;
From planets it gains naught but a small trace
    But then the sun shines down on it warm grace.
But how was this connection first begun
    Inside the womb with the most gorgeous sun?
A hidden route beyond our human sight
    Provides a path to that celestial light,
That route by which all hidden gold's refined   3795
    And stones turn into jewels that are mined,
That route which gives each ruby its red shade
    And sends a spark where every horseshoe's made,
That route which ripens fruit while on the tree,
    That route which gives the timid bravery.

'Tell all, great falcon, with your blazing wing,
    Who's been trained on the forearm of the king,
O phoenix-catching falcon, make it known,
    You who defeat vast armies on your own—
You are yourself *my whole community*,   3800
    Since I'm your prey, great falcon, please tell me!
Mercy in wrath's place! I don't understand
    Why you would choose to shake a dragon's hand!'

The Commander of the Faithful answers, saying what the reason
was for dropping his sword in that situation*

He said, 'I use my sword the way God's planned,
    Not for my body but by God's command;
I am God's lion, not the one of passion—
    My actions testify to my religion:
"*You did not throw when you threw,*"* God has said:
    I'm just a sword the Sun swings at your head;
I've moved the baggage of my self away,   3805
    "All but God's non-existent," I now say,
My Lord's the Sun and I'm the shadow seen,
    For I'm His servant this side of the screen;
Adorned with jewels of union like a knife,
    While fighting I don't kill but grant new life.
My diamond-bright blade blood can never stain—
    How can the wind drive off my clouds again?
A mountain of forbearance and deep calm
    The fiercest winds can't blow away or harm;
That which is swept by wind is trash, no more,   3810
    And there are many winds like this in store!
The wind of rage and that of greed and lust
    Blow those who don't pray at the time they must!
I am a mountain, He's my solid base,
    Like straw I'm blown just by thought of His face;
My longing changes once His wind has blown,
    My captain is the love of Him alone,
Rage may rule kings but I have conquered it;
    I've tied up anger to my horse's bit,
The sword of my forbearance chopped my rage,   3815
    God's anger is a mercy at my stage;
Although my roof's been wrecked I'm drowned in light:
    Father of Dust's* a garden blooming bright!
A reason had emerged in that attack
    For me to choose to draw my sabre back,
So "*he loves for God's sake*" should be my name,
    "*He hates for God*" my sole desire and aim,

"*He gives for God*" my liberality,
  "*He clings to God*" my being, as you see;
I'm mean or generous too for God alone,   3820
  I'm His possession, not what men can own.
My deeds for God are not based on opinion
  Or mere conformity, but through His vision,
Reasoning and calculation I have fled
  To tie my sleeve to God's cloak hem instead;
While flying I can see the realm I'm in,
  While whirling the sole point round which I spin;
If I should drag a load I know to where,
  For I'm the moon—my chief's the sun up there!
I can't tell any more humanity,   3825
  A narrow river can't contain the sea!
I speak thus for their brains are limited,
  This isn't wrong, it's what the Prophet did,
So hear my evidence, I'm free from lust,
  The word of slaves is worth much less than dust.'
The testimony of a slave's worth naught
  According to the law upheld at court,*
Though thousands of slaves be your witnesses
  The court still won't give you allowances;
The slaves of lust are much worse in God's view   3830
  Than men they've captured, bound, and auctioned too.
The latter type can be set free again
  While lust's slaves live with joy but die in pain—
The slave of lust has no means of release
  Except the grace of God which doesn't cease.
He's fallen in hell's pit now, it's too late
  And it's his own fault—it's not down to fate:
He's thrown himself inside such a deep pit
  That I can't measure the full depth of it.
I'll stop here, for if this speech should extend   3835
  Not only hearts but stones would bleed, my friend;
Not due to hardness would their hearts not bleed
  But through distraction and not taking heed—
They'll only bleed that day when blood's worth naught
  But you must bleed when blood is worth a lot.

Slaves' testimonies are void as a rule—
    Find witnesses who aren't slaves of the ghoul;
'*We've sent you as a witness,*'* God has said
    Since he was free, from being's grip he'd fled.

'Rage can't enslave me,' said Ali, 'I'm free,   3840
    There's naught here but God's attributes—come see!
Enter! God's grace has liberated you!
    His mercy comes before His anger too!
Come in! Now you've fled danger that you've known
    You're like a jewel that was once a stone;
You've fled the thorn of unbelief and doom
    So in the rose-bed of '*He*'* you will bloom!'
'Illustrious one, I'm you and you are I,
    Ali, how could I cause Ali to die!
Your sins surpass good deeds of the obedient   3845
    And you've traversed the heavens in an instant.'
Sins of such men excel their piety,
    Rose leaves can grow from thorns for all to see:
The Prophet once Omar approached to kill—
    This led him to Islam's acceptance still,*
And pharaoh ordered magic from his men
    But fortune helped them save themselves again;
If magic and denial they'd not been taught,
    To stubborn pharaoh would they have been brought?
Why did they witness Moses's famed rod?   3850
    Their sin became obedience thus to God.
God has chopped off the thick neck of despair
    For sin's turned to obedience everywhere,
Since he can change round evil acts this way
    To righteous deeds, despite what whisperers say,
Cursed Satan now gets stoned in strong attacks
    And out of jealousy he finally cracks;
To us a sinful act he'll try to sell
    In order thus to lead us down to hell,
But when he sees that sin's now piety   3855
    All he has left is sheer anxiety!

'Enter! The door is open for you now—
    You spat but I gave favours anyhow;
I grant such gifts to those who torture me
    And bow my head down in humility,
Imagine what I give men who are loyal—
    Treasures and kingdoms that are all eternal!'

*The Prophet said in the ear of the stirrup-holder of the
Commander of the Faithful Ali: 'Ali will be slain
by your hand, I swear to you!'*

'The honey of my generosity
    Won't turn to poison if you murder me;
Into my servant's ear the Prophet said   3860
    That he would one day chop off my sweet head,
God's Messenger thus made him understand
    That in the end I'd be slain by his hand.
That servant now begs, "Kill me for my sake
    So I won't make this dreadful, vile mistake!"
I say, "Since you must bring about my end
    How can I try to dodge God's will, my friend?"
He falls before me, pleading, "Noble lord,
    Split me in two, for God's sake, with your sword,
So fate will not decree this as my role,   3865
    That my soul won't burn pining for your soul."
I tell him, "Go! The ink's already dry,
    That pen's foiled giants who could touch the sky.
There is no hatred in my soul for you
    Since this is not an act you choose to do;
You are God's instrument with which He'll write—
    With God's own instrument should I now fight?"'
The warrior asked, 'Then what's revenge about?'
    Ali said, 'It's a mystery God's set out:
Should He now counter His own act, you'll see   3870
    A garden grow from His change of decree;
To change His own acts suits God for He's one:
    He holds both grace and wrath in union,

He's the commander of phenomena,
    In every realm He is the emperor.
If He breaks His own instrument, He'll then
    Repair that broken instrument again:
We made it be forgotten*— comprehend
    That better things replace them in the end!
God abrogates laws for our benefit: 3875
    He takes grass but gives flowers in place of it,
The day's activity is stopped at night—
    Watch stillness now bestow true wisdom's light,
But then the night is cancelled by the day,
    The fire of which makes stillness burn away.
Though sleep and rest in darkness may abound
    The Water of Life* too in there is found,
And aren't minds refreshed while resting here
    As pauses help a voice sound loud and clear:
From opposites thus opposites alight—   3880
    Inside your heart's dark core He's shone this light.'

The Prophet's wars brought peace which all had sought,
    Our peace these days stems from the wars he fought;
Though he slew thousands who showed enmity
    This was so men could gain security:
The gardener trims the branches that cause harm
    To cultivate a straight and tall date-palm,
And any weeds he finds he will uproot
    So that the garden thrives and bears much fruit;
The dentist pulls out teeth that show decay   3885
    So that the patient's pain will go away—
Loss therefore can hide many gains inside
    As martyrs gain new life once they have died;
Once cut, the throat that ate its daily bread
    Receives God's bounty and feels joy* instead:
When throats of animals are lawfully slit
    Men's throats grow and from grace they benefit,
But what if one should stab another man?
    Guess by analogy now if you can!

A third throat grows, one nurtured day and night   3890
    With tonic from God and His rays of light—
The throat that's cut drinks tonic He lets flow,
    The throat that dies in '*Yes!**' has just fled '*No!*'

Say, 'That's enough!' You miserable, vile troll,
    How long will you choose bread to feed your soul?
You bear no fruit just like the willow tree
    For you have given bread priority—
If your base sensual soul can't give up bread
    To turn to gold try alchemy instead!
Since you would like your garments cleaned today   3895
    From all the washers why now turn away?
Although you break your fast with bread, my friend,
    He mends what's broken, He'll help you ascend,
Since He mends what is broken, be aware:
    If He breaks things, in truth it is repair,
But if you break things He will say to you:
    'Now fix it!' But you won't know what to do!
He has the right to smash things up, for He
    Knows how to mend what's broken instantly:
He who knows how to sew can tear as well,   3900
    He'll buy a better thing than what He'll sell;
He'll wreck a house so its roof hits the floor
    And then rebuild it better than before;
Should He decapitate a man, His grace
    Would bring a thousand heads soon in its place—
If He had not decreed a confrontation,
    Saying: '*There's life through your retaliation,*'*
Who would have had the gall to strike His sword
    At someone else and claim it's from the Lord!
For anyone with open eyes can tell   3905
    That killer is a fool of fate as well;
If by the Lord's decree a fool is led,
    He'll even strike against his own child's head—
Don't curse the evildoers, but beware
    You're impotent too in God's ruling snare.

Adam is surprised at the accursed Satan falling astray and shows conceit

Once Adam looked at Satan with disdain
  Filled with contempt and scorn, when he was vain;
Self-conscious, he thought he was in the right
  And laughed at wretched Satan's awful plight.
The Lord's possessiveness cried, 'Who are you?   3910
  About the hidden truths you have no clue!'
If He should turn your waistcoat inside out,
  He'd lift a mountain from its base no doubt,
He would unveil a hundred Adams then
  And cause cursed Satans to be born again:
Adam said, 'I repent now for that glance,
  I won't presume again with arrogance.
Now that I've begged, please lead me to decide
  That wealth and knowledge don't deserve our pride;
*Don't let a heart you've blessed now go astray!**   3915
  Make evil fates decreed now fade away!
Please spare our souls from meeting wretched ends,
  Don't separate us from pure-hearted friends.
There's nothing worse than life apart from You,
  Filled with anxiety, and helpless too.'

Our worldly goods steal what is spiritual,
  Our body likewise strips our precious soul:
Our own hands broke our legs—if not for You
  To save their souls what can mere humans do!
If he should save his soul from dangers here   3920
  He will have stopped calamity and fear,
For if the soul's deprived of unity
  It blindly mourns alone eternally—
Since You won't grant admission though he tries
  To save his soul, that exiled lover dies.
Call heaven and God's Throne contemptible,
  Say seas and mines are poor and miserable—
Compared with Your perfection that's correct
  For transitory things You can perfect.

If You should curse Your slaves, You have the right,   3925
    For You that's fine, successful source of light!
The sun and moon You can call worthless things
    And say that cypress trees are bent like springs,
From non-existence and from harm You're free,
    To non-existence You grant strength to Be:
Shedding is known by those who cause to grow,
    Since those who tear know also how to sew.
Each autumn He makes gardens disappear
    Then causes glorious roses to grow here,
Saying: 'You'd withered; come back fresh and bright!   3930
    Bloom beautifully and fill men with delight!'
Once the narcissus' eye went blind, He then
    Healed it; a broken reed He fixed again.
We're not the Maker but the objects made,
    Content though weak—this is the way we've stayed,
Saying: '*Myself! Myself!*'* repeatedly;
    We'd all be demons if You should decree.
Escape from demons due to this we find:
    You have redeemed our souls from being blind;
You show the way to all who are alive—   3935
    Without their sticks how can the blind survive!
Whatever's sweet or bitter, all but You,
    Burns humans up and is fire's essence too,
Whoever's refuge and support's a flame
    As Zoroastrians has become the same,*
For *everything but God is foul and vain;*
    God's grace is that cloud which pours down much rain.

Resumption of the story about Ali and his leniency towards his own killer

Think of Ali and his vile murderer,
    The kindness he showed his inferior:
He said, 'I see my foe by day and night   3940
    But I nurse no bad feelings, nor feel spite,
For, just like manna, death to me tastes sweet
    Since Resurrection's what I'm bound to meet.'

This deathless death is lawful for us now,
     Lack of provisions feeds us anyhow:
Though it may look like death on the outside
     There's life through which we will live on inside,
As birth for foetuses seems like death too
     Though in the world they are thus born anew.
Because I yearn for death so eagerly   3945
     '*Don't cause yourself to perish*'* speaks to me:
We all know sweet fruit's banned, and we take heed
     But to ban bitter fruit there is no need;
This berry with sour skin and flesh you see
     Is banned for sourness and dishonesty,
The fruit of death though tastes sweet once it's peeled—
     For me '*Now they're still living*'* was revealed!
Kill me, my trusty friends! I will live on:
     Eternal life awaits once I have gone;
There's life in my death, so please understand,   3950
     How long must I stay exiled in this land!
If I were not in exile here today,
     '*We will return to God*'* why would He say?*
Returners go back to their home again,
     To unity from separation's pain.

Ali's stirrup-holder falls before him, saying, 'Commander of the Faithful, kill me and release me from this fate!'

He said, 'Ali, please kill me straight away
     So I won't live to see that awful day!
Please shed my blood—it will be lawfully—
     So that the final hour my eyes won't see!'
'Should every atom be a murderer   3955
     And aim their daggers at your jugular,
They couldn't harm a hair or make you bleed
     Because that isn't what the Lord's decreed.
So don't you grieve! I'll be your intercessor,
     Not body's bondsman, I'm the spirit's master:
The body has no worth for me, it's clear
     Without one I'm a noble chevalier—

The killing sword's sweet basil now instead,
  My death a banquet and narcissus-bed!'
The one who breaks his body in this way   3960
  Desire for leadership can never sway;
Though he may strive for power outwardly
  That's just to show how rulers ought to be—
To breathe life into leadership anew,
  Grow fresh fruit on the caliphate's tree too.*

In explanation of how the Prophet's efforts to conquer Mecca and other towns was not out of love for power, for he has said: 'The world is a carcass.' Rather it was by God's command

The Prophet strove to conquer Mecca, though
  Power was not his aim—still some don't know;
He whose pure breast ignored the treasure-chest
  Of all the heavens when put to the test
(When they were filled with treasure to the brim   3965
  And houris* and the spirits looked at him,
Having adorned themselves just for his sake)
  Has no desire but God—make no mistake!
God's glory filled him so much it was clear
  Even those close to God could not come near.
No prophet can fit in that place, my friend,
  *Nor angels even—try to comprehend!**
'We're not distracted and we're not like carrion,'
  He said, 'We're drunk with God and not His garden.'
The treasures of the heavens though he saw   3970
  The Prophet judged it worthless just like straw—
What then are Mecca, Syria, and Iraq
  For him to covet and wish to attack!
If you think this you must be sick indeed,
  Comparing him with your own stupid greed!
Put yellow glass up right in front of you
  And everything will then look yellow too—
To smash such coloured lenses is a must
  In order to distinguish Man from dust.

Dust rose behind his horse as that knight sped, 3975
 You thought the dust a man of God instead!
Satan saw dust and said, 'Things made of clay
 Cannot be better than my fire, can they?'
If God's dear friends as evil you should see,
 That thought of yours is Satan's legacy;
If you are not a child of Satan too,
 How did the dog's inheritance reach you?

'I'm no dog but God's lionheart instead,
 The cage of form God's lionheart has fled!
The worldly lion seeks prey, loves to hoard, 3980
 Death's freedom draws the lion of the lord:
A hundred lives he sees in death—his aim
 Becomes to burn moth-like within death's flame!
Desire for death's a necklace for the best
 While for the Jews it was a major test:
"*O Jewish people!*" in the book God said,
 "For the sincere there's gain in being dead:
While profit can make men desire to kill
 Desire for one's own death is better still;
Let this desire be on your tongues now, Jews, 3985
 And thus among men honour you won't lose."
Not one Jew had the bravery to try
 And face Mohammad's challenge; this is why
He said, "If they'd accepted this, then none
 Would have continued to be Jews—not one!"
Instead they offered tax on properties,
 Begging: "Don't put us all to shame now, please!"*
This discourse looks like it can't reach its end,
 Give me your hand, since you have seen the Friend!'

The Commander of the Faithful Ali says to his own foe,
'When you spat in my face my carnal soul was aroused
and I lost the power to act sincerely, for God alone—that
was what prevented me from killing you'

The Leader of the Faithful told his foe: 3990
    'During that battle fought a while ago
When you spat in my face, my self was moved:
    I lost my temper though that's disapproved,
Thus both God and my passions had their shares
    But sharing's not allowed in God's affairs.
You were created by the Lord's own hand—
    You're His, not made by me, please understand!
Smash up forms made by God when He condones,
    Break the beloved's glass with just His stones!'
The Magian heard this, found light in his heart,   3995
    His Magian girdle then he tore apart,
Saying, 'I sowed the seed of wrong; just now
    I thought you would be different somehow.
The balance of the nature of the One,
    You are the pivot all scales hang upon;
You are my tribe and you're my origin,
    The light of my sect's candle, and my kin!'
'I'm the Eye-seeking Lamp's* most humble slave,
    The one which to your lamp its radiance gave,
The slave of that wave of the sea's light too   4000
    Which has just brought a gorgeous pearl to view.
To witness your conversion is my dream,
    For like the great ones of the age you seem.'
Then nearly fifty of his family,
    Like lovers sought the faith of certainty;
His clemency's sword had redeemed this way
    So many souls in bodies made of clay;
Sharper than iron's sword is mercy's blade,
    Much more successful than an army's raid.

Alas, for those two mouthfuls Adam chose,   4005
   The fervour of pure thought in this way froze:
Wheat thus eclipsed his sun which had shone bright
   Just like a full moon that's eclipsed at night—
One fistful thus made grace from Adam's heart
   Scatter just like the stars so far apart.*
When spiritual then food was beneficial,
   But when it was mere form it caused dismissal,
Like the green thistles that the camels eat
   And from it benefit as though it's wheat;
But when they have all dried up and turned brown   4010
   The desert camels swallow them still down—
They tear this camel's palate up, O Lord,
   A nourishing rose thus becomes a sword!
When food was spiritual it then was green
   But once mere form it turned stale, as we've seen:
In the same way you were accustomed to
   Pure, wholesome food—a gracious soul like you
Now eats this ghastly dry stuff every day,
   Since spirit has become mixed with mere clay;
Once mixed with clay it's dry and it cuts flesh—   4015
   Abstain from it now, camel, it's not fresh!

This speech flows earth-soiled, it has lost its force,
   The water's turbid—block it at its source!
God will transform it to a pure stream then—
   He made it dark, He'll make it clear again.
Patience will bring fulfilment in the end,   4018
   Have patience—*God knows best what's right*, my friend!

EXPLANATORY NOTES

PROSE INTRODUCTION
[written in Arabic prose; numbered by page and line]

3: 4 *like a niche in which there is a lamp*: Koran 24: 35, from a passage which has attracted a considerable amount of mystical interpretations.

3: 6 *known as Salsabil*: Koran 76: 18. Salsabil is the name of one of the four rivers in paradise in the Muslim tradition. See note to v. 3573.

3: 8 *and of resting places*: Koran 25: 24, referring to paradise.

3: 11 *Many He leads astray by it, while many others God will guide with it*: Koran 2: 26, referring to God's message and the different reactions (to believe or to deny) among the recipients.

3: 14 *by the hands of noble, pious scribes*: Koran 80: 15–16, where it is understood to refer to the writing down of the Koran.

3: 15 *none shall touch it but the purified, a revelation from the Lord of both the worlds*: Koran 56: 79–80, where it is understood to refer to the Koran.

3: 16 *Falsehood does not approach it from the front or from behind*: Koran 41: 42, where it is understood to refer to the Koran.

3: 17 *He is the best of guards and the most merciful of all*: Koran 12: 64, where it forms part of Jacob's response to his other sons when they ask him for permission to take Joseph out with them.

4: 2 *veracious . . . may God be pleased with him and them*: this is a formulaic prayer in Arabic which is normally used in reference to the Prophet Mohammad's Companions (see note to v. 367), one of whom, Abu Bakr, is known as 'the Veracious' (as-Seddiq). However, it is Rumi himself, rather than Hosamoddin, who is reported to have been a descendant of Abu Bakr the Veracious (for whom see the Glossary).

4: 5 *Last night I was a Kurd, but now I've woken up an Arab!*: a verse in Arabic attributed to a number of poets, none of whom, however, has been identified as an ancestor of Hosamoddin Chalabi.

4: 10 *qebla*: the direction, from any given location, towards the Kaaba in Mecca (see Glossary), which Muslims face to pray.

4: 15 *absent and present ones*: those mystics who are absent from the world and present with God.

TEXT
[numbered by verse, or couplet]

9 *then you should die!*: the original means literally 'be non-existent!' Therefore, *'then you should die!'* is to be understood here not simply as a dismissal, but rather, at the same time, as an instruction to become consumed like the reed by the fire of divine love.

24 *Like Plato here with Galen*: Plato (d. 347 BCE), the influential Greek philosopher who founded the Academy at Athens, was familiar to Muslims primarily through his Neoplatonic interpreters, and therefore was remembered as a mystic and metaphysician. In this way, he complements Galen (see Glossary), who is remembered as the representative *par excellence* of Greek medicine.

26 *Moses fell and swooned*: Koran 7: 143, in the context of Moses's request to God to reveal Himself; in response, God reveals Himself to a mountain, flattening it. On witnessing this, Moses himself collapses and faints.

29 *The nightingale*: in classical Persian poetry the nightingale and the rose are stock images symbolizing the lover and the beloved, respectively.

72 *moon-faced ones above*: an allusion to the houris, or female denizens of Paradise.

77 *You're Mostafa and I'm Omar your friend*: Mostafa ('the appointed one') is one of the names of the Prophet Mohammad, while Omar (see Glossary) was one of his most devoted companions.

80–5 *A feast was sent down . . . you'll not run out of it*: references to the many accounts in Muslim tradition of God's provision of food to Moses and Jesus and their followers, including in the Koran (2: 61, 5: 115–18).

88 *zakat*: a tax for the benefit of the poor on certain categories of wealth possessed by fellow Muslims. It is considered a religious obligation to God, and is traditionally counted as one of the 'five pillars' of Islam. The relationship between *zakat* and rainfall as well as that between fornication and the spread of disease are derived from the sayings attributed to the Prophet Mohammad.

100 *if he does not refrain*: Koran 96: 15, where it refers to those who prevent Muslims from praying. It is usually understood to be a reference to the opponents of the first Muslims in Mecca (see Glossary).

118 *The moon was split*: Koran 54: 1, usually interpreted as a reference to the miraculous splitting of the moon by the Prophet Mohammad, though it has also been considered a reference to a portent of the end of time.

123 *Shamsoddin*: the first direct reference in the *Masnavi* to Rumi's teacher, Shams-e Tabrizi; *shams* means 'sun', hence the word-play.

125 *So I can breathe in scent from Joseph's shirt*: the scent of Joseph's shirt was perceived by his father Jacob before it even reached him, informing him that Joseph was still alive and restoring sight to his eyes after he had gone

blind through weeping over his favourite son's disappearance (see further Koran 12: 93–6).

130 *drunkenness*: this term is used in Sufi literature to mean intoxication due to love.

225 *Think of the child whose jugular Khezr slit*: a reference to part of the story in the Koran (18: 65–82) about Moses's failed attempt to follow Khezr (see Glossary) as a disciple without questioning him about his actions. Khezr shocks Moses by, among other things, killing a boy. This act is later revealed by Khezr to have been in accordance with the wishes of God, who wanted to give the boy's pious parents a better child in his place.

228 *Like Ismail*: Ismail, the forefather of the Arabs, is the son whom Abraham was ready to sacrifice in the Muslim version of this well-known story, rather than his brother Isaac, who plays this role in the Judaeo–Christian tradition.

229 *Ahmad's*: Ahmad, meaning 'most praised', is one of the names of the Prophet Mohammad. It is used in the Koran (61: 6) where Jesus announces that a messenger of God called Ahmad will come after him.

238 *Moses stayed veiled*: Moses was 'veiled' (i.e. ignorant) in his Koranic encounter with Khezr (see Glossary), in that he doubted the correctness of his guide's actions, including the destruction of a boat which was the property of others (see note to v. 225).

245 *barber's blade*: this is probably a reference to the Muslim practice of circumcision, which was normally carried out by barbers in Rumi's time.

277 *a man who's tasted truth*: mystical knowledge is often described by Sufis as 'tasting the truth', indicating that it is an immediate, experiential form of knowledge which gives greater certainty than theoretical knowledge.

279 *Magicians challenged Moses, friend of God*: a reference to the Koranic story (20: 62–76) about the help given by God to Moses, so that he could meet the challenge of Pharaoh to perform a miracle greater than the sorcery of his magicians. By magic they make their rods move about, while through God's help the transformation of Moses's rod is even greater (according to tradition, it changes into a snake).

289 *like those from Merv and Reyy*: Merv and Reyy were prosperous towns in the east and west of medieval Persia. This expression is the equivalent of 'like chalk and cheese'.

297 *the Mother of the Book*: Koran, 13: 39, where it can be understood to signify the source in heaven of all books of revelation, or, more universally, the source of all knowledge.

298 *a gap they don't encroach upon*: Koran, 55: 20, where it describes the way in which different kinds of water (salt and sweet) are kept separate, as one of a long list of signs in nature of God's favours to mankind.

322 *Bu Mosaylem's name*: in Muslim tradition, Bu Mosaylem was a contemporary of the Prophet Mohammad who claimed falsely to be a

prophet himself. He was known, like the Prophet Mohammad, as 'Ahmad', the name associated in particular with the foretelling of the latter's mission (see note to v. 229).

323 *those who know well*: Koran, 38: 29, where it is used to describe those who appreciate revelation.

367 *Companions*: the Companions, or contemporary followers, of the Prophet Mohammad. In Sunni Islam, the tradition to which Rumi belonged, the Prophet's Companions are the first generation of his religious successors.

394 *They're sleeping*: Koran 18: 18, taken from the story of the Companions of the Cave (see note to v. 406).

401 *He who makes each dawn break*: Koran 6: 96, in a passage describing God's qualities. Rumi compares the break of dawn with the signalling of the Resurrection (see note to v. 1925) on Judgment Day by the angel Esrafil (see Glossary).

406 *Companions of the Cave*: seven companions who, together with their dog, are described in the Koran (18: 9–26) as hiding in a cave during the reign of a cruel tyrant, and praying to God for protection. They sleep there for some 309 years before waking up and returning to the outside world, though it seems to them like a single night. Their experience is referred to in the Koran as a demonstration to sceptics of God's power both to protect His faithful servants and to resurrect men on Judgment Day. In the earlier Christian version of this Koranic story, they are known as the 'Seven Sleepers of Ephesus'.

410 Heading   *The caliph*: this title, traditionally understood as meaning 'political successor to the Prophet', has been held by various rulers who could trace their ancestry back to the tribe of the Prophet.

417 *houri*: female denizen of paradise.

428 *How he makes shadows stretch*: Koran 25: 45, where it serves to describe one of the signs of God's management of His ordered creation. The shrinking and extension of shadows inform of the motion of the planet in relation to the sun, while saints inform of the light of God.

429 *don't love the ones that set*: Koran 6: 76, in the Koranic account of Abraham's search for a god truly worthy of worship – he worships in turn a star, the moon, and the sun, until he witnesses that each one of these is transient, at which point he declares: 'I don't love the ones that set.' This search leads him ultimately to worship none but the Eternal Creator.

437 *Sanctify my house*: Koran 2: 125, God's command to Abraham and Ismail to purify the Kaaba (see Glossary) for the sake of His worshippers.

504 *Not seeing Jesus's one-colouredness . . . he didn't guess*: this refers to traditions that can be found in works of the Islamic 'Stories of the Prophets' genre, which present Jesus as an apprentice of a dyer. In one version, he

miraculously dyes a pile of multi-coloured garments pure white. Rumi associates one-colouredness with the purity and selflessness of Jesus.

514 *the primordial trust*: this refers to the Koranic 'Covenant of Alast' (7: 172), when Mankind testified that God is the Lord by saying 'Yes!' in response to his question 'Am I not (*alasto*) your Lord?' This is understood to have taken place when mankind was pure spirit in the presence of God, before entering the world.

524 *And if from mourning it has not turned blue*: dark blue was the colour of mourning in the Persian tradition of Rumi's time.

532 *Jesus's breath*: Koran 3: 49 describes Jesus's breath as giving life to a bird of clay.

539 *Sins made a woman's olive face . . . Venus shining bright*: this alludes to the story of Harut and Marut (see Glossary), two angels who tried to seduce a beautiful woman. They were punished as a result, while the woman was turned into Venus.

544 *But then snubbed Adam, the most honoured one*: this alludes to Koran 2: 30–4, where God instructs the angels to prostrate themselves before Adam, His vicegerent on earth. All of them obey except Satan (known also as Eblis).

551 *Like saving Abraham from flames that roar*: an allusion to God's rescue of Abraham from Nimrod's fire (see further 'Nimrod' in the Glossary).

572 *'Return!'*: Koran 89: 28, meaning 'Return to God!'—an instruction to the righteous on Judgment Day. Rumi refers to the Sufi return to God during this life through the mystical path.

578 *Water of Eternal Life*: a miraculous stream or fountain which grants eternal Life. It is found usually in darkness and with the help of Khezr (see Glossary).

611 *Nor take away the wine and drinking-cup*: wine is a common symbol in Sufi literature for the intoxicating love of God and remembrance of Him.

619 *When you threw you did not throw!*: Koran 8: 17, in a passage describing the Prophet Mohammad's actions in battle as being in reality God's actions. This is one of the most frequently cited Koranic verses in Sufi discussions of annihilation in God.

721 *a mercy to the world of men*: Koran 21: 107, where it refers specifically to the Prophet Mohammad. Rumi frequently chooses not to make a distinction between God's representatives from among the prophets and the Sufi saints.

740 *Their faith was tampered with*: this alludes to the Muslim belief that although Jesus (like the prophets before him) delivered his message faithfully to his followers in the form of the holy book that he brought with him, it was tampered with and distorted. It is therefore not represented accurately in the New Testament.

745 *By heaven and its zodiac!*: the first verse of Koran 85: 1, which refers to the massacre of the faithful in pits of fire by tyrants.

750 *the trumpet blast*: according to Muslim eschatology, the Resurrection (see note to v. 1925) is signalled at the end of time with the blast of a trumpet (see also 'Esrafil' in the Glossary).

751 *To the good the Book we send*: Koran, 35: 32, which is interpreted as God's gift of divine knowledge to a chosen élite among the faithful.

770 *The colouring by God*: Koran 2: 138. Rumi uses this allusion to imply that positive human qualities are of divine origin.

784 *Drowning . . . followers*: a reference to the story of Moses's escape from the pharaoh and his army. See further v. 1196.

794 *And Abraham's well-hidden mysteries*: see note to v. 551.

798 *Jesus's pure breath*: see note to v. 532.

860 *Shayban the Shepherd*: a Muslim ascetic of the eighth century who is mentioned as a hero of the tradition in the medieval works of Sufism.

865 *And Abraham from fire felt no alarm*: see note to v. 551.

868 *Korah*: a biblical figure (Num. 16) who is also mentioned in the Koran (28: 76–82, 29: 39, and 40: 24). As a punishment for behaving arrogantly towards Moses and hoarding his wealth, he was swallowed up by the earth.

869 *Jesus's breath made water mixed with clay*: see note to v. 532.

871 *Moses's light made Sinai dance and spin*: see note to v. 26.

881 *His mother's called Hawiya, which means 'hell'*: Koran 101: 9, where Hawiya is said to be the mother of evildoers, whose final abode will be hell. Rumi thus includes the Jewish king among this group.

886 *From us sweet perfumed words shall rise*: Koran 35: 10, which is usually interpreted as referring to the Muslim testimony of faith: 'There is no deity but God.' This statement is often chanted in Sufi worship.

903 *Kalila and Dimna*: the famous book of Indian fables which was popular in Rumi's time in the form of an Arabic translation.

915 *the Lord of every dawn*: Koran 113: 1, one of the epithets of God.

930 *Go down*: God's order to leave paradise in the Koranic description (2: 36, 38) of the fall of Adam and Eve.

956 *the tops of mountains might be moved*: Koran 14: 46, which asserts that even if men should learn how to make mountains move, among other impressive accomplishments, ultimately only what God decrees will happen.

1017 *But the good name of angels . . . who God's own word would doubt*: see note to v. 544.

1026 *The dog of the Companions of the Cave*: see note to v. 406.

1032 *For donkey's ears are just for simpletons!*: the Persian word for 'hare' is *khargush*. Individually, *khar* means donkey, and *gush* means ear. Thus

Rumi plays on the form of the word in this dismissive comment addressed to the hare.

1072 *The student's tablet turns to one 'preserved'*: in Muslim theology, the Preserved Tablet is where all knowledge is recorded and the source of all revelation, of which the Koran is one part.

1074–5 *The intellect repeats . . . Sultan of the Soul!'*: this alludes to the story of the Prophet Mohammad's ascension. He is led by the Angel Gabriel before proceeding by himself in the final stage, which is beyond Gabriel's endurance, to the closest possible proximity to God.

1085 *the moon was split*: Koran 54: 1. See note to v. 118.

1111 *All rulers' glories and their sermon-praise*: this refers to a significant form of confirmation of political authority in Islamic societies, namely the mention of the ruler's name during the Friday sermon at the main mosque.

1143 *He sees*: Koran 6: 103, where it is stated that God sees and knows all things.

1149 *We return to Him*: Koran 2: 156, where this is presented as the response of God's patient devotees in the face of adversity. Rumi uses this as a confirmation that the soul returns, ultimately, to its source in God.

1164 *ass-eared beast*: see note to v. 1032.

1193 *like water under straw*: a proverbial expression in Persian to describe someone whose ill intent is masked by false politeness and friendship.

1197 *Just like the gnat . . . the skull of Nimrod*: according to tradition, though Nimrod (see Glossary) tried to hide from God and protect his body, a gnat entered through his nostrils and destroyed his brain.

1199 *For Pharaoh heeded what Haman conveyed*: in the Muslim tradition, Haman is remembered as an adviser to Pharaoh, and is mentioned in the Koran alongside Korah (see note to v. 868).

1243 *He taught the Names*: Koran 2: 31, concerning God's establishment of Man as His vicegerent on earth, and His bestowal of knowledge which is superior even to that of His angels.

1249 *For Moses simply called his stick 'a rod'*: see note to v. 279.

1250 *Alast*: see note to v. 514.

1263 *'O Lord, we've erred!'*: Koran 7: 23, the confession by Adam and Eve in the Koranic description of their fall from paradise.

1322 *When God's help comes*: Koran 110: 1, where it is understood to be foretelling the success of the Prophet Mohammad's mission through God's help against all the odds.

1323 *birds in flocks*: from the Koranic story (105: 3) which is understood to refer to the help given by God to the Prophet Mohammad's tribe when Mecca was being invaded by an army from south Arabia which made use of an elephant. God sends birds which throw stones down at them and thus destroy their enemies. This is traditionally believed to have taken place shortly before Mohammad's birth in the very same year, and thus serves as a sign that God provided help to pave the way for His prophet's future success.

1337 *'Believers are each other's mirrors'*: a saying of the Prophet Mohammad, which Rumi uses to assert that the faults we see in others are really a reflection of our own faults.

1353–4 *'It sprouts'*... *tall and straight*: Koran 48: 29, where the sprouting of strong and healthy plants is used as a metaphor for the success of the faithful.

1359 *'Faith's Pride'*: this name or title, Fakhroddin, means 'the Pride of the Religion', or 'Faith's Pride'. It has been suggested that this is a reference to the theologian and philosopher Fakhroddin Razi, who is depicted as a rival to Rumi's father at the court of the Khwarazmshah rulers of Persia. See further, Nicholson, vii (Commentary), 103.

1382 Heading *'We have returned from the lesser jihad to the greater jihad'*: part of a well-known saying of the Prophet Mohammad after a successful battle. In the full version, it identifies 'the greater jihad' as the war against one's own self and its desires. See further Nicholson, vii (Commentary), 103.

1389 *'Is there not still another bit?'*: Koran 50: 30, where it similarly represents hell's response to the question 'Are you full yet?'

1390 *Placelessness*: this signifies the realm of Unity beyond the dimensions of space.

Be! And it was: the divine fiat; the way in which God is repeatedly described as granting created things existence, before which they are described as non-existents in a storehouse. See Koran 16: 40, 15: 21.

1399 Heading *Commander of the Faithful*: an alternative title for the caliph, used especially by the caliphs Omar and Ali, for whom see the Glossary.

1407 *God's face*: Koran 2: 115, where it is stated that God's face can be seen everywhere.

1414 *beneath their clothes their heads they hide*: Koran 71: 7, where it describes vividly the actions of those who reject Noah's warnings. They also block their ears so as not to hear his message.

1424 *God's Shadow*: a traditional epithet for Muslim rulers.

1425 Heading *Commander of the Faithful*: see note to v. 1399.

1437 *'First say salaam, then talk!' the Prophet said*: Muslims are instructed to greet each other by saying 'Peace (*salaam*) be upon you!' when they meet.

1439 *'Don't fear!'*: Koran 41: 30, as part of the angels' address to the faithful, whom they reassure with the promise of paradise.

1445 *The state ... with her inside*: 'state' and 'station' are technical terms, respectively for temporary experiences of ecstasy due to inspiration bestowed by God and stages on the Sufi path traversed by the mystic through his own effort.

1456 *Commander of the Faithful*: see note to v. 1399.

1473 *'compulsion'*: the specific Arabic term for 'compulsion' (*jabr*) is used in Islamic theological discourse to mean predestination, which is the sense intended here.

1475 *commanding self*: The 'commanding self' is the literal translation of the most common Arabic term used for the carnal soul. It is derived from Koran 12: 53, where one finds the more complete version: '*the soul commanding to evil*'.

1488 *He split the moon*: Koran 54: 1. See note to v. 118.

1490 Heading   '*O Lord, we've wronged ourselves!*': Koran 7: 23, the response of Adam and Eve to God after they are blamed for eating from the forbidden tree.

'*Since you have sent me astray!*': Koran 7: 16, 15: 39, Satan's contrasting response after being banished by God from heaven as a punishment for refusing to bow down to Adam (see note to v. 544).

1492 *Each act of ours is God's manifestation*: an allusion to the theological position that God creates our actions, only after which Man acquires them. In this way the belief in predestination is upheld, while Man is also responsible for his actions.

1505 *For whose sake are good women? For good men!*: Koran 24: 26, where it is asserted that the good are meant for each other just as the impure are meant for each other.

1519 Heading   *He is with you wherever you may be*: Koran 57: 4, emphasizing God's omnipresence.

1539 Heading   '*Let whoever wants to sit with God sit with the Sufis*': this is a repeated message in Sufi literature, which emphasizes the benefits of associating with Sufis. See further Nicholson, vii (Commentary), 111.

1575 *Delights me more than musical audition*: musical audition is the most common translation of the Sufi practice of sama', or meditative listening to music while unaware of oneself and immersed in the remembrance of God, which sometimes also involves dance. This was one of Rumi's favourite activities, and consequently became the most distinctive practice of the order of Sufis which his disciples later formed, the Mevlevis or 'Whirling Dervishes' (see further the Introduction).

1588 *He cries, 'O Lord!' God says, 'I'm always here!'*: from a saying of the Prophet Mohammad about God's immediate answer to the prayers of his faithful servants. See further Nicholson, vii (Commentary), 113.

1591 *No-place*: or Placelessness, see note to v. 1390.

1593 *like those four rivers ruled by heaven's fold*: the Koranic (47: 15) rivers of water, wine, milk, and honey in paradise.

1613 Heading *Commentary on the saying of 'Attar ... antidote'*: this verse is from a *ghazal* in the collection of poems, or Divan, of Faridoddin 'Attar (concerning whom, see Introduction, and *Encyclopaedia Iranica*, s.v. "Attar').

1625 Heading *The reverence of the magicians ... cast your rod first?*: see note to v. 279.

1632 *Listen!*: Koran 7: 204, where it is used to instruct attentiveness to the Koran, in order to gain God's mercy.

1638 *Enter their houses by their doors*: Koran 2: 189, a verse that is often cited as a proverb to mean that one should do things in the proper way.

1654 *Knowledge and wisdom lawful meals produce*: an allusion to the emphasis placed by the early ascetic precursors of Sufism on reliance exclusively on sustenance which is known to be lawful and not ill-gotten according to the religious law, as part of their extreme emphasis on purity.

1677 *Even though God created all the pain!*: an allusion to the theological doctrine that God is the creator of all acts.

1683 *A verse we cause you to forget*: Koran 2: 106, concerning the abrogation of certain verses in the Koran by other ones that are revealed later.

1684–7 *They caused you to forget ... they made you forget recite*: Koran, 23: 110, where the unbelievers are warned that their mockery of the righteous caused them to forget God's message.

1719 *'I swear' until 'in hardship', for relief!*: Koran 90: 1–4, the last verse of which asserts that without God's help Man is helpless in the face of the challenges before him.

1722 *God's jealousy*: the notion that God possessively demands our exclusive attention and devotion.

1743–4 *Even ... maa?*: in Persian *maa* is the relative pronoun meaning 'we/us/our', which is the way that it is used in v. 1743. However, in Arabic it is a particle serving, in different contexts, to either negate or affirm, and this is the sense intended in v. 1744.

1769 *When I say 'none', read: 'but' the Deity!*: wordplay involving parts of the Muslim testimony of faith: '*There is no deity but God.*' Rumi is suggesting that he cannot mention directly his intended subjects (God, the sea of spirituality), which are too lofty and would therefore burn up his tongue (v. 1768).

1773 Heading *Sa'd is truly jealous*: Sa'd ebn 'Obada was a Companion of the Prophet remembered for his jealous disposition.

1799 *the order 'Be!'*: see note to v. 1390.

1805 *Pay tax on your fair face*: this implies that your face is so fair that it should be counted as precious wealth on which one must pay tax.

1817 *It's dawn . . . all night*: a reference to the process of composition of the *Masnavi*. Rumi would recite verses when inspired with them, even if that meant staying up all night, and Hosamoddin would write down what he recited.

1819 *We sit and drink Mansur's most potent wine*: Mansur al-Hallaj (d. 922) was a Sufi who died on the gallows. He is famous for having made the utterance 'I am the Truth' while experiencing mystical ecstasy, and later traditions identify this as the reason why he was executed, although this is contradicted by the earliest sources (see further 'Hallaj' in *Encyclopaedia Iranica*). 'Mansur's wine' therefore refers to a particularly intoxicating love for God.

1831 *Each day He's busy with a new affair*: Koran 55: 29, where it refers to God's constant activity, as He bestows favours on His creation.

1853 *The mountain beckoned John the Baptist near*: this alludes to a tradition among the 'Stories of the Prophets' which relates that a mountain opened itself up to protect John the Baptist from his pursuers.

1882 *Just like the beardless youth whom they call 'lord'*: a reference to the practice by some Sufi groups of contemplating divine beauty in the form of pre-pubescent boys. Rumi strongly disapproves of this practice.

1913–14 *While Joseph's scent . . . be like Jacob–cry!*: see note to v. 125.

1915–17 *Listen to this advice from Sana'i*: Here Rumi quotes verses from a *ghazal* from the collection, or Divan, of Hakim Sana'i (concerning whom, see Introduction).

1925 *The Resurrection*: this refers to the end of time when the dead are resurrected and the truth is revealed. Rumi uses this Koranic image frequently to represent the experience of mystical enlightenment, through which reality can be witnessed in this life.

1934 *Recite: 'Community of jinn and men . . . if you can pass beyond, go then*: Koran 55: 33, where God challenges His creatures to transcend heaven and earth, in order to point out that they are unable to do so without His authority.

1936 *not*: the negative particle and word for 'no' in Arabic, with which begins the Muslim testimony of faith (There is no deity but God). Rumi urges the reader to pass beyond negation to the affirmation of God expressed in the second part of this testimony, as exemplified by the saints in v. 1935.

1943 *God's blast*: see note to v. 750.

1944 *that which in Mary was revealed*: meaning the Divine Spirit.

1948 *through me you hear and see*: part of a Sacred Tradition, or saying of the Prophet in which he presents a message from God in his own words, which is frequently cited in Sufi literature. God affirms that his worshippers continue to draw close to Him through extra acts of devotion until they eventually see and hear through Him, and thus become annihilated in Him. See further Nicholson, vii (Commentary), 131.

1949 '*God's for him*': from a saying of the Prophet Mohammad which states that God is there for whoever should devote himself to Him. It is used here to allude to subsistence in God after self-annihilation. See further Nicholson, vii (Commentary), 131.

1967 *the Prophet's heavenly tree*: the tree of paradise called 'Tuba' in the Islamic tradition.

1969–70 *But they refused to shoulder it . . . they shrank from it*: Koran 33: 73, concerning the primordial trust accepted by Man to be His vicegerent in creation, after the heavens and the earth had shrunk from such a weighty responsibility (see note to v. 514).

1972 *For just a bite Loqman is held at bay*: Rumi plays on the similarity between his name and the Arabic word for bite or morsel (*loqma*). For Loqman, see Glossary.

1983 *redhead*: the name the Prophet gave to his wife Aisha (see Glossary).

1984 '*And throw a horseshoe in the fire as well*': this refers to the use of horseshoes as charms, by, for instance, writing the name of the object of one's desire on a horseshoe and throwing it in a fire, in order to bring that person under one's control (see further, Nicholson, vii (Commentary), 135). It is used here primarily because of the association with things red: rubies, redhead, glowing horseshoe in a fire.

1997–9 *Mohammad said, 'Belal, refresh us all . . . dazed!*': Belal was a freed Abyssinian slave, who became a Companion of the Prophet Mohammad. On account of his attractive and powerful voice, he was chosen by the Prophet to serve as the first muezzin.

2001 *His dawn prayer thus was subject to delay*: allusion to the tradition that the Prophet and his followers once woke up only after the time for the dawn prayer had already passed.

2005 *the Invisible*: the unseen spiritual world.

2015 *Salt made . . . more eloquent*: essentially a play on the Arabic and Persian words for 'salt', cognates of which can also mean 'excellent' and 'well-formed', respectively. A *hadith* is a report about what Prophet Mohammad said or did. For the full text of the *hadiths* that have been identified as the ones referred to here, see Nicholson, vii (Commentary), 137.

2046 Heading *Commentary on the verse of Hakim Sana'i*: the two couplets cited here are taken from the *Hadiqat al-haqiqat* of Sana'i, concerning whom see the Introduction.

2047 *feel doubt as to a new creation*: Koran 50: 15, where it is understood to refer to bodily resurrection on Judgment Day (see note to v. 1925). Rumi uses it here as an example of the error of scepticism concerning what one cannot perceive for oneself.

2090 *the Last Day's trumpet blast*: see note to v. 750.

2107 *Job's fount which cleanses and serves as a drink*: allusion to Koran 38: 41–2, which describes the spring provided by God to Job for both washing and drinking.

2121 *Am I not your Lord?*: Koran 7: 172, God's question in the tradition of the establishment of the covenant between God and Mankind (see further note to v. 514).

2135 *Be!*: Koran 2: 117 etc.; see note to v. 1390.

2140 *The Pole of each age*: meaning the supreme Sufi saint of each age, who is the spiritual axis of the universe.

2152 *The miracles of Moses and Mohammad*: referring to the miracle of Moses's rod turning into a snake (for which see note to v. 279 above), and the miracle of the moaning pillar described in the preceding passage.

2153 *They strike five times a day*: rulers would have drums beaten at the palace gates five times each day to proclaim their sovereignty.

2241 *The Meccans who reviled the Prophet*: at the start of his mission the Prophet Mohammad was reviled by his fellow citizens, and eventually migrated to Medina (see Glossary).

2245 *'Show us the straight path!'*: Koran 1: 6, part of the first *sura*, or chapter, of the Koran, which is repeated during ritual prayer.

2255 Heading   *Hatem Ta'i*: the subject of a popular biographical tradition which is thought to stem from a chivalrous pre-Islamic poet by this name. He represents the epitome of generosity in the Arabo–Persian literary tradition.

2262 *Water of Life*: see note to v. 578.

2269 *Sameri*: the 'Samaritan'. He is identified in the Koran (20: 87–97) as the man who led the Jews to worship the golden calf.

2286 *Yazid*: Yazid ebn Mo'awiya, the second Omayyad caliph, succeeding his father, Mo'awiya, who had been a Companion of the Prophet from a prominent Arab family. He is universally reviled for having ordered the beheading of the Prophet's grandson Hosayn and the massacre of his followers in Kerbala.

2296 *qebla*: the direction, from any given location, towards the Kaaba in Mecca (see Glossary), which Muslims face to pray.

2318 *But you've reversed the way rope-makers plait*: a reference to the way rope is traditionally made, with one sequence of plaiting being followed by another in the reverse direction. The bedouin in this way describes his wife as having become worse over the years rather than improving.

2326 Heading   *'Why preach what you don't practise' ... 'more abhorred by God'*: both these citations are from the same passage in the Koran (61: 2–3).

2353   *Poverty's pride*: part of a well-known saying of the Prophet Mohammad, in which he singles out poverty as a characteristic in which he takes pride for having surpassed the level of all previous prophets.

2368   *poverty's my pride*: see note to v. 2353.

2376   *Hashemites*: the Prophet Mohammad was born amongst the Banu Hashem, or Hashemite, clan of Meccan Arabs.

2392   *If strangers enter . . . all their hair*: Muslim women traditionally cover their hair in the presence of people who are not closely related.

2436   *It's beautified for men*: Koran 3: 14, in reference to the attractive things provided in this world, which are counted as inferior to nearness to God.

2437   *he's consoled by her*: Koran 7: 189, in reference to the creation of woman.

2439   *'Please redhead, speak to me!'*: representing the words of the Prophet to his wife Aisha; see note to v. 1983.

2464   *But it's for the eclipse men beat their bowls*: a traditional way of reacting to the eclipse of the moon, which was thought to have been caused by a dragon that must be driven away.

2477   *Be! And it was*: Koran 2: 117 etc.; see note to v. 1390.

2485   *donkey-sellers' fights*: fights staged by the owners in order to deceive potential customers.

2493   *Like changing footprints so you can't be tracked*: deliberately planting footprints that face towards the opposite direction of one's actual path, in order to mislead trackers.

2494   Heading   *He has lost this world and the hereafter*: Koran 22: 11, in reference to fickle people who follow God for rewards and turn away when they experience adversity.

2508   *O my servants!*: Koran 39: 53, as part of an instruction to the Prophet Mohammad to tell his people to repent and start to follow true guidance.

2521   Heading   *He belittled you in their eyes so that God could bring to pass something that needed to be done*: Koran 8: 44, where it refers to the rejection of Prophet Mohammad by his own tribesmen in Mecca (see Glossary).

2525   *God's she-camel, her share*: Koran 91: 13, in a passage about the mission of Saleh to the Thamud (for both, see Glossary).

2551   *jathemin*: Koran 7: 78, an Arabic term meaning 'falling prostrate' which is used in a passage describing the Thamud (see Glossary) after they are destroyed by an earthquake for rejecting the Prophet Saleh.

2570   *Why should I feel bad for the wicked's sake*: Koran 7: 93, where it represents the thoughts of the Prophet Shoaib after the people who rejected him are destroyed.

2582 Heading   *He let the seas meet each other with a gap which they don't encroach upon*: Koran 55: 19–20. See note to v. 298.

2607–8 *Water of Life/Draught of Life*: see note to v. 578.

2615 Heading   *That God may forgive you your past and future sins*: Koran 48: 2, as part of a speech addressing the Prophet Mohammad and recounting the favours he has received from God.

2616–18 *Lord grant me . . . It is not suitable . . . After me*: Koran 38: 35, as part of Solomon's appeal to God to grant him a unique form of sovereignty that no one after him would be blessed with.

2646 *see by the light of God*: part of a saying of the Prophet Mohammad about the miraculous insight of the true believer, who sees by the light of God.

2657 *Love makes men turn deaf and blind*: a saying of the Prophet Mohammad.

2660 *The Tablet's contents*: this refers to the Preserved Tablet, for which see the note to v. 1072.

2661 *He taught the names*: Koran 2: 31. See note to v. 1243.

2668 *Come here . . . a paradise of images of me*: Koran 39: 29–30, where God addresses the perfect souls, described as being at peace.

2684 *Much more than wrathful I'm compassionate*: an allusion to a Sacred Tradition (see note to v. 1948), in which God states that His mercy precedes His wrath.

2700 *veracious*: the epithet commonly used to refer to Abu Bakr (see note to p. 4, line 2, and Glossary).

2706 *Say, come!*: Koran 3: 61 and 6: 151, meaning 'Come and worship God!'

2715 Heading   *Commander of the Faithful*: see note to v. 1399.

2721 *the Lord has bought!*: Koran 9: 111, where it is used to mean 'bought' in the sense that the faithful serve God and He rewards them with paradise.

2726 *Lower your lustful gaze!*: Koran 24: 30, in a passage instructing modesty in dress and conduct. Rumi cites it here to convey the importance of renouncing sensual pleasure.

2730 *beneath them rivers flow*: Koran 2: 25, among many occurrences, where it describes the gardens of paradise.

2753 *the final blast*: see note to v. 750.

2759 *By the morning*: Koran 93: 1, the start of a *sura*, or chapter, of the Koran, the tenth verse of which instructs Prophet Mohammad not to drive beggars away.

2770 *He was not begotten*: Koran 112: 3, in a passage usually interpreted as a succinct definition of monotheism aimed polemically at Christians.

2790 *Ja'far's gold*: it is unclear whether this refers to the coinage of an Abbasid vizier called Ja'far, or to Ja'far al-Sadeq, the sixth Shi'ite

Imam and important Sufi authority, to whom are attributed works on alchemy.

2792 *see by God's light*: see note to v. 2646.

2799 *One drew the Draught of Life from Joseph's face*: this alludes to Koran 12: 19, which describes how Joseph was discovered in a well after being trapped there by his jealous brothers. For Draught of Life, see note to v. 578.

2800 *To watch a fire . . . escape from hell this way*: this alludes to Koran 28: 29–30, which describes how a fire stole Moses's attention and led him to witness God.

2801 *Jesus jumped . . . took him to heaven instantly!*: this alludes to Koran 4: 157, which presents the Muslim belief that Jesus was not crucified but rather rescued by God and taken directly to heaven.

2806–7 *A war of vengeance . . . all the same*: this refers to the Prophet Mohammad's uncle Abbas, who at first fought against him, but later became a follower. The much celebrated Abbasid caliphate was named after him, as they looked back to him as their ancestor.

2813 Heading *A gulf is fixed between them and what they desire*: Koran 34: 54, where it refers to a punishment dealt out to those who deny God and the unseen realm.

2817 Heading *'If you fornicate, do it with a free woman; if you steal, steal a pearl!'*: Rumi uses this Arabic proverb to urge the reader to have a high aspiration.

2840 *Kawsar*: see Glossary.

2875 *A hidden treasure*: this alludes to a Sacred Tradition (see note to v. 1948), in which God tells David that the reason He created the world was that He was a hidden treasure and wanted to be known. See further Nicholson, vii (Commentary), 176.

2907 *Hajj*: the pilgrimage to Mecca which all Muslims are required to perform once in their life if they have the means.

2915 *They've turned away from it*: Koran 51: 9, where the singular 'he' is used instead, in describing those who deny revelation because of their own wickedness.

2949 *the lamp and glass*: this alludes to Koran 24: 35, which uses the same terms and has attracted much attention from mystic commentators. Rumi reinforces in this couplet the message of the previous one, which emphasizes the need he feels for Hosamoddin.

2955 *the drink that is divine*: see note to v. 611.

2961 *Heed the Koran on those who went astray*: the Koran contains many stories about communities who failed to heed God and went astray, with the result that they were destroyed (e.g. see 'Aad' and 'Thamud' in the Glossary).

2969 *Consult them . . . regretting it*: this is the infamous advice given in a saying attributed to the Prophet Mohammad with regard to the opinion of women, but Rumi uses it here to refer to the urging of the carnal soul.

2970 *It leads you off the path towards the Lord*: Koran 38: 26, in a passage which represents God's speech to David, warning him against following his own desires.

2972 Heading *'Since everyone . . . all the rest'*: this refers to a saying of the Prophet Mohammad to Ali (see Glossary), urging him to seek wisdom as a means of gaining proximity to God, rather than mere pious deeds, which others preoccupy themselves with in order to reach the same goal. See further Nicholson, vii (Commentary), 181–2.

2972 *Lion of God*: the most common epithet of Ali, concerning whom see the Glossary.

2975 *Mount Qaf*: see Glossary.

2982 *Khezr*: see Glossary.

2983 *Here's where we split!*: Koran 18: 79, in the story about Moses and Khezr (see Glossary). After Moses fails for the third time to have faith in Khezr, he is told that they have reached the point where they must part ways.

2985 *Up above their hands rests God's alone*: Koran 48: 10, in a passage where taking an oath with the Prophet is said to be the same as taking an oath with God, so the Prophet's hand represents God's hand.

2994 *Qazvin*: a city located north-west of Tehran in northern Iran. It is unclear why the inhabitants of this town in particular should be associated with tattoos.

3019 *Turning thus from the cave*: Koran 18: 17, in the story of the Companions of the Cave (see note to v. 406). The sun's light is diverted from them by God's will, so that they are spared the discomfort of its heat.

3032 *Consult them too!*: Koran 3: 159, in God's address to the Prophet advising him to consult his followers.

3050 *Those who think ill of God*: Koran 48: 6, in a passage referring to those bound for hellfire because of unbelief.

3065 *All perishes*: Koran 28: 88; see note to v. 3067.

3067 *'There is no' for 'except' he's left aside*: allusion to Koran 28: 88, where one is instructed not to pray to any other gods, because *There is no god other than He* and *Everything perishes apart from His face*.

3078 *For camels, needle eyes are much too small!*: this metaphor found in the Gospel of Matthew is also found in the Koran (7: 40), where it describes how unlikely it is for unbelievers to enter heaven.

3080 *Be!*: Koran 2: 117; see further the note to v. 1390.

3084 *He works on something new each day*: Koran, 55: 29, see note to v. 1831.

3092 *Be!*: see note to v. 3080. Here Rumi refers to the two consonants that form the single word for 'Be!' in Arabic (*kon*). Vowels are not normally written in Arabic script.

3104 *under which the rivers flow*: Koran 2: 25; see note to v. 2730.

3113 *Be!*: see notes to vv. 1390 and 3092.

3116 *So we took vengeance on them*: Koran 7: 136, 15: 79 and 43: 25, concerning the punishment dealt out to the disobedient.

3146 *We took revenge*: see note to v. 3116.

3160 *A mirror for believers*: see note to v. 1337. In this context, however, Rumi uses the same saying of the Prophet Mohammad to make the point that the Sufi master can read the disciple's thoughts as clearly as looking into a mirror.

3169 *their hearts have goodness*: Koran 22: 32, where it describes the faithful servants of God.

3181 *Farmers rejoice*: Koran 48: 29, in a passage where believers are compared with strong and tall plants, which fill farmers with delight.

3185 *For at the Gathering . . . Resurrection Day*: the Gathering and Resurrection Day are different names for Judgment Day at the end of time (see note to v. 1925).

3186 *Are you alone . . . as I created you*: Koran 6: 94, in a passage describing unbelievers on the Day of Judgment.

3192 *sleep little when they sleep . . . seek His forgiveness*: Koran 51: 17–18, in describing the qualities of the righteous who will be admitted to heaven.

3195 *God's land is vast*: Koran 39: 10, where it emphasizes the abundant rewards that the righteous can hope to receive.

3200–2 *they're asleep . . . First right, then left . . . right side . . . The left*: Koran 18: 18, in the story of the Companions of the Cave (see note to v. 406), where it is asserted that, though they moved to the left and to the right, this was by God's will and they remained asleep.

3208 *I'm taking cumin to Kerman*: this is the equivalent Persian expression to 'taking coals to Newcastle'. The best cumin comes from the city of Kerman in south-eastern Iran.

3229 *I'm better*: Koran 7: 12, where this represents Satan's answer to God upon being asked why he had refused to bow in obeisance to Adam (see note to v. 544).

3241 *There was a scribe . . . would recite*: the Prophet Mohammad is traditionally believed to have been illiterate, so when he recited the revelations inspired in him it was his companions who would record them in writing.

3255–6 *Shackled, they must keep their heads up . . . Behind a barrier, and above a screen*: Koran 36: 8–9, where those who cannot be made to heed the truth are described as being impeded from the truth, with the implication that it is God's will that they should not believe.

3289–90 *it will be forced to quake ... it will say publicly*: Koran 99: 1–4, describing one of the signs of the end of time as being when the earth quakes and tells what it has witnessed.

3320 *from Thamud and from Aad*: see Glossary entries.

3327 *wild, frightened asses*: Koran 74: 50, in a passage describing sinners on Judgment Day.

3393 *Suppress your rage*: Koran 3: 134, in a passage describing the qualities of the righteous, which include the ability to control one's anger.

3405 *Guide us!*: Koran 1: 6. See note to v. 2245.

3413 *There shall be no more kinship then*: Koran, 23: 101, in a passage describing Judgment Day, when kinship will no longer avail anybody.

3416 *Bu Jahl's son ... those astray*: the son of Bu Jahl (see Glossary) was at first an enemy of the Prophet, but later became a Muslim. In contrast, the Prophet Noah's son eventually went astray.

3418 *qebla*: see note to v. 2296.

3421 *God's bird*: this seems to be used here as a metaphor for prophets and saints who serve as spokesmen for God.

3429 *those who stand in ranks*: Koran, 37: 165, in a passage describing those devoted to the service of God.

3445 *The world is just a toy ... Are merely children*: this Persian passage alludes to Koran 29: 64 and 57: 20, which express the same sentiment.

3454 *Spirits and angels to Him will ascend*: Koran 70: 4, in a passage referring to Judgment Day.

3456 *Opinion does not free you from all need*: Koran 10: 36, where it is asserted that mere opinion is of no avail when faced with the truth.

3462 *Like asses carrying their books*: Koran 62: 5, in a passage describing those who were entrusted with the law revealed to Moses, but failed to live in accordance with it.

3467 *'He!'*: the Arabic word for 'he' is commonly used by Sufis as the name representing the essence of God, and is often chanted in worship.

3478 *Water of Life*: see note to v. 578.

3479 *So understand 'Last night I was a Kurd, Now I'm an Arab though!'*: this is also cited in the prose introduction of the *Masnavi* (see note to p. 4, l. 5).

3500 *the hand of Moses*: this refers to the Koranic description of Moses's hand turning white owing to the light of God (see e.g. Koran 7: 107).

3513 *Seat of Certainty*: Koran 54: 55, where the righteous are assembled in heaven.

3514 Heading '*How are you ... God*': This refers to a saying of Prophet Mohammad in response to Zayd's (see Glossary) saying that he had woken up 'a true believer'. When the Prophet asks him further about this, Zayd relates his experiences, including staying awake all night and witnessing visions of God's throne and the people in heaven and hell. See further Nicholson, vii (Commentary), 204–5.

3525 *The day their faces will turn black or white*: Koran 3: 106, referring to Judgment Day.

3526 *Inside its womb*: the womb of the soul signifies the body.

3527 *The damned ... identify*: this alludes to a saying of the Prophet Mohammad in which it is stated that people are either blessed or damned already in their mother's womb. The second hemistich alludes to Koran 55: 4, which expresses the same assertion that the guilty can be identified by signs on them. See further Nicholson, vii (Commentary), 205.

3534 *By the light of God*: see note to v. 2646.

3536 *those of highest stature*: Koran 95: 4, where it describes the lofty form in which Man was originally created before having been reduced to the lowest depths as earthly creatures. Only those who believe in God and do good deeds regain the highest stature.

3538 *The Turks from Indians then we can discern*: in Persian literature Turks represent fair-skinned people while, in contrast, Indians represent dark-skinned people.

3542 *the Resurrection*: see note to v. 1925.

3550 *Kawsar*: see Glossary.

3558 *God feels no shame*: Koran 33: 53, where it means that God does not hesitate to tell the truth about your inappropriate behaviour, though the Prophet Mohammad does.

3573 *Like Salsabil and Zanjabil*: the names of two of the four streams in heaven, which the inhabitants will drink from (Koran 76: 17–18).

3589 *King Solomon's ring*: in the Sufi tradition this is associated with God's Greatest Name, which has power over all things, including the bodily senses.

3613 *That day when all the secrets are revealed*: Koran 86: 9, referring to Judgment Day.

3614 *Draughts of hot water ... poured*: Koran 47: 15, describing what those sent to hell receive.

3618 *Bad women to the bad men*: see note to v. 1505.

3621 *Prostrate before him, move near constantly!*: Koran 96: 19, in encouragement of those keen to worship God.

3622 *Boraq*: see Glossary.

3639 *qebla*: see note to v. 2296.

3642 *Believers in what is unseen*: Koran 2: 3, describing the believers, those to whom the Koran has been sent.

3643 *Does it look cracked to you?*: Koran 67: 3, which is found in the context of describing the heavens as examples of God's perfectly formed creation, in which cracks cannot be seen.

3666 *And different wings of light—some four, some three*: Koran 35: 1, describing the angels. The number of wings is usually seen as referring either to pairs of wings or having a purely symbolic significance, as it is used in this passage by Rumi.

3670 *My followers are stars*: part of a saying of the Prophet Mohammad about his Companions (see note to v. 367).

3673 *I have been inspired*: Koran 18: 110, as part of God's instruction to Mohammad about what to say about his own status as a mere human who has been chosen to be God's messenger.

3679 *The Merciful sits on the throne*: Koran 20: 5, describing God on the heavenly throne as ruler of heaven and earth.

3686 *stand before us*: Koran 36: 32, 53, describing Judgment Day.

3688 *with slavery's earrings on*: slaves in Persia traditionally wore earrings to indicate their status and the identity of their masters.

3689 *O Lord, You have revived us*: Koran 40: 11, describing Judgment Day.

3697 *large bowls like troughs*: Koran 34: 13, in a passage describing the powers and favours which Solomon was granted by God, including the making for him of large bowls like troughs by demons placed under his control.

3701 *Water of Eternal Life*: see note to v. 578.

3720 *fear of the Divine*: Koran 22: 32, where it represents the humility felt by the pious before God.

3735 *Commander of the Faithful*: see note to v. 1399.

3752 *Why herbs . . . in its place*: an allusion to Koran 2: 61, which describes the ingratitude of Moses's community towards God who had provided them with food. See also vv. 80–5.

3754 *He said 'I was with God the night before*: this alludes to a saying of the Prophet Mohammad in which he explains that he is nourished by God at night and so he has no need to break his fast as his followers do. See further Nicholson, vii (Commentary), 214.

3777 *Since you're 'the gate to where God's knowledge is'*: this is taken from a famous saying of the Prophet Mohammad in which he describes himself as 'the city of knowledge' and Ali (see Glossary) as 'the gate' to the city.

3779 *There is none like Him*: Koran 112: 4. See note to v. 2770.

3802 *Commander of the Faithful*: see note to v. 1399.

3804 *You did not throw when you threw*: Koran 8: 17. See note to v. 619.

3816 *Father of Dust*: One of the nicknames of Ali.

3828 *The testimony of a slave ... at court*: According to Islamic Law, the testimony of a witness is valid only if he is free and not a slave.

3839 *'We've sent you as a witness'*: Koran 33: 45, addressing the Prophet Mohammad, who is described as 'a witness' in the sense of a warner to His community about their duty to God and Judgment Day.

3843 *'He'*: see note to v. 3467.

3847 *The Prophet once Omar ... acceptance still*: Omar is said to have approached the Prophet to kill him, but ended up returning from his house a convert to Islam.

3874 *We made it be forgotten*: Koran 2: 106. See note to v. 1683.

3878 *The Water of Life*: see note to v. 578.

3887 *Receives God's bounty and feels joy*: Koran 3: 169–70, describing those who have died serving in God's way.

3891 *Yes!*: Koran 7: 172. See note to v. 514.

3903 *'There's life through your retaliation'*: Koran 2: 178, in a passage concerning the legal issues related to punishment for murder.

3915 *Don't let a heart you've blessed now go astray*: Koran 3: 8, where it occurs in the context of a prayer.

3933 *'Myself! Myself!'*: this is part of a tradition which reports that the Prophet Mohammad will be able to intercede for Muslims, while the other prophets will be unable to intercede for their own communities. When asked for intercession the other prophets respond by saying 'Myself!' which is taken to mean that they feel concerned about their own welfare and therefore cannot intercede for anyone else.

3937 *Whoever's refuge ... as Zoroastrians has become the same*: in medieval Persian Sufi literature Zoroastrians, or Magians, are associated (negatively) with the worship of fire and dualism, the characteristics which Rumi refers to in this verse.

3945 *'Don't cause yourself to perish'*: Koran 2: 195, where it refers to spending one's wealth excessively for God's sake.

3948 *'Now they're still living'*: Koran 2: 154 and 3: 169, concerning those who have been slain serving in the way of God as martyrs.

3951 *'We will return to God'*: Koran 2: 156. See note to v. 1149.

3961–2 *Though he may strive ... the caliphate's tree too*: the final two couplets of this section allude to the controversy over successorship to the Prophet Mohammad. Ali was only the fourth to become his political successor, as caliph, despite a large following who considered him to be clearly the best qualified

3965 *houris*: female denizens of Paradise.

3968 *No prophet can ... comprehend!*: this is taken from a saying of the Prophet Mohammad in which he describes his unique privilege of 'spending time' with God, a privilege which no other prophet, nor the angels, has been given.

3983–8 *'O Jewish people!' in the book God said . . . 'Don't put us all to shame now please!'*: this anecdote alludes to Koran 2: 94 and 62: 6–8, where the Jews are challenged to wish for death if they truly believe that they alone are favoured by God and will go to paradise.

3999 *Eye-seeking Lamp*: used here as an image to represent God, who seeks out discerning eyes so He can be known.

4005–7 *Alas . . . so far apart*: in the Muslim tradition the forbidden food that Adam ate is usually identified as grains of wheat (or barley), rather than an apple.

GLOSSARY OF PROPER NAMES

Aad (pronounced 'Od' in Persian) one of the vanquished nations referred to in the Koran (e.g. 7: 69). They lived just after Noah's time and became proud because of their prosperity, which led them to reject the prophet HUD, who had been sent to them. They were destroyed in the end by a roaring wind.

Abu Bakr Abu Bakr as-Seddiq ('the Veracious'), the first successor of the Prophet Mohammad as caliph, and thus considered by Sunni Muslims to have been the first of the four Rightly-guided Caliphs. See OMAR, OSMAN, and ALI.

Abu Jahl (lit. 'Father of Ignorance'), the name traditionally given by Muslims to a mortal enemy of the Prophet in MECCA whose original name was Abu'l-Hakam, which implies that he became ignorant after having been wise (the cognate '*hekma*' means wisdom).

Abu Yazid Abu Yazid al-Bestami (or Bayazid Bestami; d. 261/874), an eminent Sufi from what is now north-central Iran. He is a highly popular figure in Persian Sufi literature, in particular because of the many bold and controversial statements he is reported to have made, such as 'There is nothing under my cloak but God.'

Aisha a wife of the Prophet Mohammad and the daughter of his companion and successor ABU BAKR as-Seddiq. She is the source of a large number of reports about the sayings and deeds of the Prophet, or *hadith*.

Ali Ali ebn Abi Taleb, often referred to as 'the Lion of God', cousin and son-in-law of the Prophet Mohammad, who was brought up in the same household. He is presented in Sufi literature as the first Sufi saint, on account of being the disciple of the Prophet. In Sunni Islam he is revered as the fourth Rightly-guided Caliph, while in Shi'i Islam he is the first Imam, or religious and political successor of the Prophet.

Azrael the Angel of Death, who appears in many stories to signal to individuals the imminence of their death. This is represented memorably in one of the shorter stories in Book One of the *Masnavi* (see vv. 960–74).

Baghdad the capital in Iraq of the Abbasid caliphate.

Bal'am son of Ba'ur the Bil'am ben Be'or of the Old Testament (Num. 22, 23, 24), who is the archetypal sage led astray by pride and lust. He is believed by exegetes to be referred to in Koran 7: 175.

Bayazid see ABU YAZID.

Boraq the name given in tradition to the Prophet's fabulous steed during his Night Journey from MECCA to Jerusalem, which was followed by his ascension to heaven (see further vv. 1081–2).

Bu Jahl see ABU JAHL.

Bu'l-Hakam see ABU JAHL.

Esrafil the angel who, according to Muslim eschatology, signals Judgment Day at the end of time with the blast of a trumpet.

Gabriel the Archangel Gabriel, who revealed the Koran to the Prophet Mohammad, and guided him on his spiritual ascent.

Galen Greek physician and authority on medicine of the second century CE, whose works came to symbolize Greek medicine in the medieval Middle East.

Hamza the subject of a popular biographical tradition exemplifying bravery which is traditionally understood to have stemmed from the biography of the Prophet Mohammad's paternal uncle, Hamza ebn Abd al-Mottaleb.

Harut and Marut a pair of fallen angels referred to in the Koran (2: 102). They looked down on Man for his sinful nature, but, when put to the test on earth, they became prone to lust. They tried to seduce a beautiful woman. That woman became Venus, while Harut and Marut were imprisoned in a well in Babylon forever as punishment.

Hosam Hosamoddin Chalabi (d. 1284), Rumi's disciple and deputy, who wrote down the *Masnavi* as Rumi recited it (see further the Introduction).

Hud an Arab prophet after whom chapter 11 of the Koran has been named, as it recounts (11: 50–60) his career as the prophet sent to the nation called AAD. While this nation was vanquished because of its disbelief, Hud and his followers were saved by God.

Jonayd Abu'l-Qasem al-Jonayd (d. 297/910), Sufi who was widely recognized as the supreme authority of his generation. He lived in Baghdad, though he was born and brought up in Persia.

Kaaba the approximately cube-shaped building in MECCA which Muslims face to pray and around which they circumambulate during the pilgrimage. According to Muslim tradition, it was constructed by Abraham and Ishmael for the worship of God, but was subsequently turned into an idol temple. Mohammad's later mission to establish Abrahamic monotheism is symbolized by his destruction of the idols at the Kaaba after the Muslim conquest of Mecca.

Kawsar the heavenly fount of divine grace mentioned in Koran 108: 1.

Khezr figure usually identified with Enoch/Elias, described in the Koran

(18: 65) as someone who has been taught knowledge by God's presence. He is the archetypal spiritual guide in the Sufi tradition. The Koranic story about Khezr (18: 65–82) describes Moses as seeking to become his disciple in order to learn some of his special knowledge. Moses is warned that he does not have the patience required, but is finally accepted on the condition that he should not question Khezr about anything. Moses fails to live up to his promise to be patient three times, after witnessing Khezr make a hole in someone else's boat, kill a boy for no apparent reason and repair a wall in a village after they are both abused by the inhabitants. Khezr dismisses Moses, but reveals to him the reasons for his actions, each of which was the fulfilment of God's will and the means of bringing about a better outcome for His devout followers.

Layli the object of MAJNUN's excessive love. Layli (also known as Layla) and Majnun are the archetypal pair of lovers in the Arabo-Persian literary tradition.

Loqman a sage and ascetic, after whom Koran 31 has been named, since he is mentioned there. He is attributed in particular with various proverbs and fables and has often been identified with Aesop.

Majnun (lit. 'the madman'), the name given to Qays, the lover of LAYLI, after he fell madly in love with her.

Mecca city in western Arabia where the KAABA is located and the Prophet Mohammad was born. After the start of his mission, Mohammad and his followers were ridiculed and persecuted by the Meccans, and so eventually, in 622 CE, they migrated northwards to MEDINA. Towards the end of his life Mohammad led his army in a successful conquest of MECCA, during which the KAABA was rid of its idols and reclaimed as a monotheistic place of worship.

Medina city to the north of MECCA to which the Prophet Mohammad and his early followers migrated in 622 CE after suffering persecution in their home town. This migration marks the start of the Muslim, or *hejri*, lunar calendar. Mohammad became the political leader of Medina, and from this base took control of the whole of western Arabia, including Mecca itself.

Mount Qaf in medieval Islamic cosmology, Qaf refers to a range of mountains that surrounds the world and marks the border with the spiritual realm.

Nimrod a ruler who declared war on God and had Abraham thrown into a massive fire. Abraham was miraculously protected by God, who turned the fire into a comfortable rose garden for his sake, while Nimrod was killed by an army of flesh-eating and blood-sucking gnats sent by God, including one which entered his brain through his nostrils.

Omar Omar ebn al-Khattab, the second successor of the Prophet as caliph, and thus one of the four Rightly-guided Caliphs. He became a follower of the Prophet Mohammad though he had been one of his fiercest enemies among the polytheists in Mecca. The account of his surprising conversion relates that he had originally intended to kill the Prophet, but was moved on hearing the Koran being recited at his sister's house. Although his career as caliph was highly successful militarily, he is none the less portrayed as a pious ruler who lived simply and expressed concern especially to distribute alms to the poor as fairly as possible.

Osman Osman ebn Affan, the third successor of the Prophet as caliph, and thus one of the four Rightly-guided Caliphs. His greatest achievement is generally thought to be overseeing the compilation of the authoritative edition of the Koran.

Rostam the heroic Persian king whose feats are recounted in Ferdowsi's *Shahnama* (*Book of Kings*).

Saleh Arab prophet mentioned several times in the Koran (e.g. 7: 73–9), who was sent to the THAMUD.

Samarkand city in Central Asia, near Rumi's birthplace, which was of major cultural importance in Rumi's time.

Saqi the cup-bearer. In Sufi poetry the Saqi can also represent the Sufi master or God.

Solomon the prophet and king, who is described in the Koran as possessing deep wisdom and having been granted power over nature as well as a legion of demons at his command (e.g. 27: 15–44). His powers were effected by means of a special ring, on which was inscribed God's greatest name. One of the demons managed to steal this ring, and thus to rule in Solomon's place until he could retrieve it.

Thamud an ancient nation referred to on several occasions in the Koran (e.g. 7: 73–9, 4: 23–31, 11: 61–8). They hamstrung the she-camel of the prophet SALEH, which had been sent miraculously by God out of a mountain to test their willingness to share water and pasture. They were destroyed as a result by either an earthquake (7: 78) or a mighty blast of noise (4: 31, 11: 67), or perhaps a combination of the two. More elaborate versions of this story describe Saleh as suggesting that they might be forgiven if they caught her foal, but it escapes and disappears into the mountain.

Yazid Yazid ebn Mo'awiya, the second Umayyad caliph, succeeding his father, Mo'awiya, who had been a Companion of the Prophet from a prominent Arab family. He is universally reviled for having ordered the beheading of the Prophet's grandson Hosayn and the massacre of his followers in Kerbala.

Zayd Zayd ebn Haretha, a freed former slave and adopted son of the Prophet Mohammad.

The Oxford World's Classics Website

www.worldsclassics.co.uk

- Browse the full range of Oxford World's Classics online

- Sign up for our monthly e-alert to receive information on new titles

- Read extracts from the Introductions

- Listen to our editors and translators talk about the world's greatest literature with our Oxford World's Classics audio guides

- Join the conversation, follow us on Twitter at OWC_Oxford

- Teachers and lecturers can order inspection copies quickly and simply via our website

www.worldsclassics.co.uk